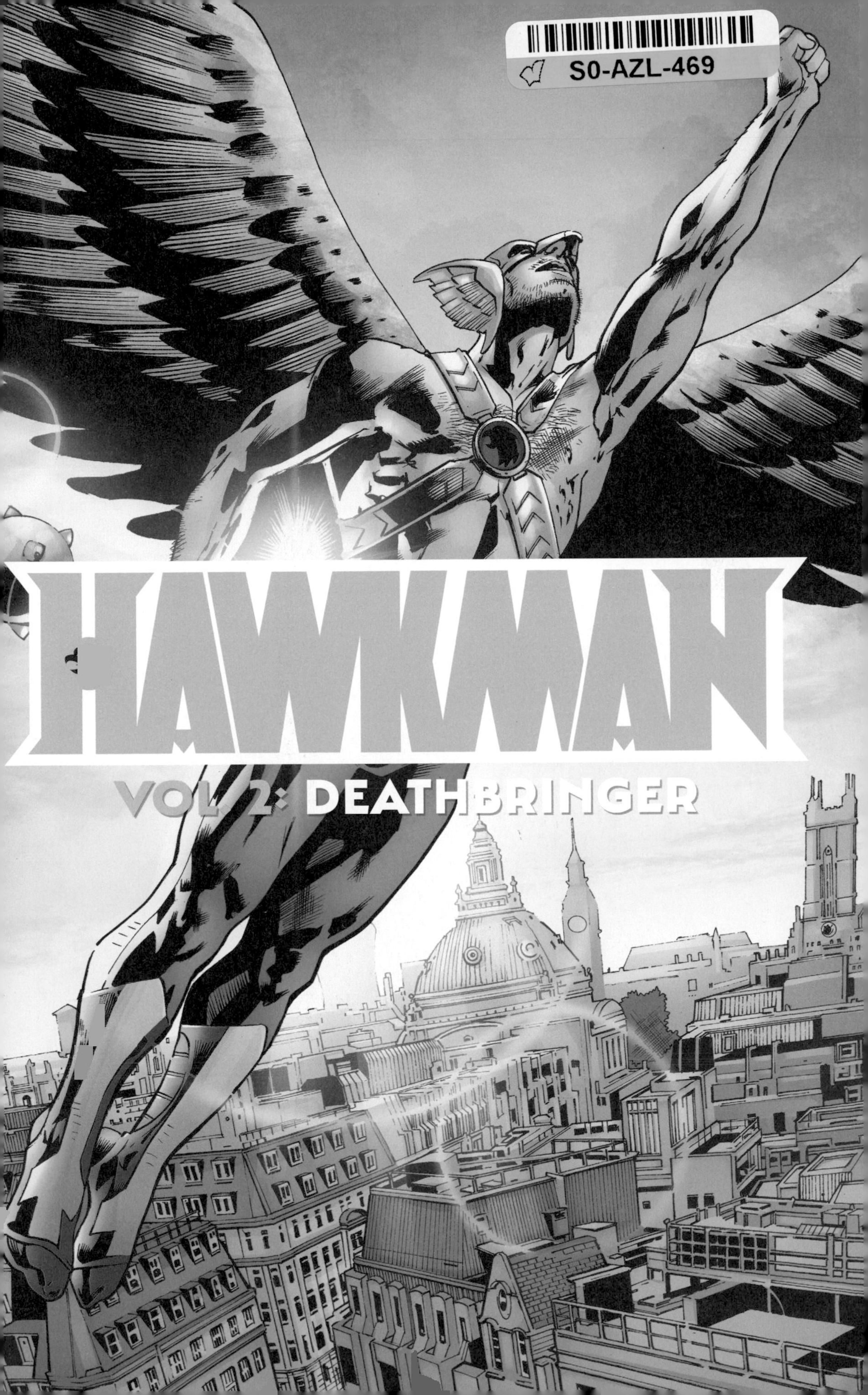
HAWKMAN
VOL. 2: DEATHBRINGER

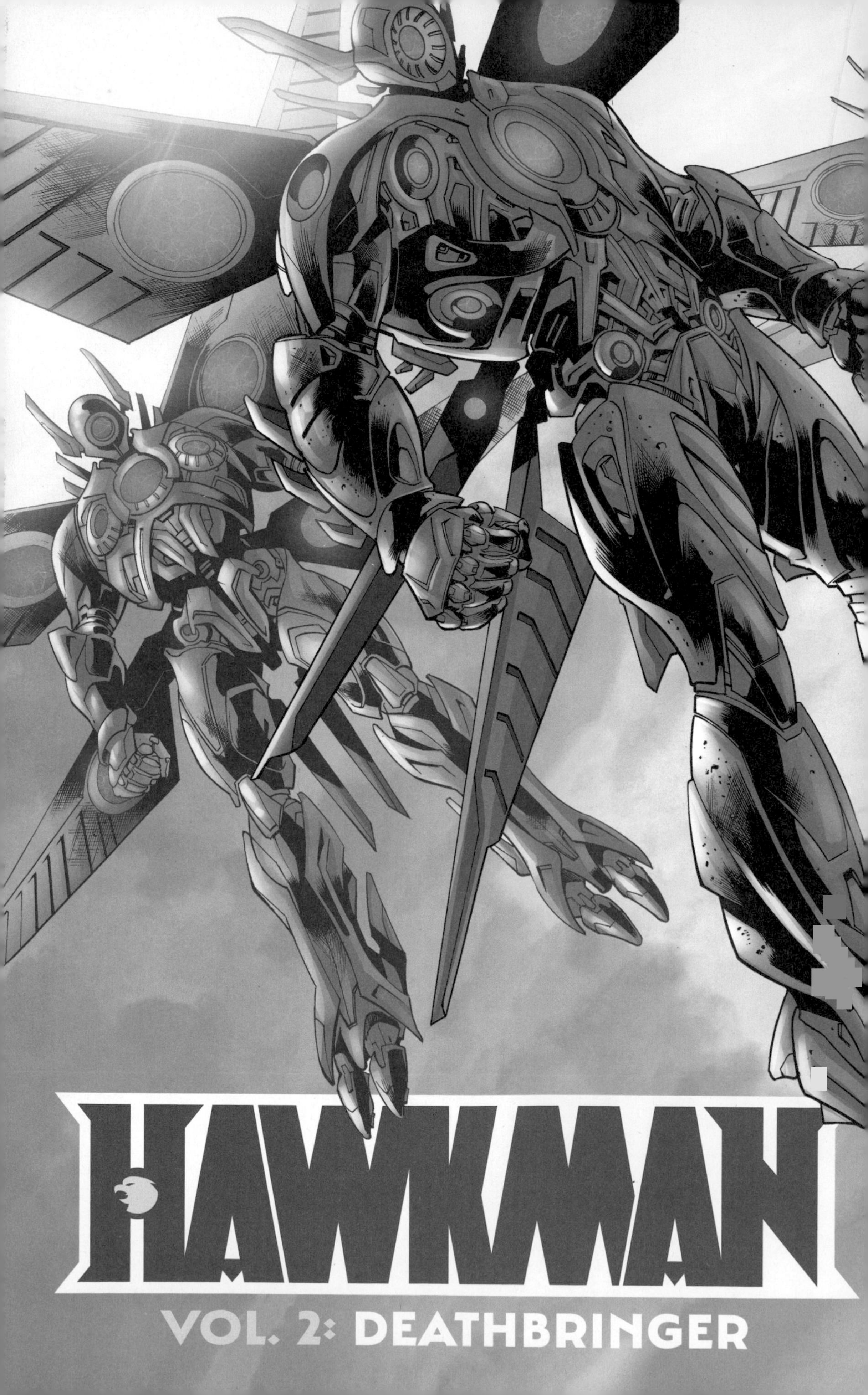

HAWKMAN

VOL. 2: DEATHBRINGER

ROBERT VENDITTI
writer

BRYAN HITCH
penciller

BRYAN HITCH | **ANDREW CURRIE**
ANDY OWENS | **NORM RAPMUND** | **SCOTT HANNA**
inkers

JEREMIAH SKIPPER
colorist

RICHARD STARKINGS & **COMICRAFT**
letterers

BRYAN HITCH & **ALEX SINCLAIR**
collection cover artists

HAWKMAN created by **GARDNER FOX**

MARIE JAVINS

ANDREW MARINO   Editors – Original Series

JEB WOODARD   Group Editor – Collected Editions

SCOTT NYBAKKEN   Editor – Collected Edition

STEVE COOK   Design Director – Books

MEGEN BELLERSEN   Publication Design

DANIELLE DIGRADO   Publication Production

BOB HARRAS   Senior VP – Editor-in-Chief, DC Comics

PAT McCALLUM   Executive Editor, DC Comics

DAN DiDIO   Publisher

JIM LEE   Publisher & Chief Creative Officer

BOBBIE CHASE   VP – New Publishing Initiatives & Talent Development

DON FALLETTI   VP – Manufacturing Operations & Workflow Management

LAWRENCE GANEM   VP – Talent Services

ALISON GILL   Senior VP – Manufacturing & Operations

HANK KANALZ   Senior VP – Publishing Strategy & Support Services

DAN MIRON   VP – Publishing Operations

NICK J. NAPOLITANO   VP – Manufacturing Administration & Design

NANCY SPEARS   VP – Sales

MICHELE R. WELLS   VP & Executive Editor, Young Reader

HAWKMAN VOL. 2: DEATHBRINGER

DC Comics, 2900 West Alameda Ave., Burbank, CA 91505
Printed by LSC Communications, Owensville, MO, USA. 11/1/19. First Printing.
ISBN: 978-1-4012-9558-5

Library of Congress Cataloging-in-Publication Data is available.

PEFC Certified

This product is from sustainably managed forests and controlled sources

PEFC/29-31-337   www.pefc.org

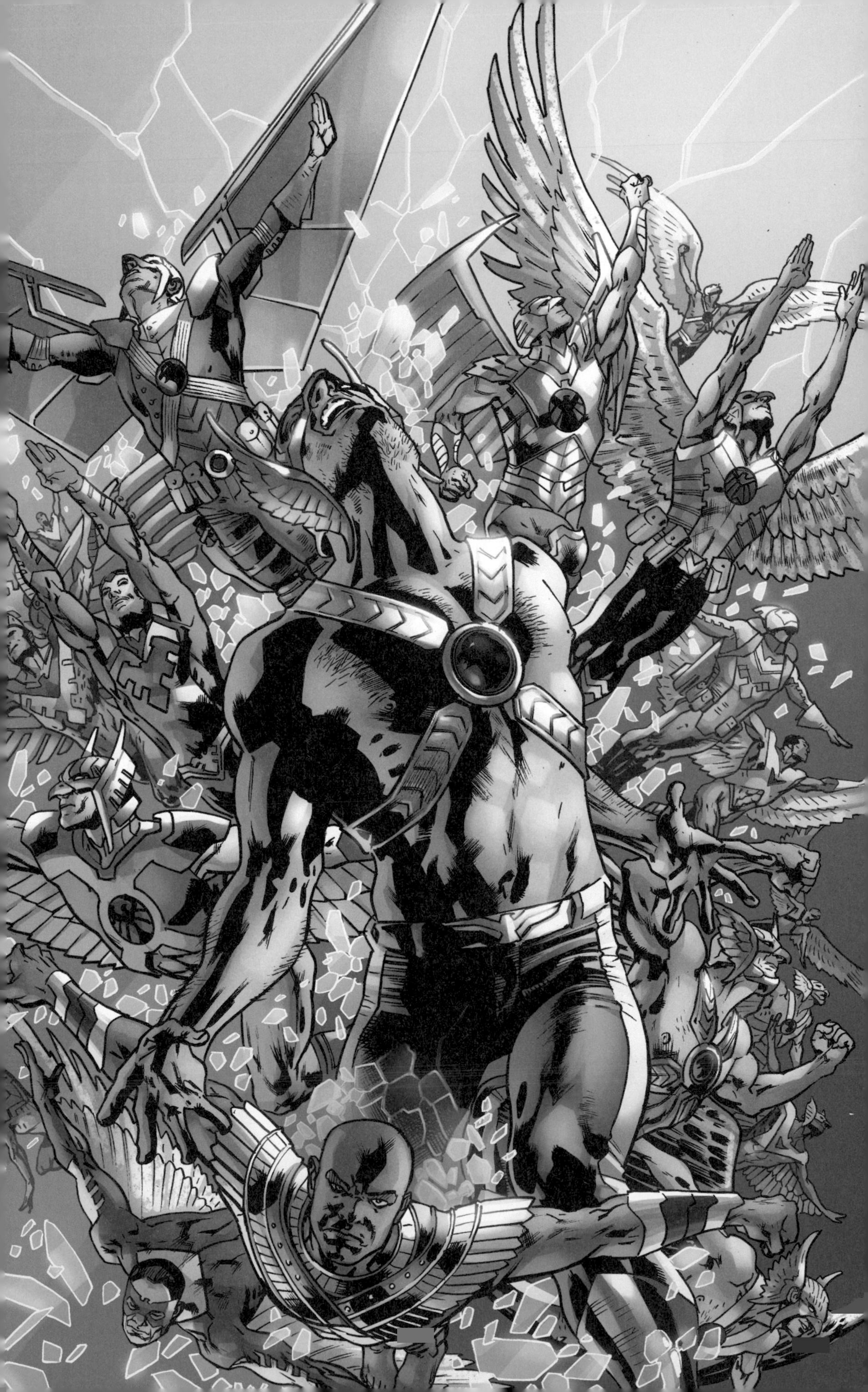

[redacted] [redacted]

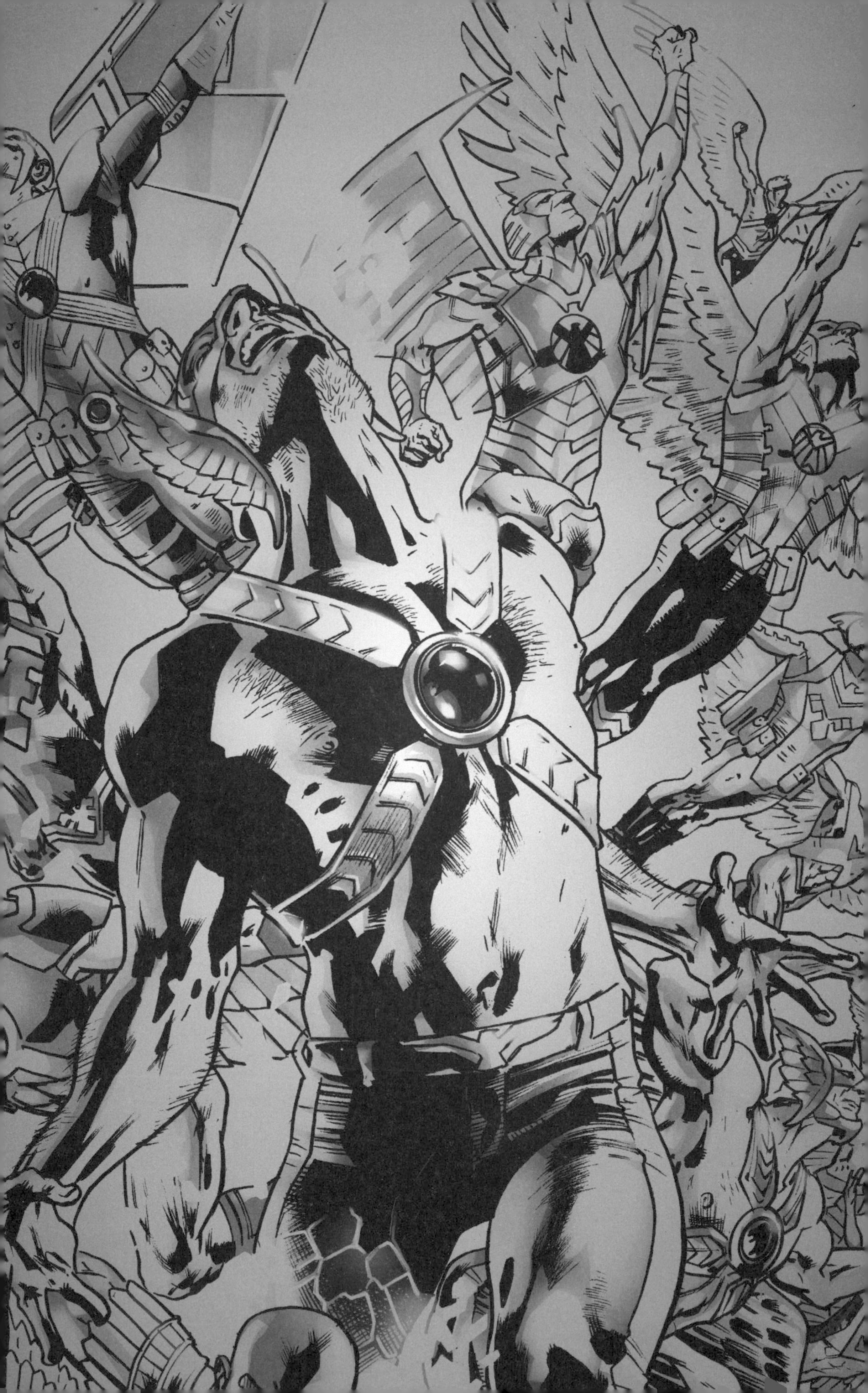

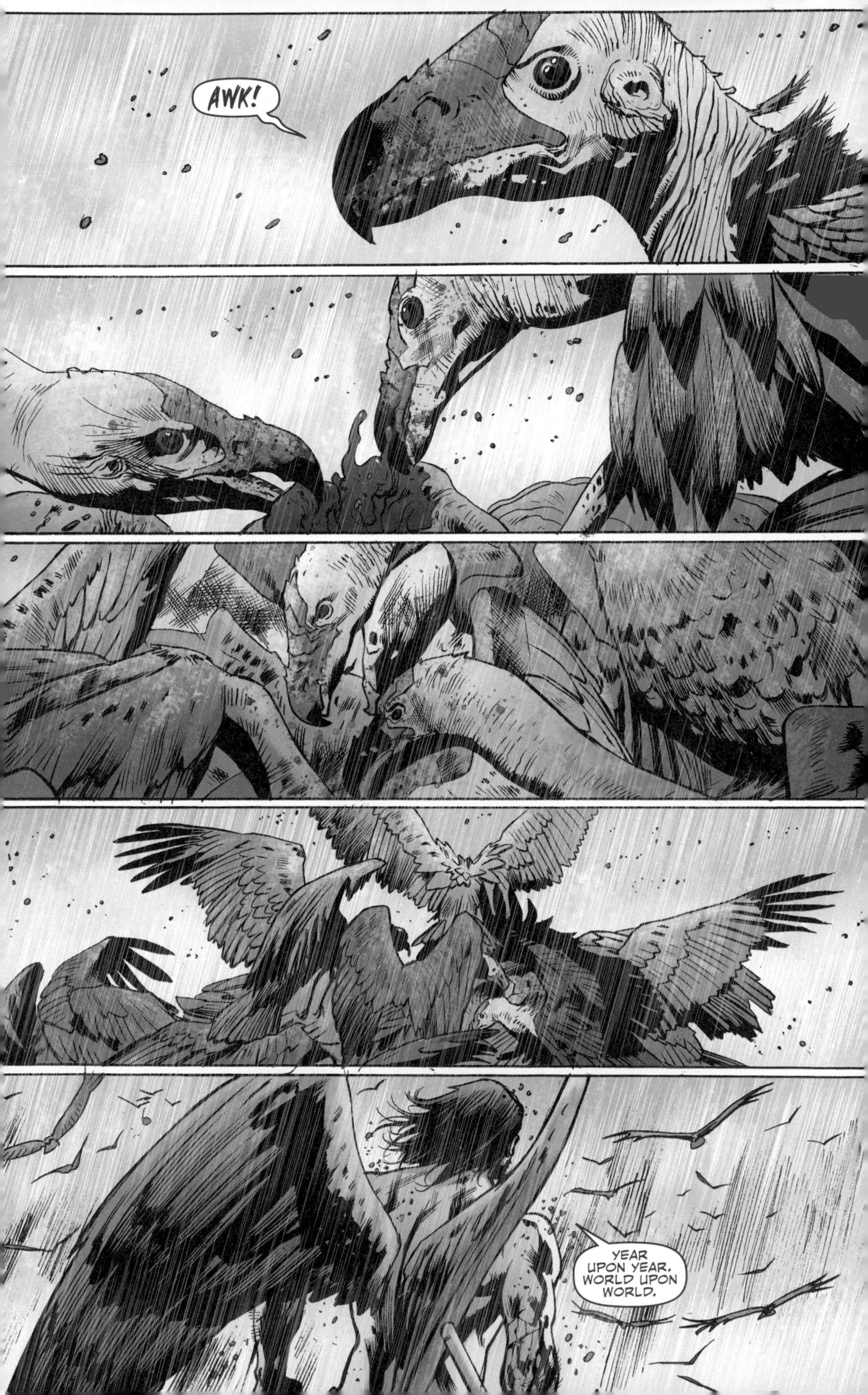
AWK!
YEAR UPON YEAR. WORLD UPON WORLD.

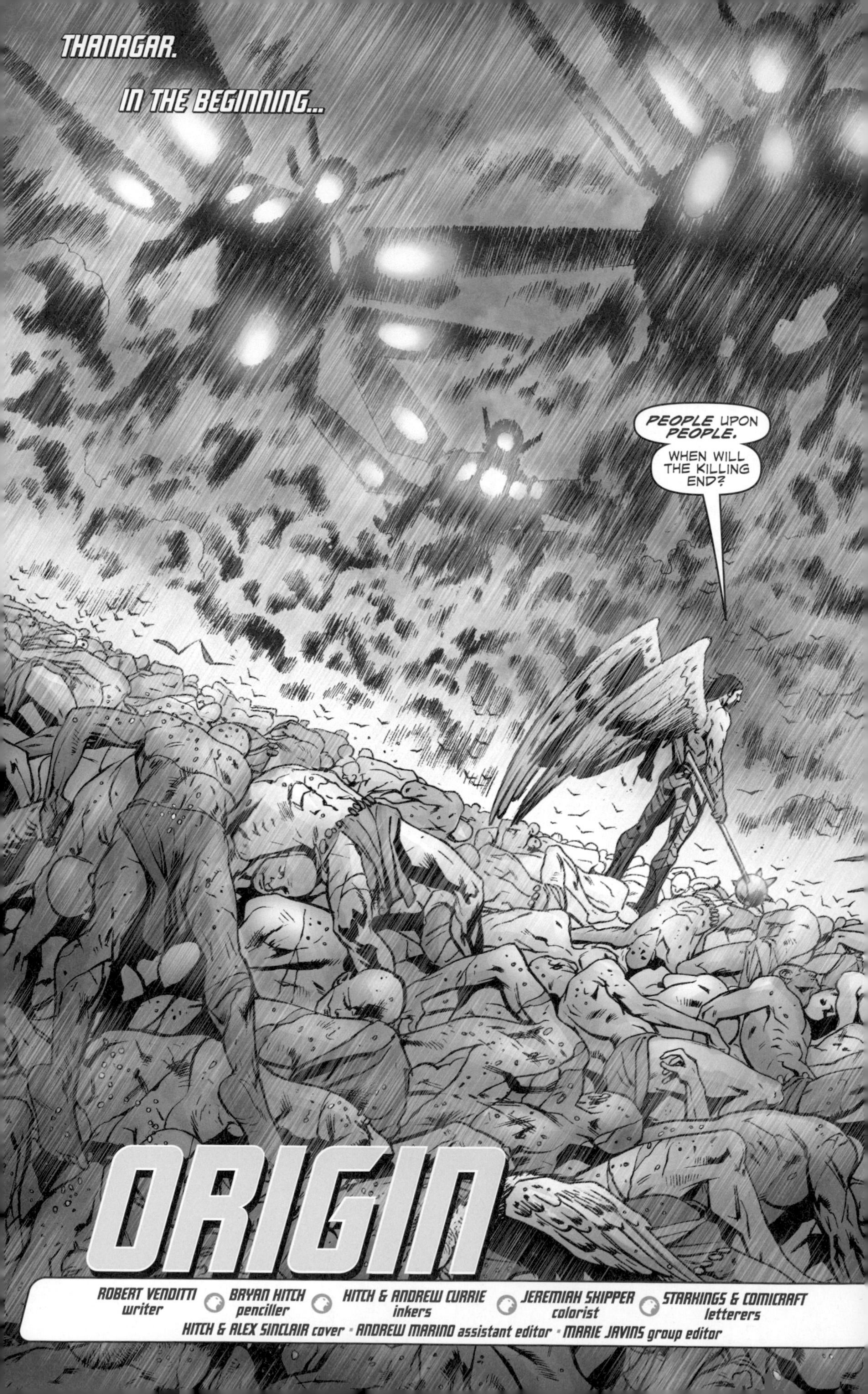

THANAGAR.
IN THE BEGINNING...
PEOPLE UPON PEOPLE.
WHEN WILL THE KILLING END?
ORIGIN
ROBERT VENDITTI writer
BRYAN HITCH penciller
HITCH & ANDREW CURRIE inkers
JEREMIAH SKIPPER colorist
STARKINGS & COMICRAFT letterers
HITCH & ALEX SINCLAIR cover • ANDREW MARINO assistant editor • MARIE JAVINS group editor

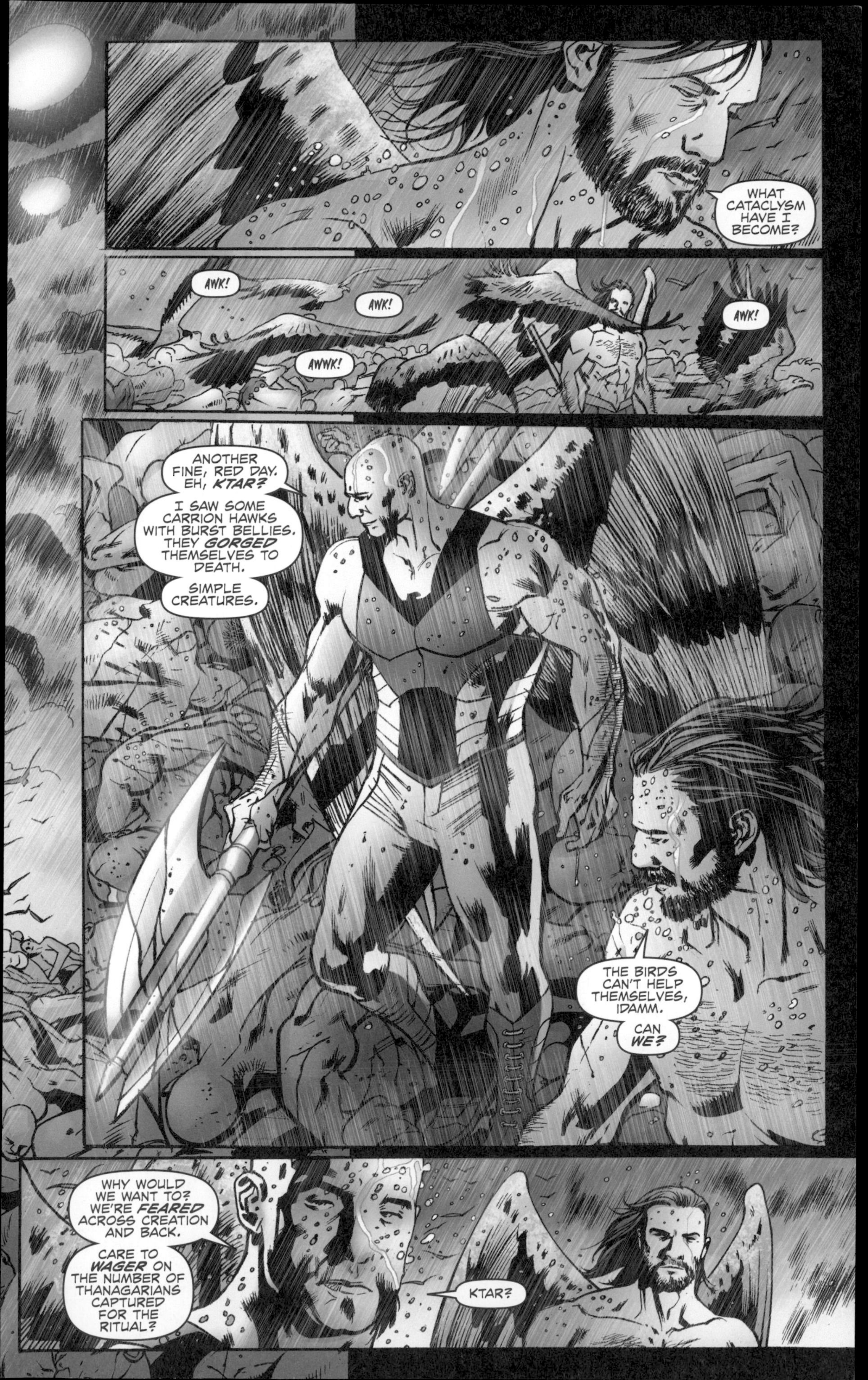
WHAT CATACLYSM HAVE I BECOME?
AWK!
AWK!
AWK!
AWWK!
ANOTHER FINE, RED DAY. EH, KTAR?
I SAW SOME CARRION HAWKS WITH BURST BELLIES. THEY GORGED THEMSELVES TO DEATH.
SIMPLE CREATURES.
THE BIRDS CAN'T HELP THEMSELVES, IDAMM.
CAN WE?
WHY WOULD WE WANT TO? WE'RE FEARED ACROSS CREATION AND BACK.
CARE TO WAGER ON THE NUMBER OF THANAGARIANS CAPTURED FOR THE RITUAL?
KTAR?

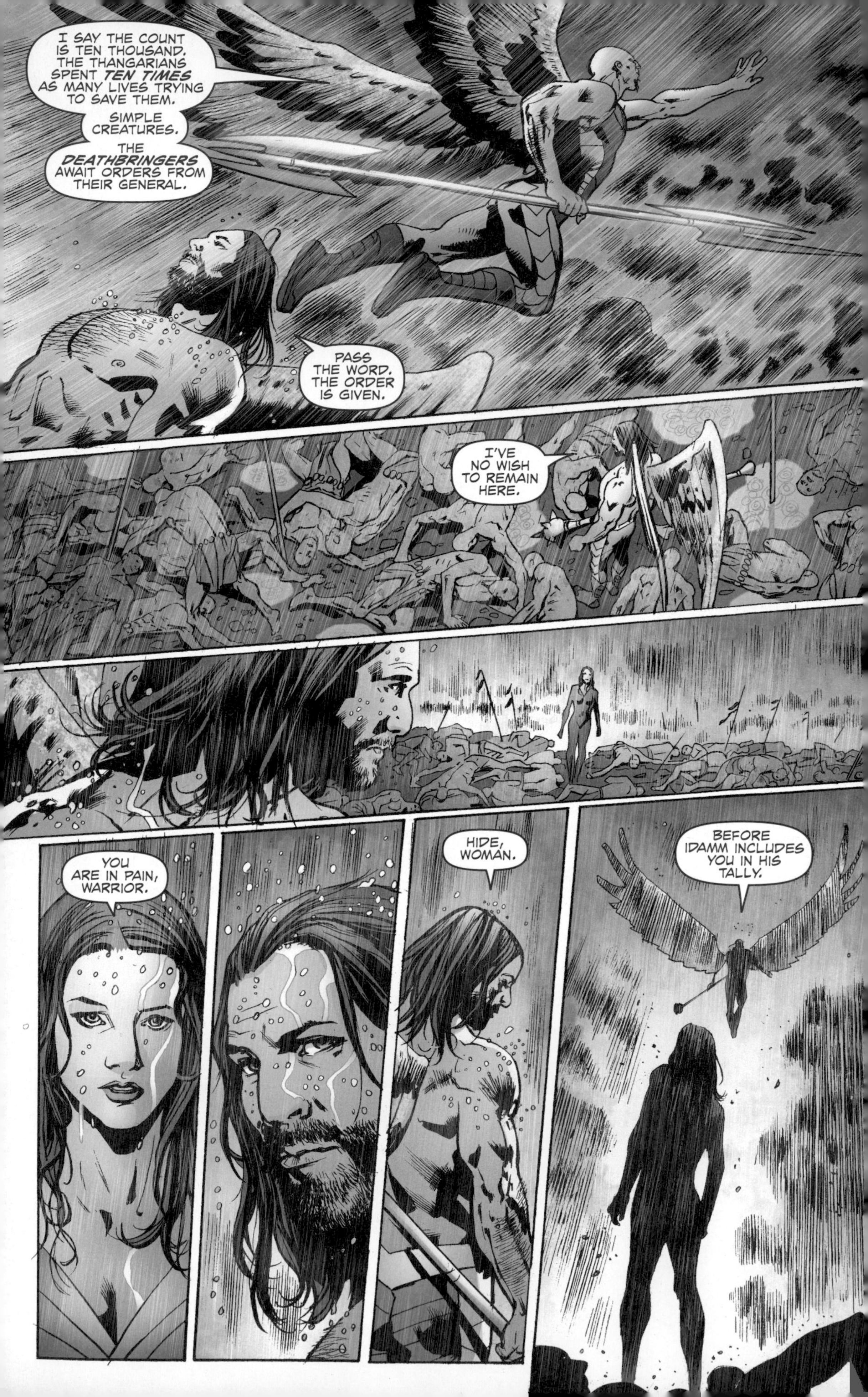
I SAY THE COUNT IS TEN THOUSAND. THE THANGARIANS SPENT *TEN TIMES* AS MANY LIVES TRYING TO SAVE THEM.
SIMPLE CREATURES.
THE *DEATHBRINGERS* AWAIT ORDERS FROM THEIR GENERAL.
PASS THE WORD. THE ORDER IS GIVEN.
I'VE NO WISH TO REMAIN HERE.
YOU ARE IN PAIN, WARRIOR.
HIDE, WOMAN.
BEFORE IDAMM INCLUDES YOU IN HIS TALLY.

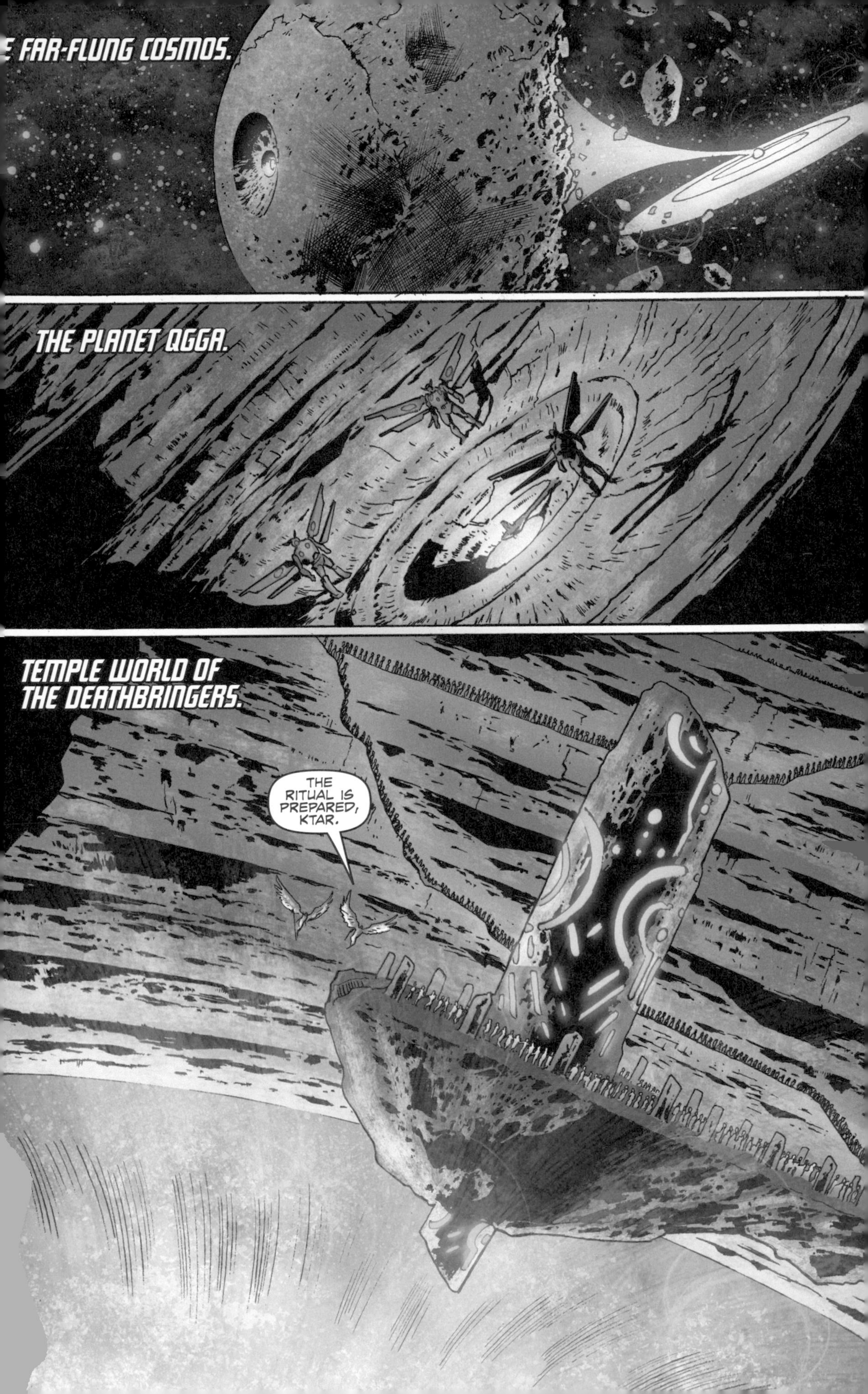
E FAR-FLUNG COSMOS.
THE PLANET QGGA.
TEMPLE WORLD OF THE DEATHBRINGERS.
THE RITUAL IS PREPARED, KTAR.

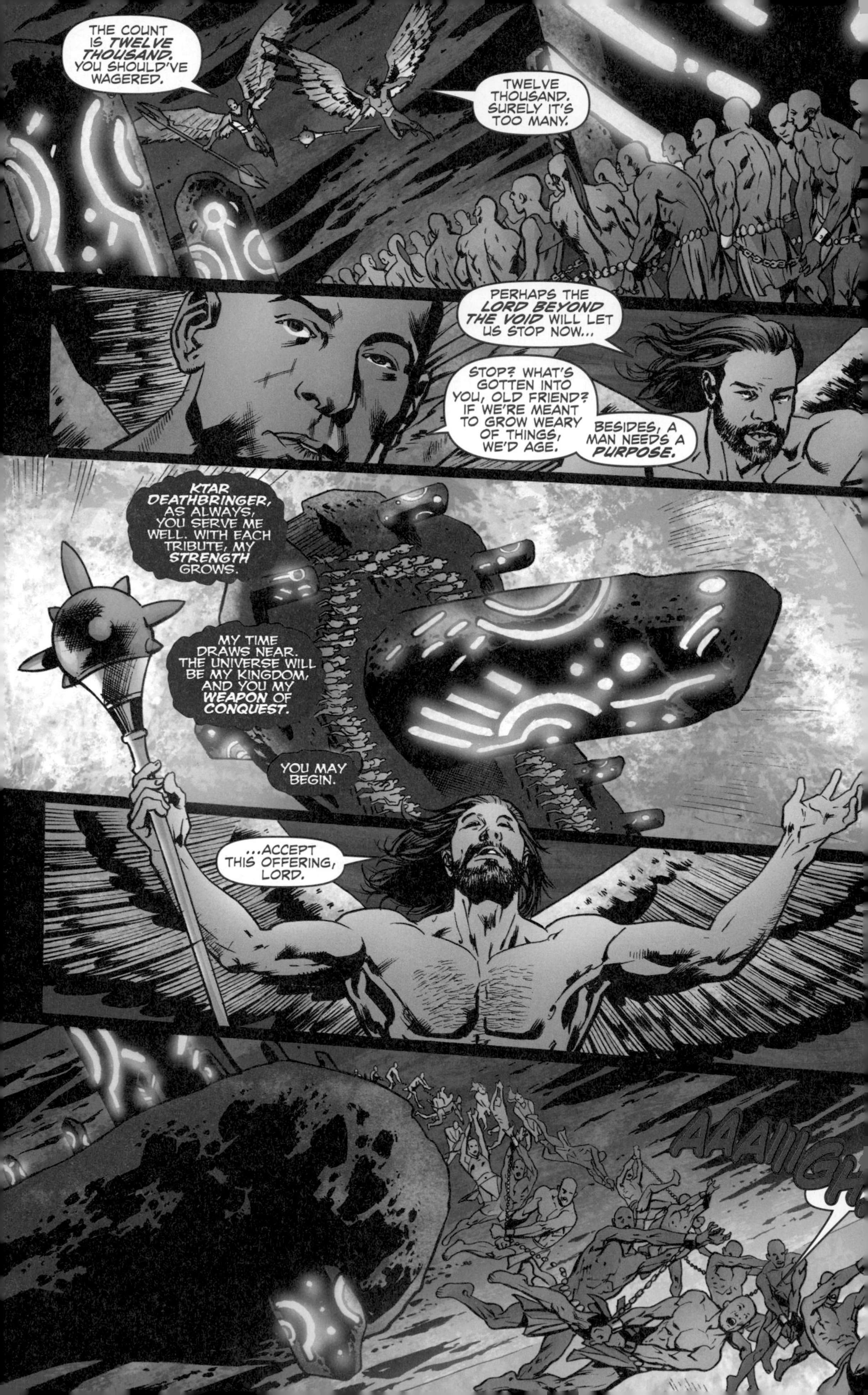
THE COUNT IS TWELVE THOUSAND. YOU SHOULD'VE WAGERED.
TWELVE THOUSAND. SURELY IT'S TOO MANY.
PERHAPS THE LORD BEYOND THE VOID WILL LET US STOP NOW...
STOP? WHAT'S GOTTEN INTO YOU, OLD FRIEND? IF WE'RE MEANT TO GROW WEARY OF THINGS, WE'D AGE.
BESIDES, A MAN NEEDS A PURPOSE.
KTAR DEATHBRINGER, AS ALWAYS, YOU SERVE ME WELL. WITH EACH TRIBUTE, MY STRENGTH GROWS.
MY TIME DRAWS NEAR. THE UNIVERSE WILL BE MY KINGDOM, AND YOU MY WEAPON OF CONQUEST.
YOU MAY BEGIN.
...ACCEPT THIS OFFERING, LORD.
AAAIIGH

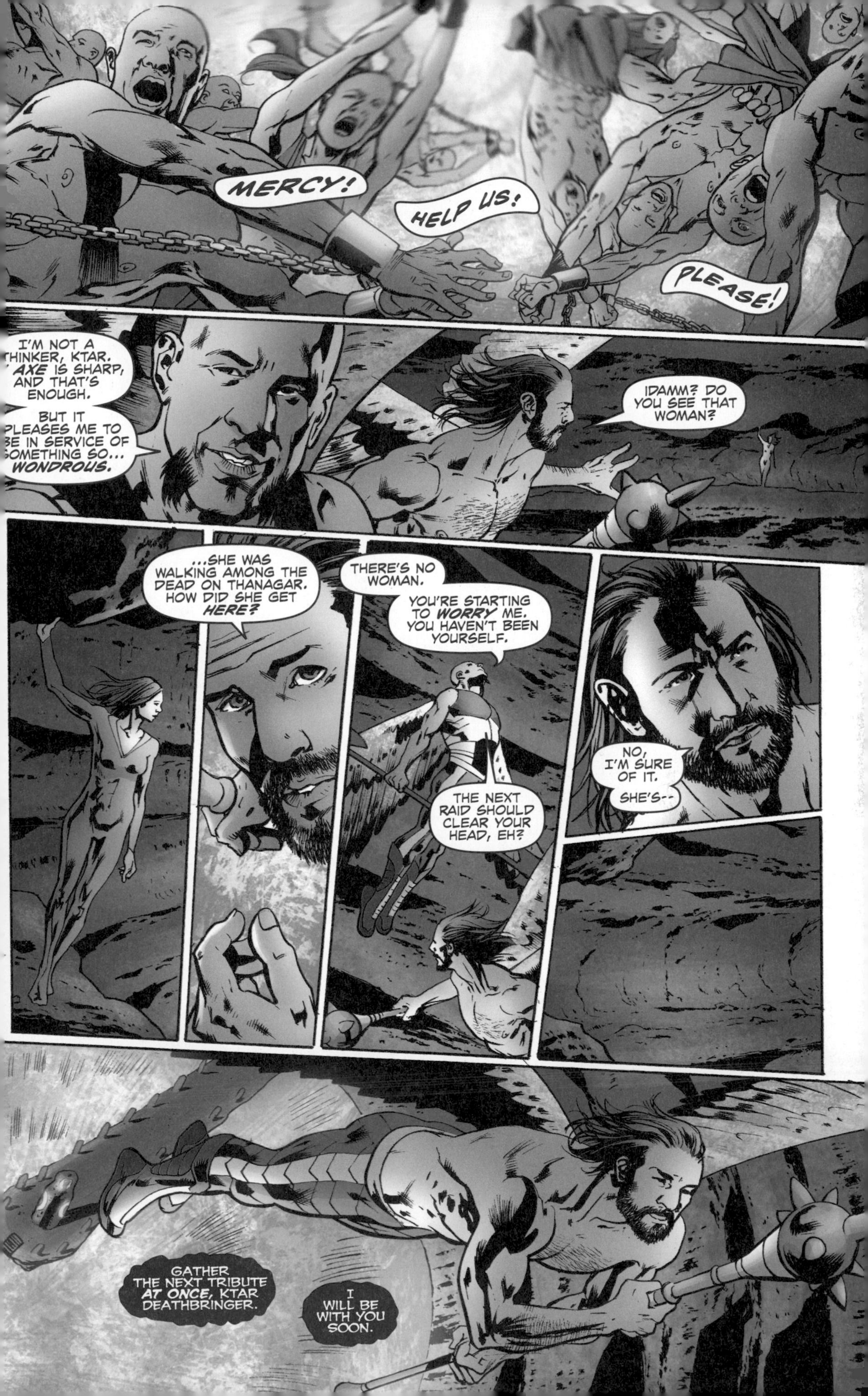
MERCY!
HELP US!
PLEASE!
I'M NOT A THINKER, KTAR. MY AXE IS SHARP, AND THAT'S ENOUGH.
BUT IT PLEASES ME TO BE IN SERVICE OF SOMETHING SO... WONDROUS.
IDAMM? DO YOU SEE THAT WOMAN?
...SHE WAS WALKING AMONG THE DEAD ON THANAGAR. HOW DID SHE GET HERE?
THERE'S NO WOMAN.
YOU'RE STARTING TO WORRY ME. YOU HAVEN'T BEEN YOURSELF.
THE NEXT RAID SHOULD CLEAR YOUR HEAD, EH?
NO, I'M SURE OF IT.
SHE'S--
GATHER THE NEXT TRIBUTE AT ONCE, KTAR DEATHBRINGER.
I WILL BE WITH YOU SOON.

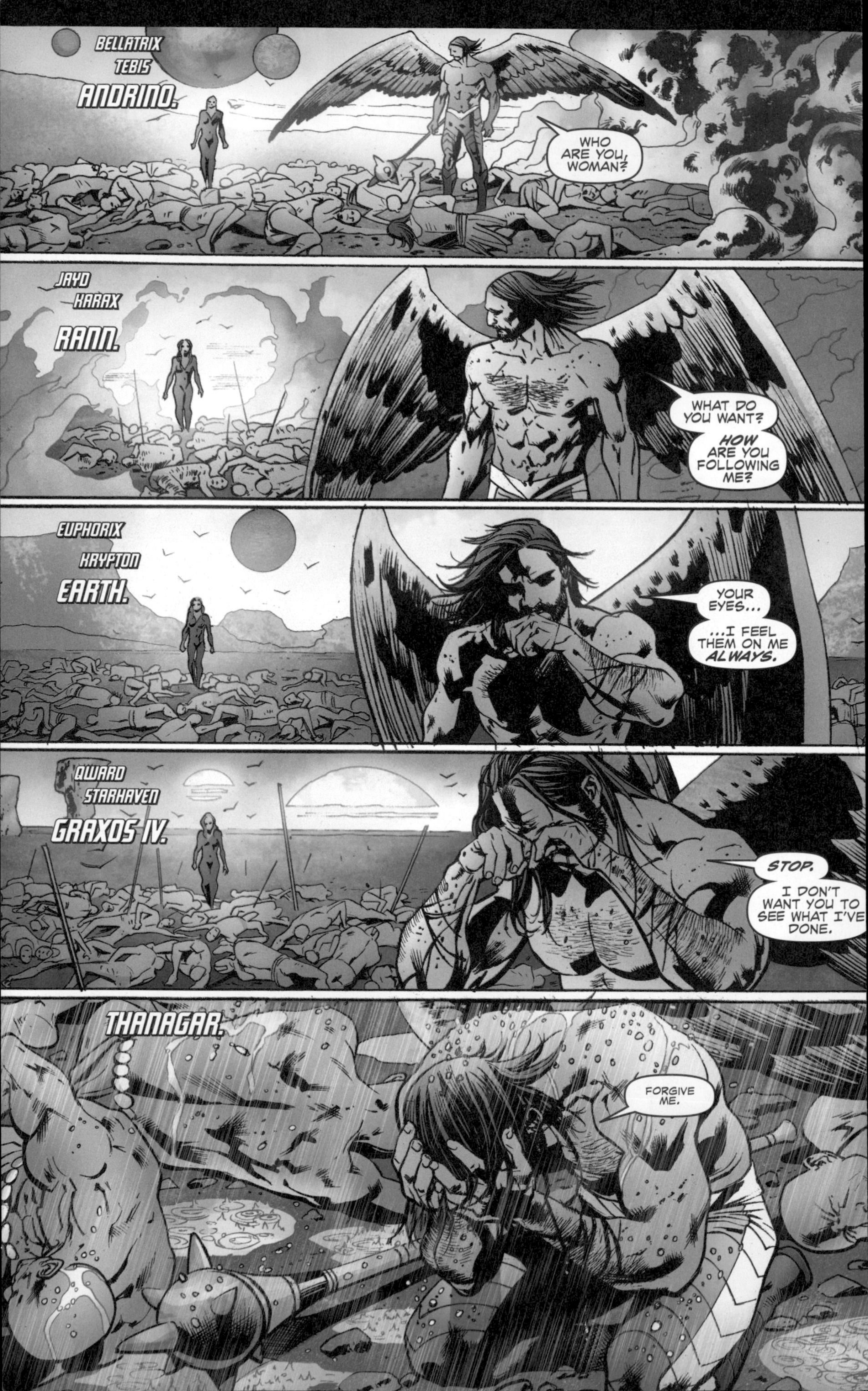
BELLATRIX
TEBIS
ANDRINO.
WHO ARE YOU, WOMAN?
JAYD
KARAX
RANN.
WHAT DO YOU WANT?
HOW ARE YOU FOLLOWING ME?
EUPHORIX
KRYPTON
EARTH.
YOUR EYES...
...I FEEL THEM ON ME ALWAYS.
QWARD
STARHAVEN
GRAXOS IV.
STOP.
I DON'T WANT YOU TO SEE WHAT I'VE DONE.
THANAGAR.
FORGIVE ME.

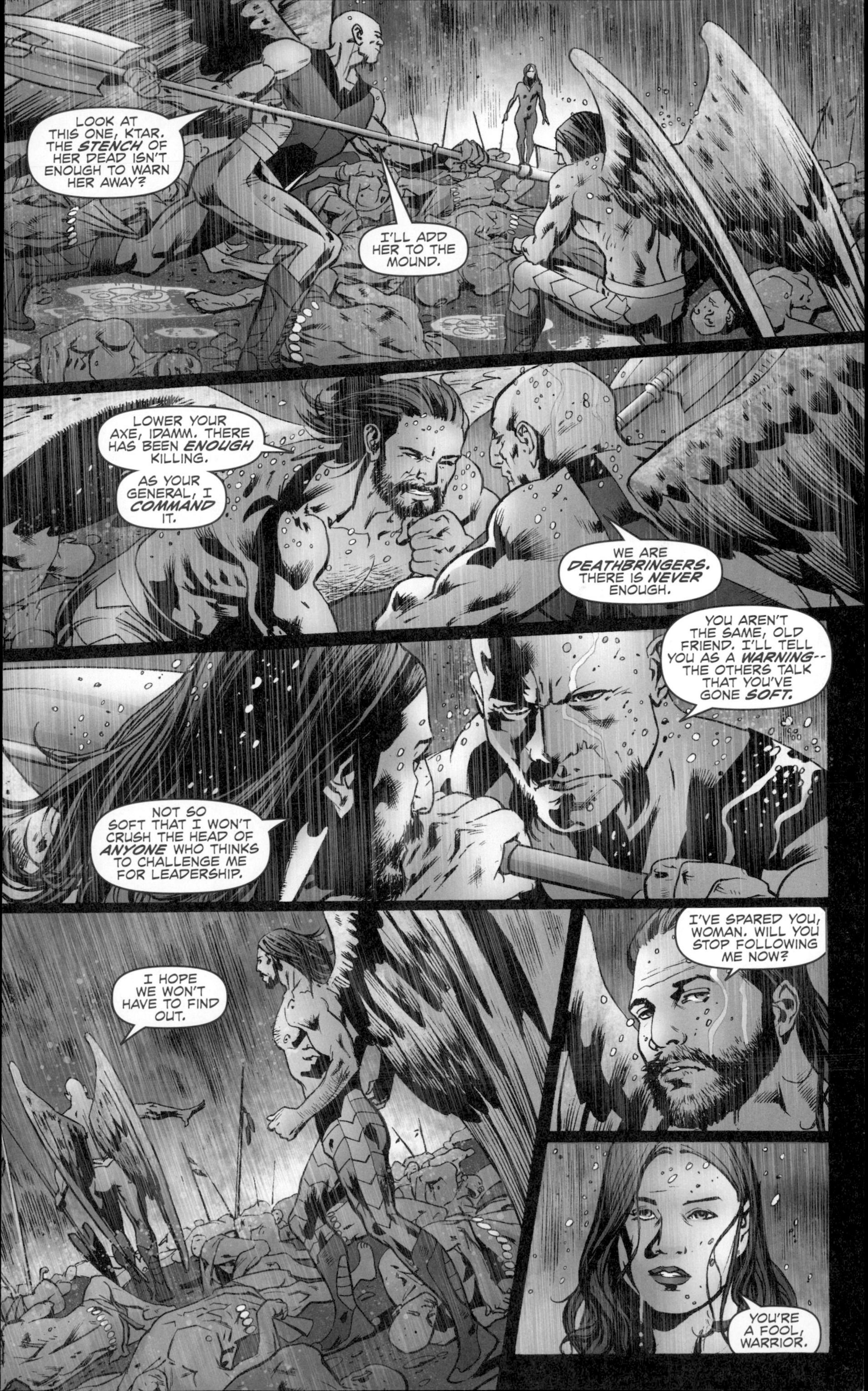
LOOK AT THIS ONE, KTAR. THE STENCH OF HER DEAD ISN'T ENOUGH TO WARN HER AWAY?
I'LL ADD HER TO THE MOUND.
LOWER YOUR AXE, IDAMM. THERE HAS BEEN ENOUGH KILLING.
AS YOUR GENERAL, I COMMAND IT.
WE ARE DEATHBRINGERS. THERE IS NEVER ENOUGH.
YOU AREN'T THE SAME, OLD FRIEND. I'LL TELL YOU AS A WARNING-- THE OTHERS TALK THAT YOU'VE GONE SOFT.
NOT SO SOFT THAT I WON'T CRUSH THE HEAD OF ANYONE WHO THINKS TO CHALLENGE ME FOR LEADERSHIP.
I HOPE WE WON'T HAVE TO FIND OUT.
I'VE SPARED YOU, WOMAN. WILL YOU STOP FOLLOWING ME NOW?
YOU'RE A FOOL, WARRIOR.

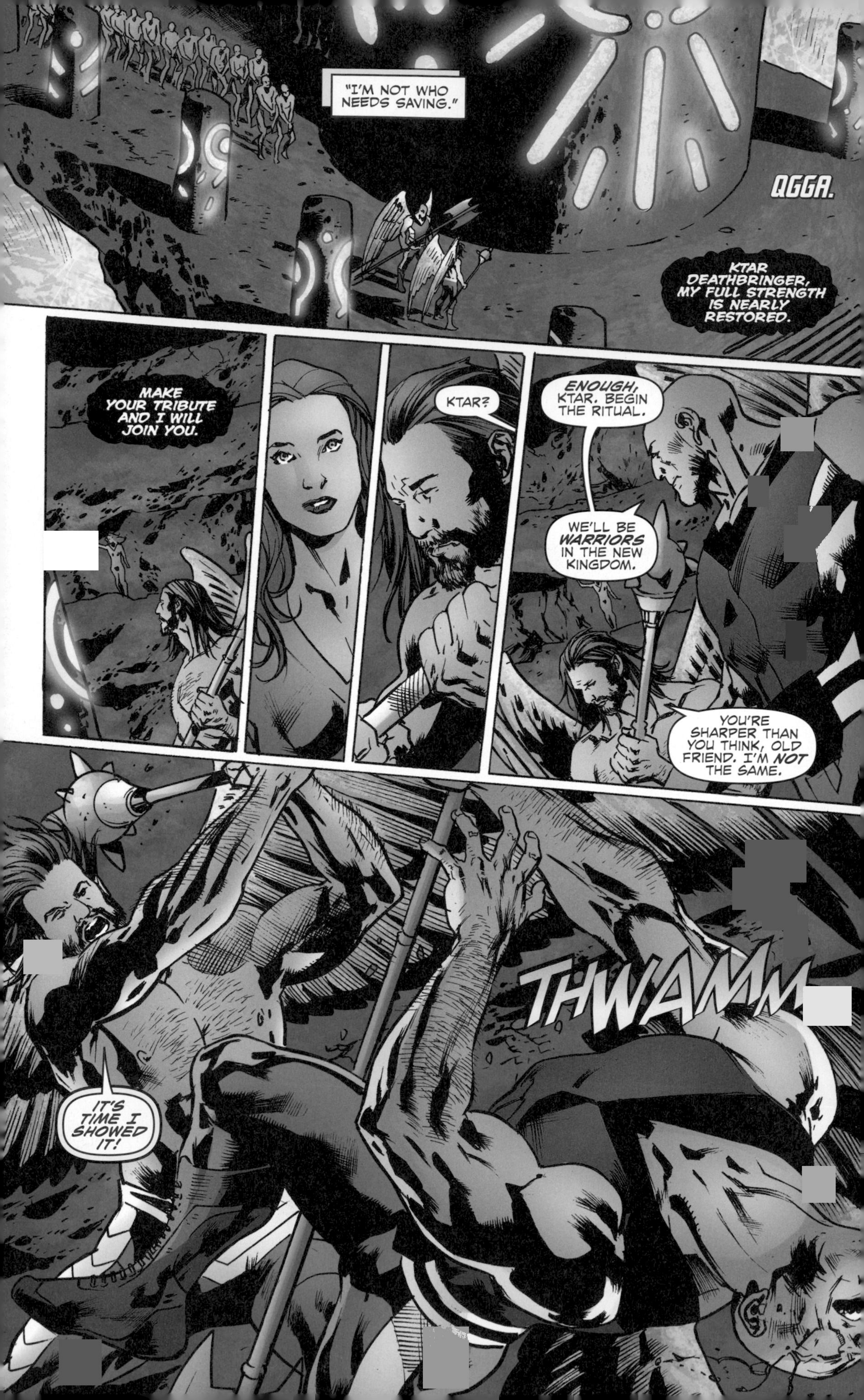
"I'M NOT WHO NEEDS SAVING."
QGGA.
KTAR DEATHBRINGER, MY FULL STRENGTH IS NEARLY RESTORED.
MAKE YOUR TRIBUTE AND I WILL JOIN YOU.
KTAR?
ENOUGH, KTAR. BEGIN THE RITUAL.
WE'LL BE *WARRIORS* IN THE NEW KINGDOM.
YOU'RE SHARPER THAN YOU THINK, OLD FRIEND. I'M *NOT* THE SAME.
THWAMM
IT'S TIME I SHOWED IT!

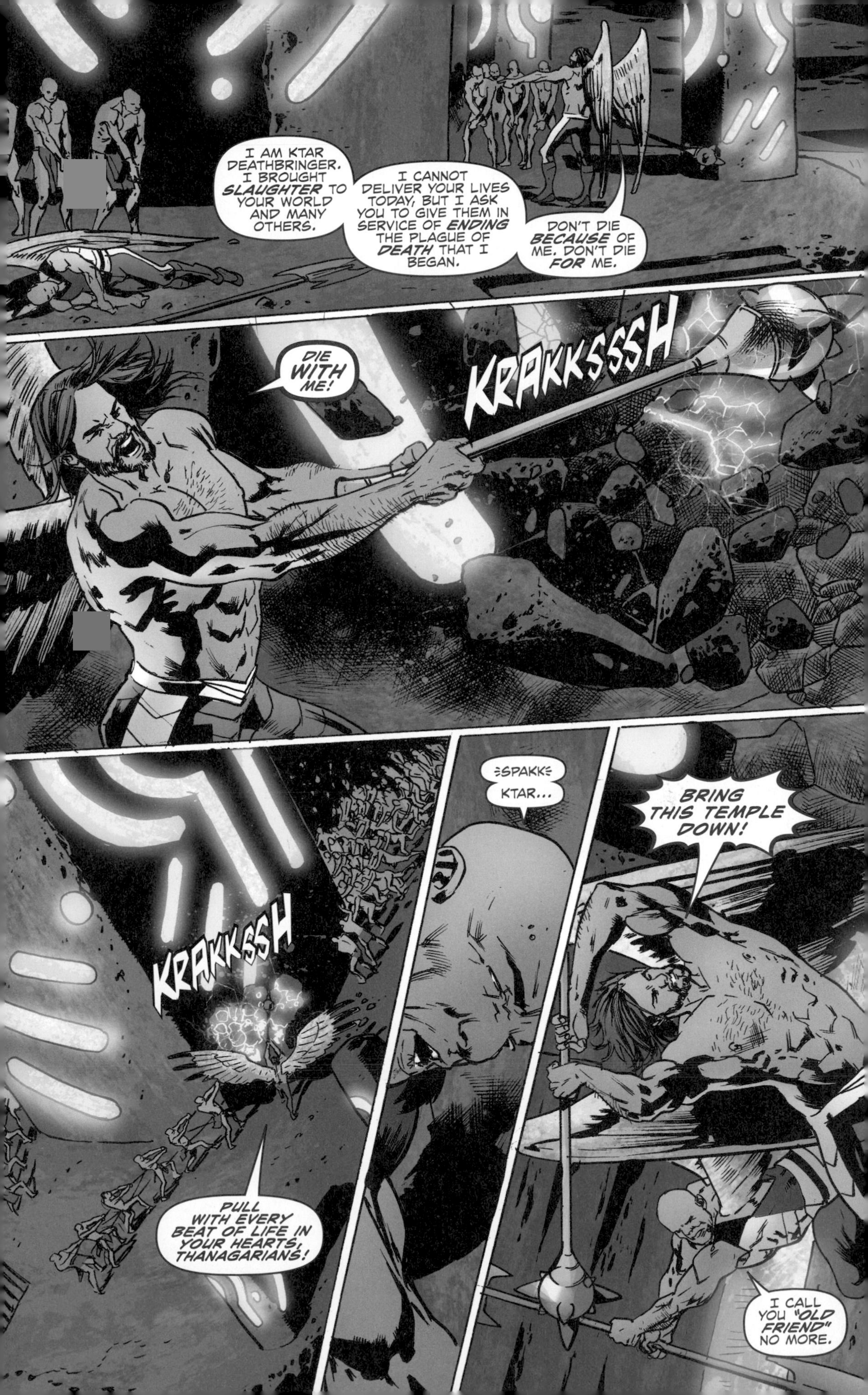
I AM KTAR DEATHBRINGER. I BROUGHT SLAUGHTER TO YOUR WORLD AND MANY OTHERS.
I CANNOT DELIVER YOUR LIVES TODAY, BUT I ASK YOU TO GIVE THEM IN SERVICE OF ENDING THE PLAGUE OF DEATH THAT I BEGAN.
DON'T DIE BECAUSE OF ME. DON'T DIE FOR ME.
DIE WITH ME!
KRAKKSSSH
KRAKKSSH
PULL WITH EVERY BEAT OF LIFE IN YOUR HEARTS, THANAGARIANS!
SPAKK
KTAR...
BRING THIS TEMPLE DOWN!
I CALL YOU "OLD FRIEND" NO MORE.

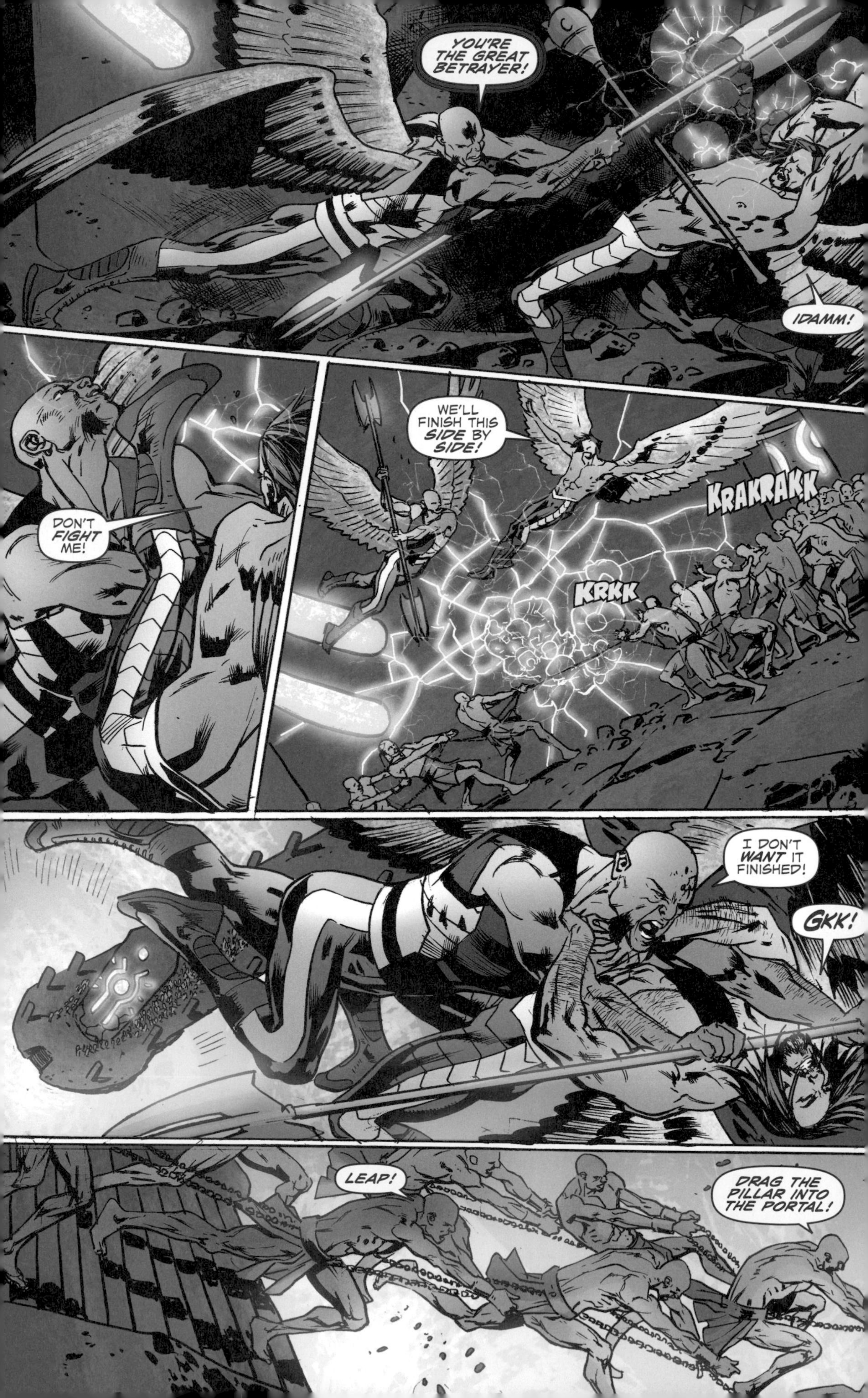
YOU'RE THE GREAT BETRAYER!
IDAMM!
DON'T FIGHT ME!
WE'LL FINISH THIS SIDE BY SIDE!
KRAKRAKK
KRKK
I DON'T WANT IT FINISHED!
GKK!
LEAP!
DRAG THE PILLAR INTO THE PORTAL!

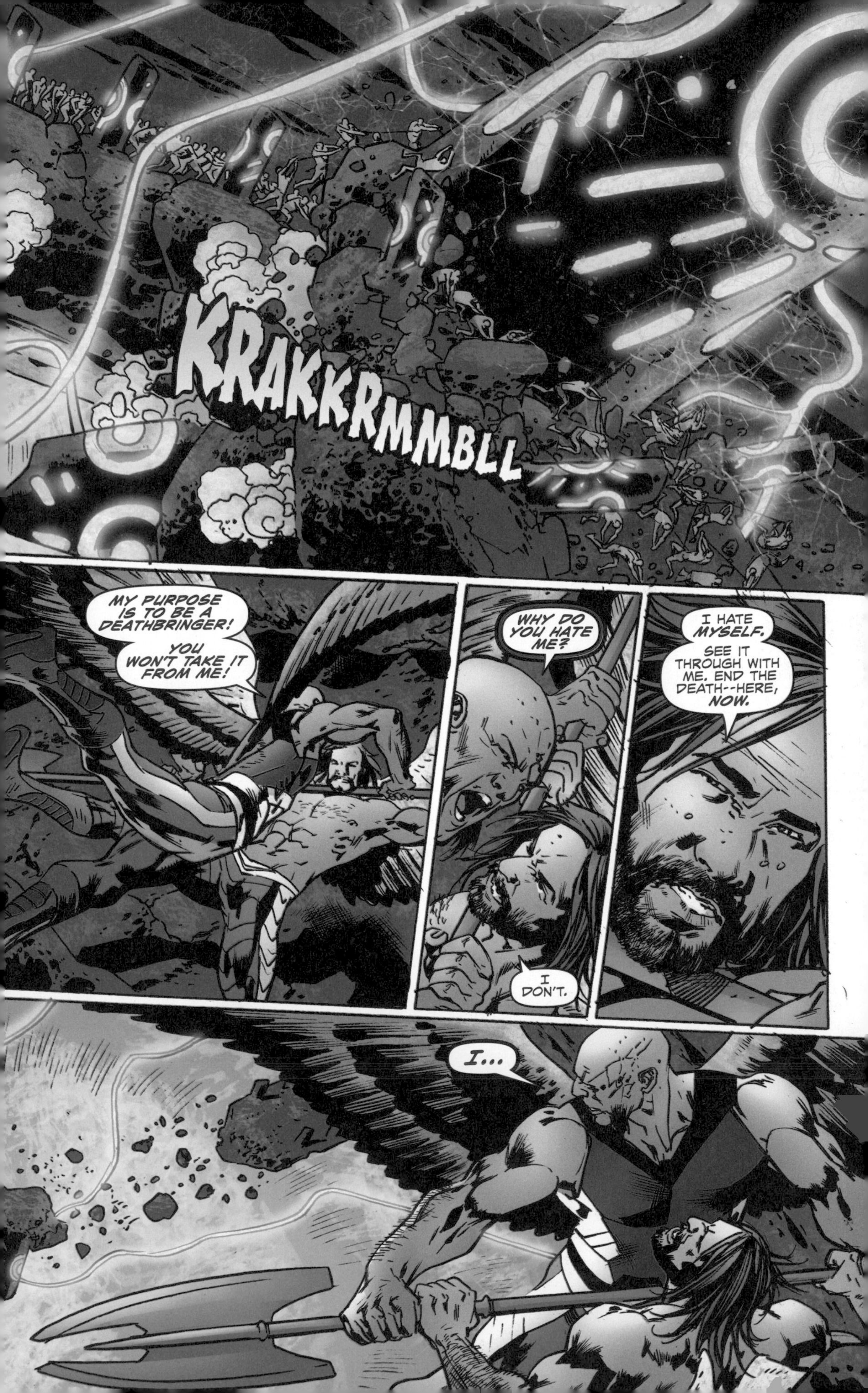
KRAKKRMMBLL
MY PURPOSE IS TO BE A DEATHBRINGER!
YOU WON'T TAKE IT FROM ME!
WHY DO YOU HATE ME?
I DON'T.
I HATE MYSELF.
SEE IT THROUGH WITH ME. END THE DEATH--HERE, NOW.
I...

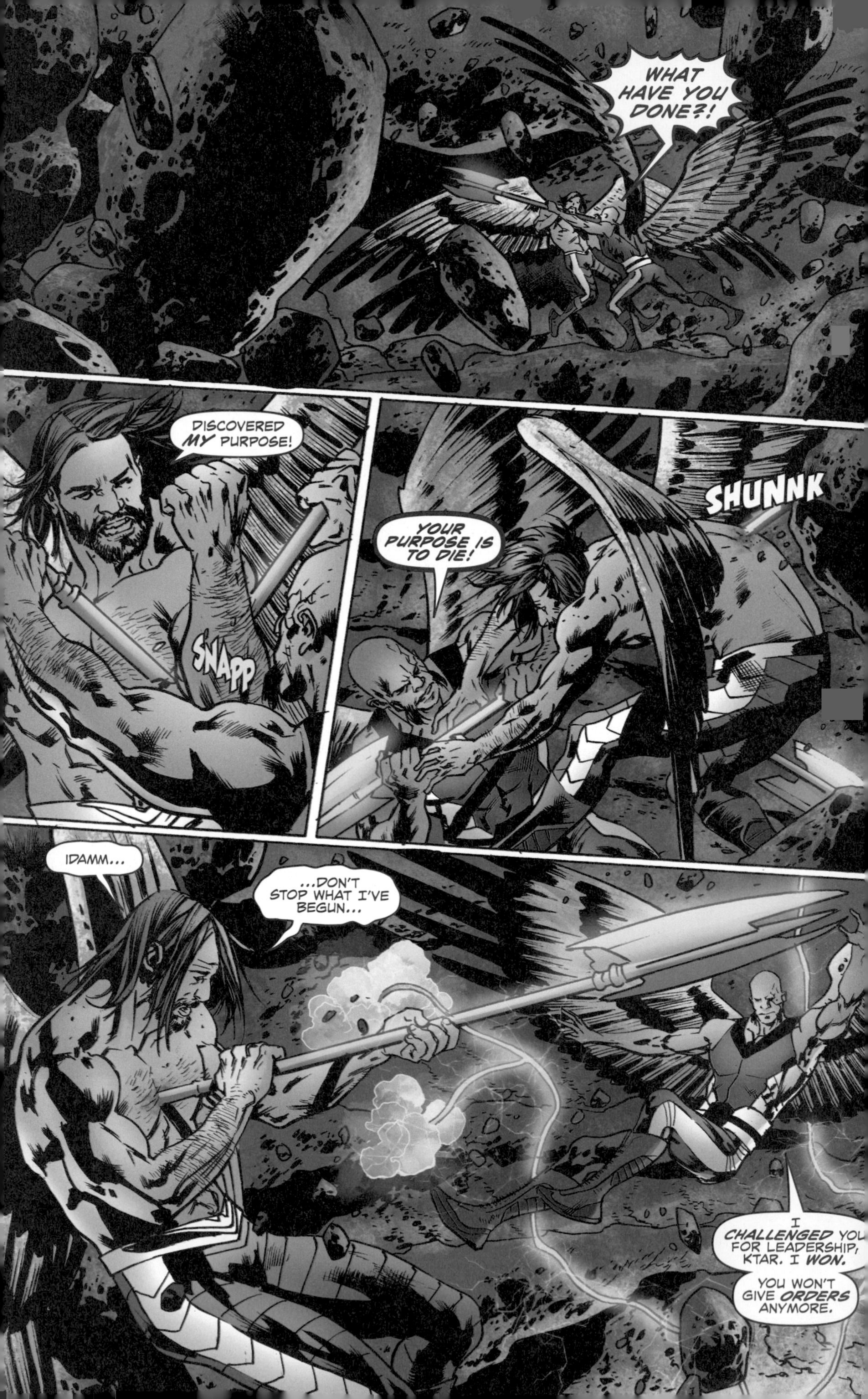
WHAT HAVE YOU DONE?!
DISCOVERED MY PURPOSE!
SNAPP
YOUR PURPOSE IS TO DIE!
SHUNNK
IDAMM...
...DON'T STOP WHAT I'VE BEGUN...
I CHALLENGED YOU FOR LEADERSHIP, KTAR. I WON.
YOU WON'T GIVE ORDERS ANYMORE.

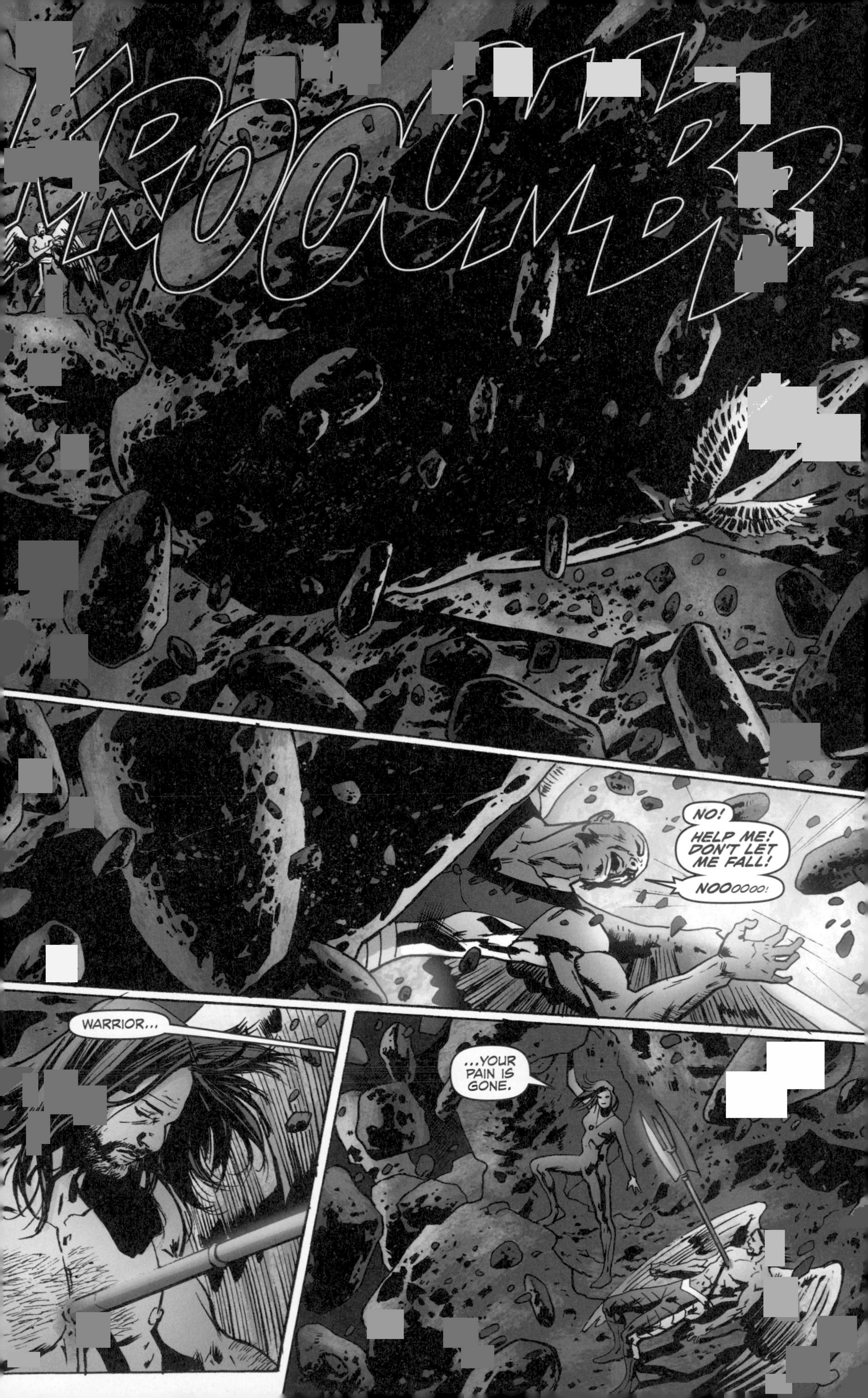
NO!
HELP ME! DON'T LET ME FALL!
NOOOOOO!
WARRIOR...
...YOUR PAIN IS GONE.

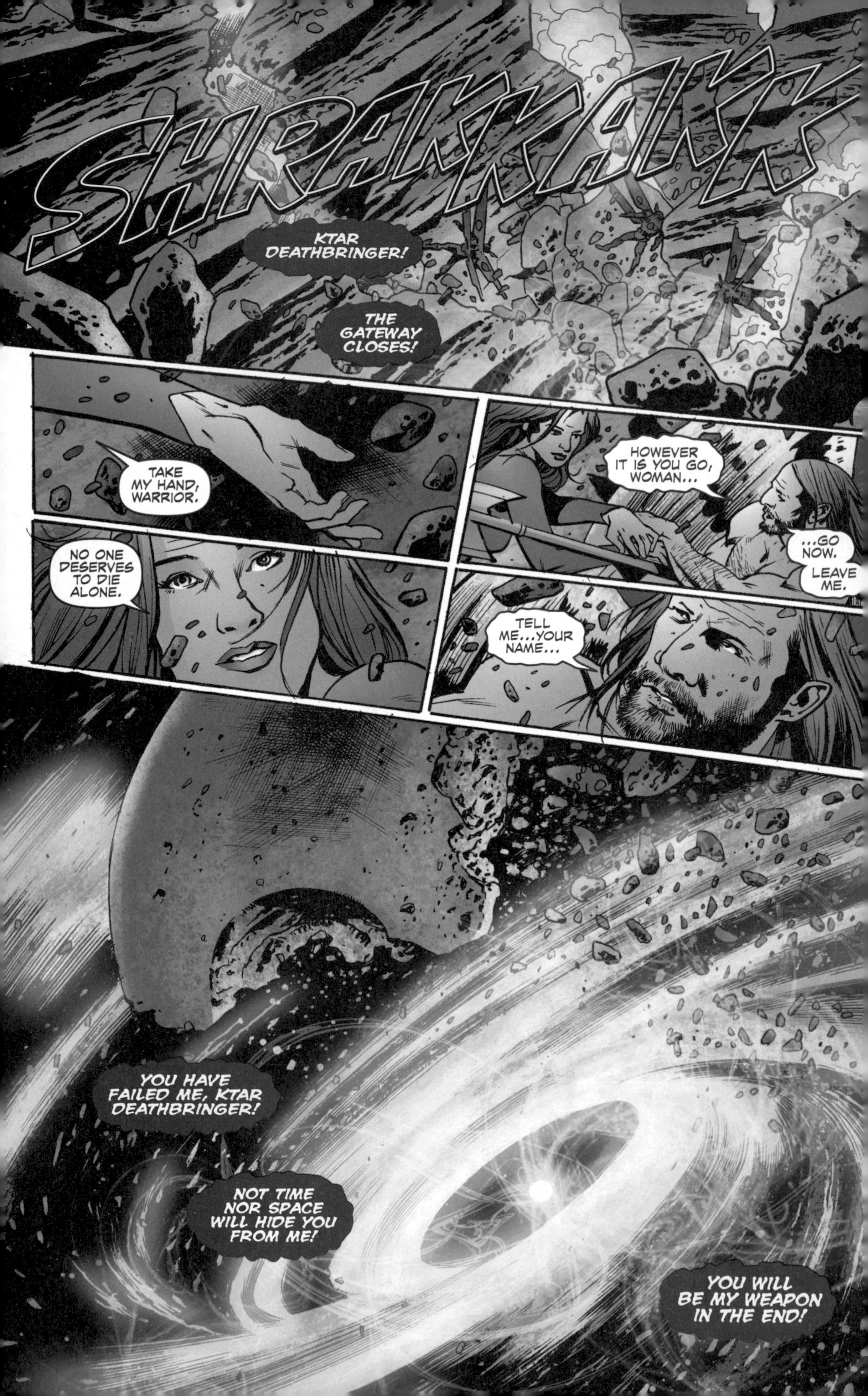
SHRAKRAKS
KTAR DEATHBRINGER!
THE GATEWAY CLOSES!
TAKE MY HAND, WARRIOR.
HOWEVER IT IS YOU GO, WOMAN...
...GO NOW.
LEAVE ME.
NO ONE DESERVES TO DIE ALONE.
TELL ME...YOUR NAME...
YOU HAVE FAILED ME, KTAR DEATHBRINGER!
NOT TIME NOR SPACE WILL HIDE YOU FROM ME!
YOU WILL BE MY WEAPON IN THE END!

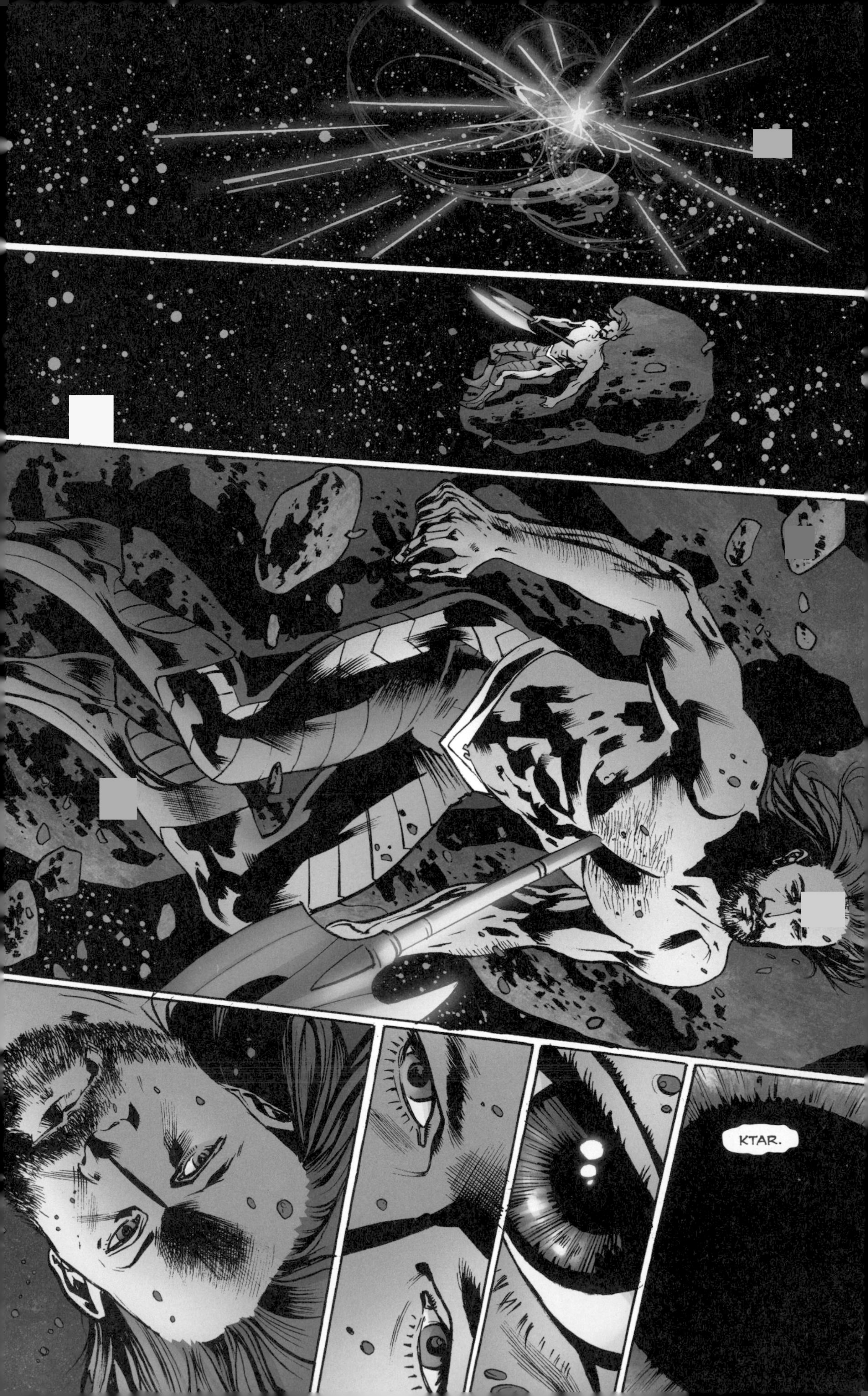
KTAR.

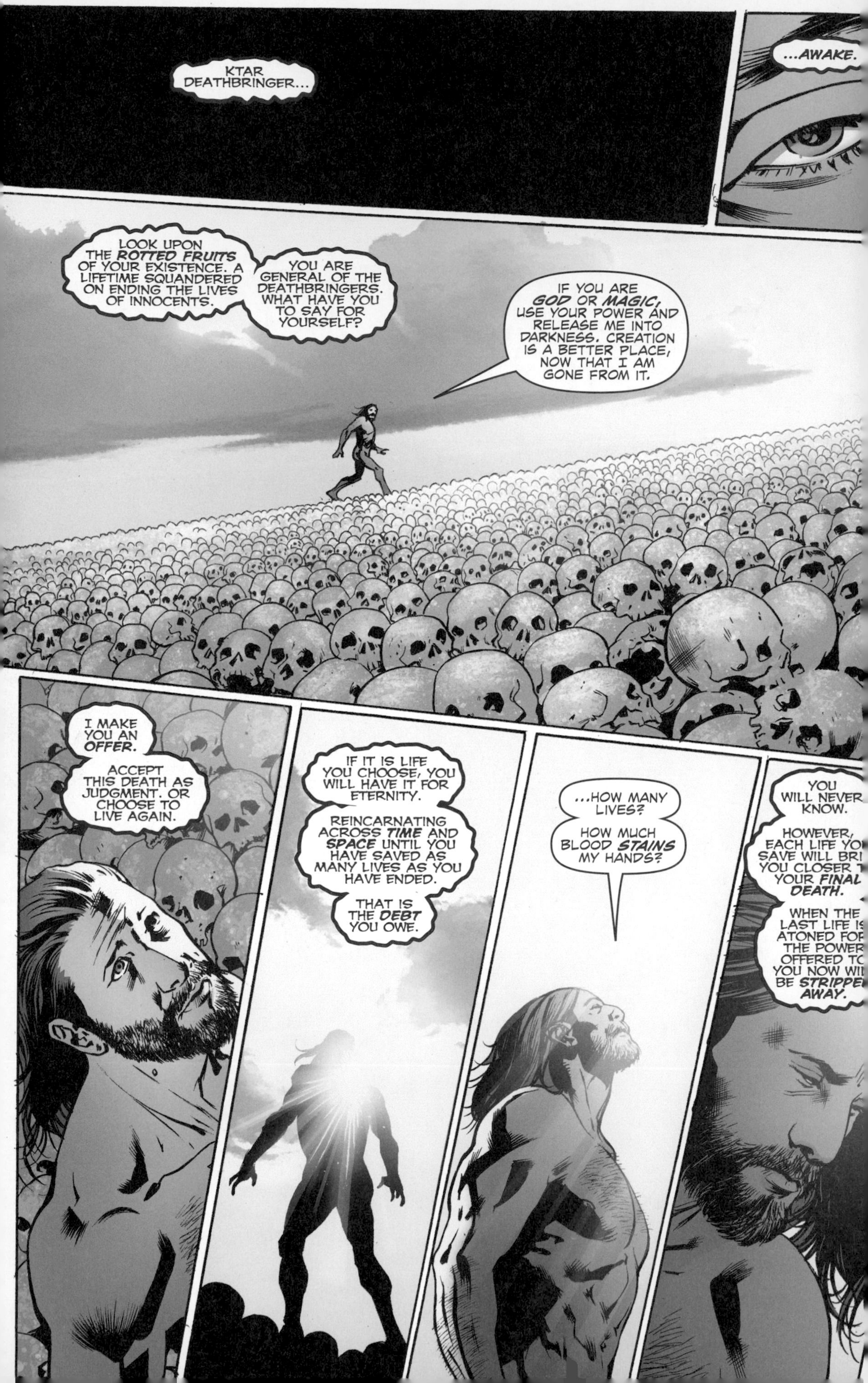
KTAR DEATHBRINGER...
...AWAKE.
LOOK UPON THE ROTTED FRUITS OF YOUR EXISTENCE. A LIFETIME SQUANDERED ON ENDING THE LIVES OF INNOCENTS.
YOU ARE GENERAL OF THE DEATHBRINGERS. WHAT HAVE YOU TO SAY FOR YOURSELF?
IF YOU ARE GOD OR MAGIC, USE YOUR POWER AND RELEASE ME INTO DARKNESS. CREATION IS A BETTER PLACE, NOW THAT I AM GONE FROM IT.
I MAKE YOU AN OFFER.
ACCEPT THIS DEATH AS JUDGMENT. OR CHOOSE TO LIVE AGAIN.
IF IT IS LIFE YOU CHOOSE, YOU WILL HAVE IT FOR ETERNITY.
REINCARNATING ACROSS TIME AND SPACE UNTIL YOU HAVE SAVED AS MANY LIVES AS YOU HAVE ENDED.
THAT IS THE DEBT YOU OWE.
...HOW MANY LIVES?
HOW MUCH BLOOD STAINS MY HANDS?
YOU WILL NEVER KNOW.

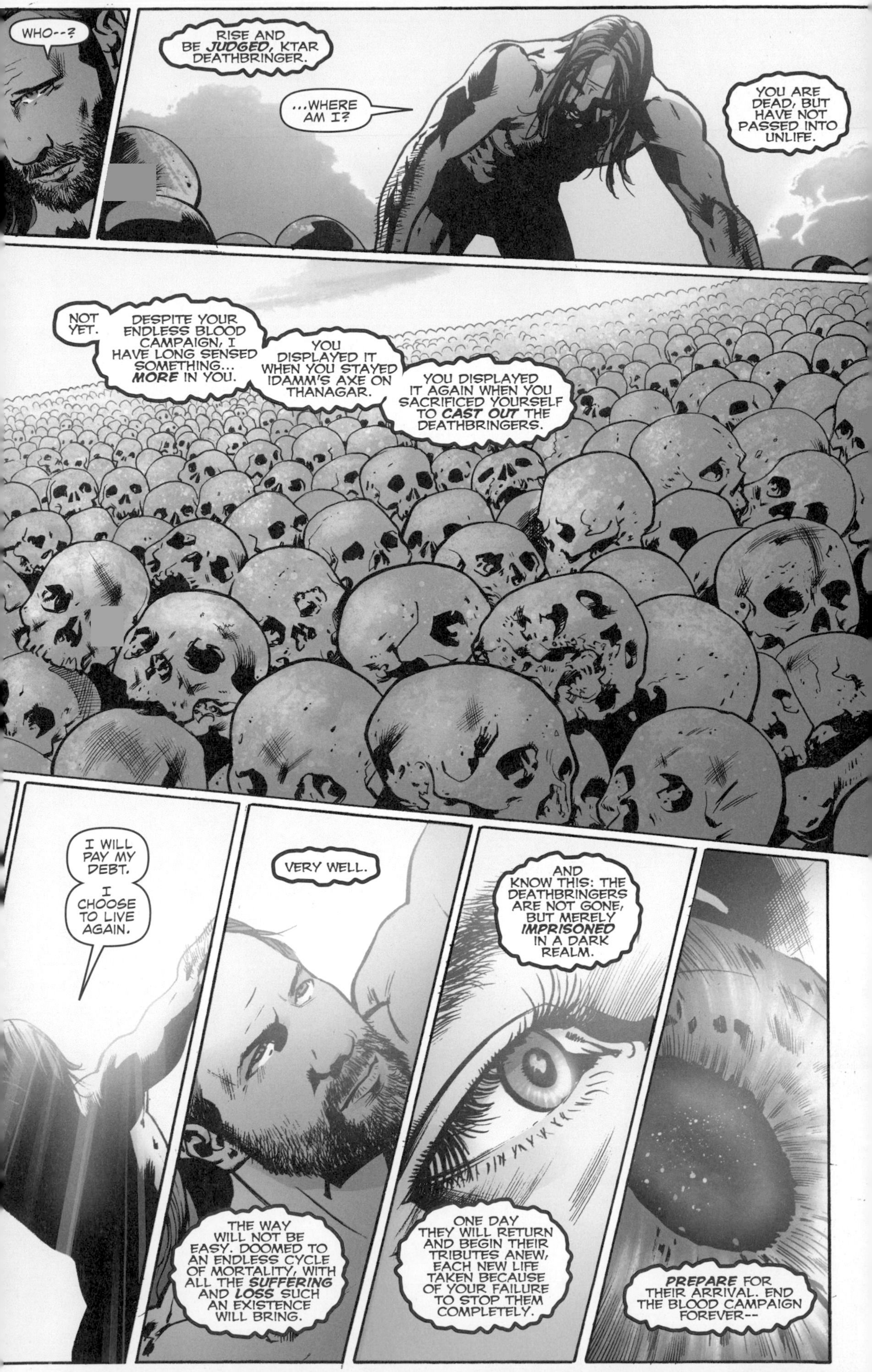
WHO--?
RISE AND BE JUDGED, KTAR DEATHBRINGER.
...WHERE AM I?
YOU ARE DEAD, BUT HAVE NOT PASSED INTO UNLIFE.
NOT YET.
DESPITE YOUR ENDLESS BLOOD CAMPAIGN, I HAVE LONG SENSED SOMETHING... MORE IN YOU.
YOU DISPLAYED IT WHEN YOU STAYED IDAMM'S AXE ON THANAGAR.
YOU DISPLAYED IT AGAIN WHEN YOU SACRIFICED YOURSELF TO CAST OUT THE DEATHBRINGERS.
I WILL PAY MY DEBT.
I CHOOSE TO LIVE AGAIN.
VERY WELL.
THE WAY WILL NOT BE EASY. DOOMED TO AN ENDLESS CYCLE OF MORTALITY, WITH ALL THE SUFFERING AND LOSS SUCH AN EXISTENCE WILL BRING.
AND KNOW THIS: THE DEATHBRINGERS ARE NOT GONE, BUT MERELY IMPRISONED IN A DARK REALM.
ONE DAY THEY WILL RETURN AND BEGIN THEIR TRIBUTES ANEW, EACH NEW LIFE TAKEN BECAUSE OF YOUR FAILURE TO STOP THEM COMPLETELY.
PREPARE FOR THEIR ARRIVAL. END THE BLOOD CAMPAIGN FOREVER--

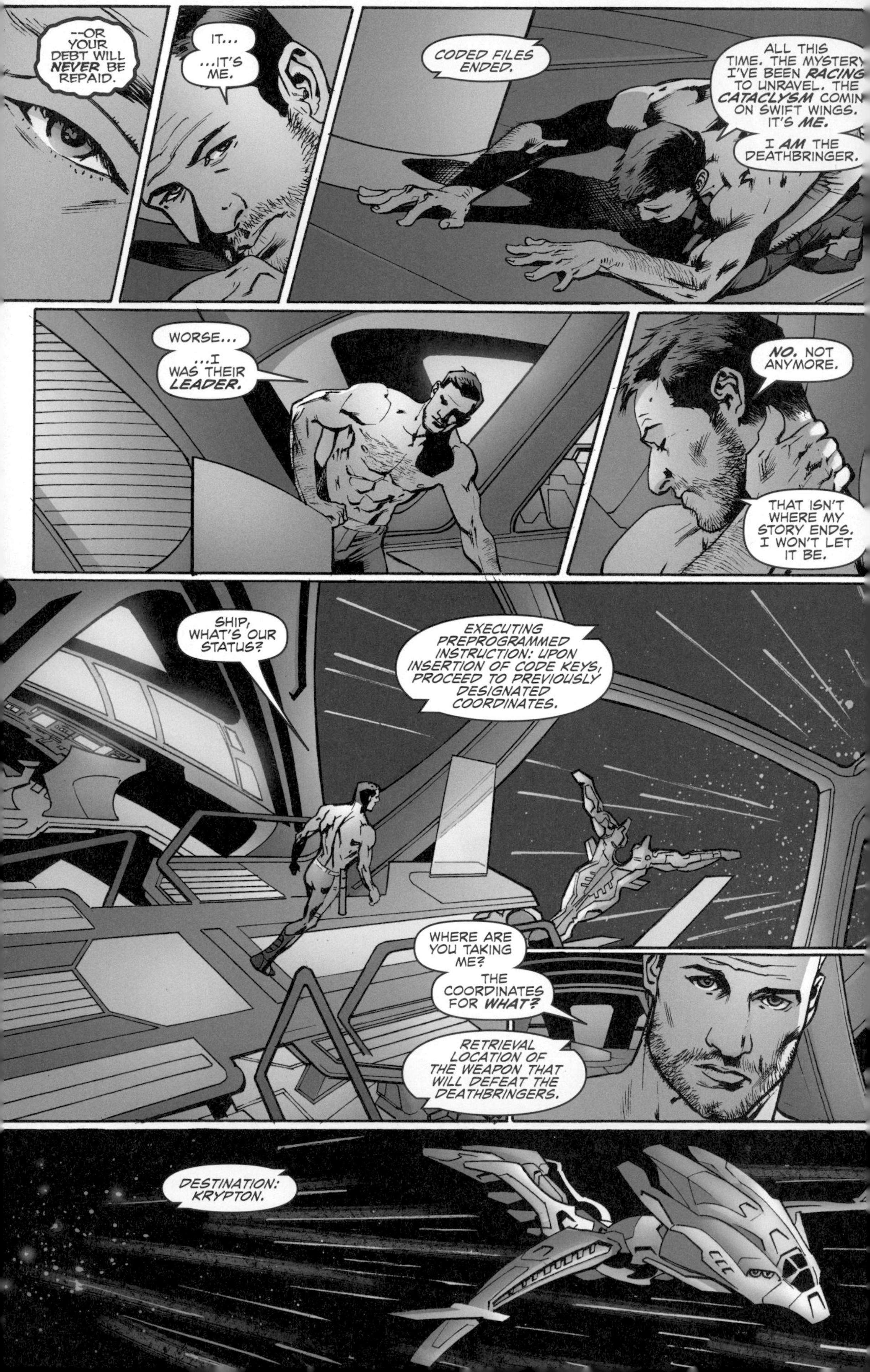
--OR YOUR DEBT WILL NEVER BE REPAID.
IT...
...IT'S ME.
CODED FILES ENDED.
ALL THIS TIME. THE MYSTERY I'VE BEEN RACING TO UNRAVEL. THE CATACLYSM COMIN ON SWIFT WINGS. IT'S ME.
I AM THE DEATHBRINGER.
WORSE...
...I WAS THEIR LEADER.
NO. NOT ANYMORE.
THAT ISN'T WHERE MY STORY ENDS. I WON'T LET IT BE.
SHIP, WHAT'S OUR STATUS?
EXECUTING PREPROGRAMMED INSTRUCTION: UPON INSERTION OF CODE KEYS, PROCEED TO PREVIOUSLY DESIGNATED COORDINATES.
WHERE ARE YOU TAKING ME?
THE COORDINATES FOR WHAT?
RETRIEVAL LOCATION OF THE WEAPON THAT WILL DEFEAT THE DEATHBRINGERS.
DESTINATION: KRYPTON.

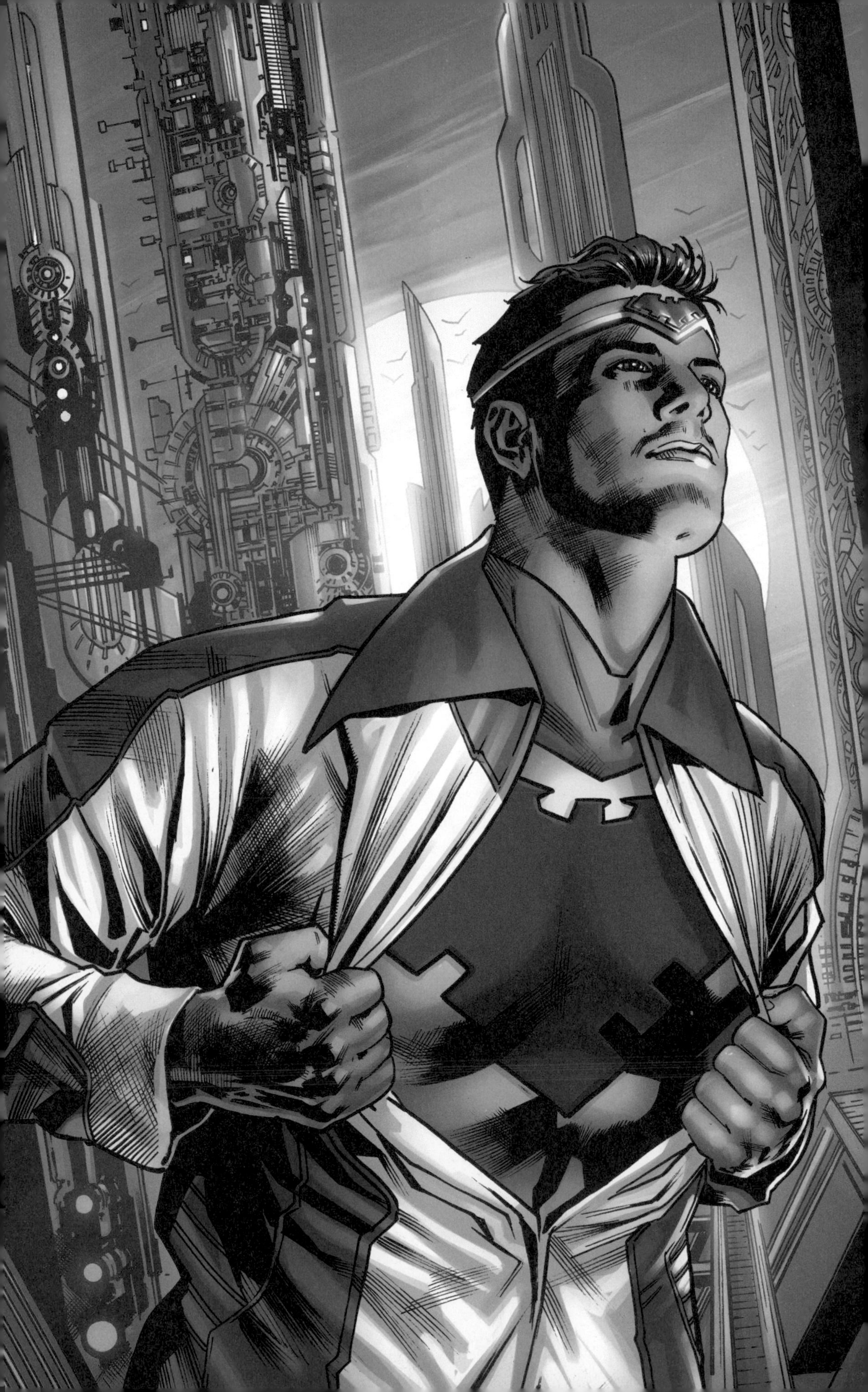

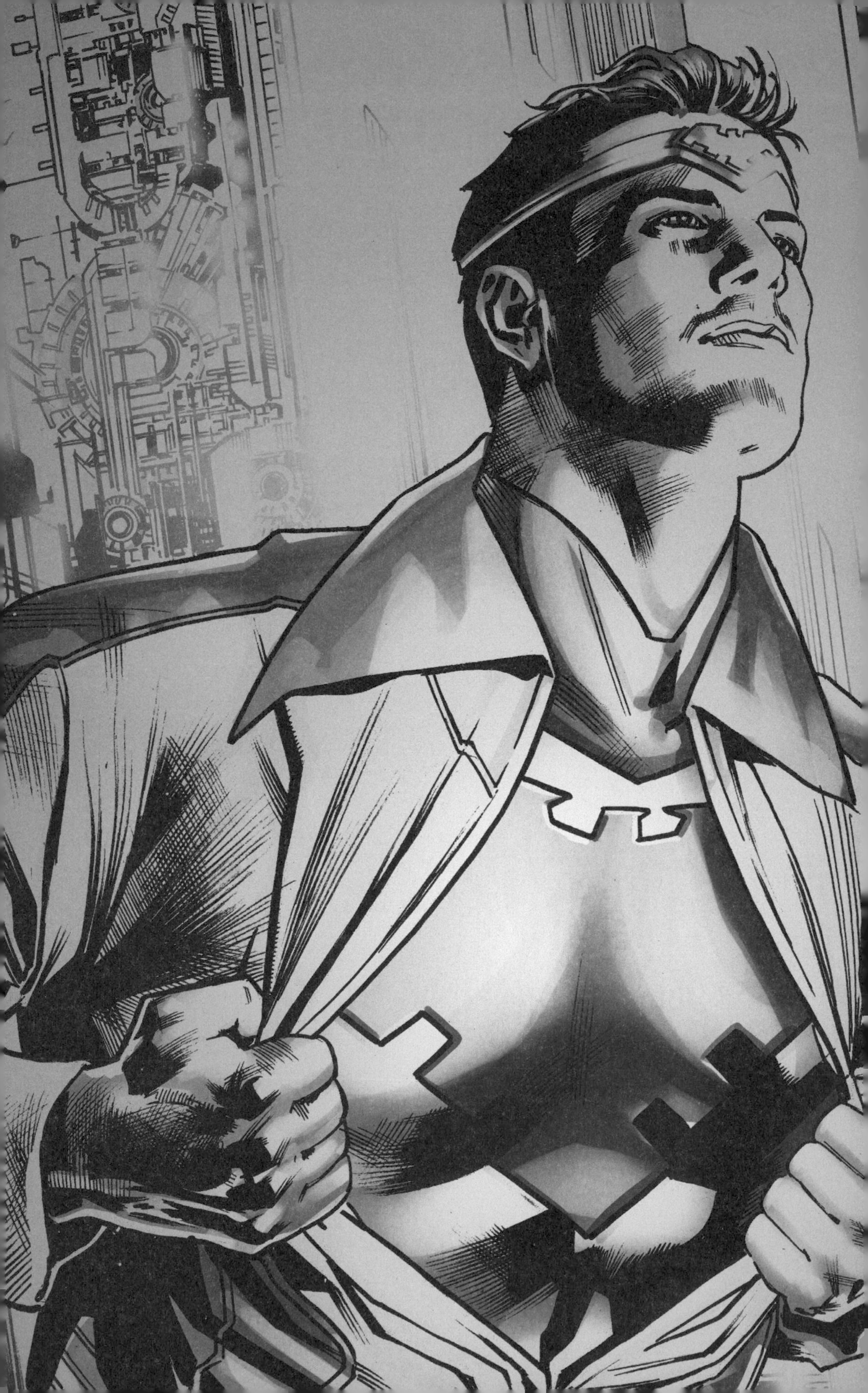

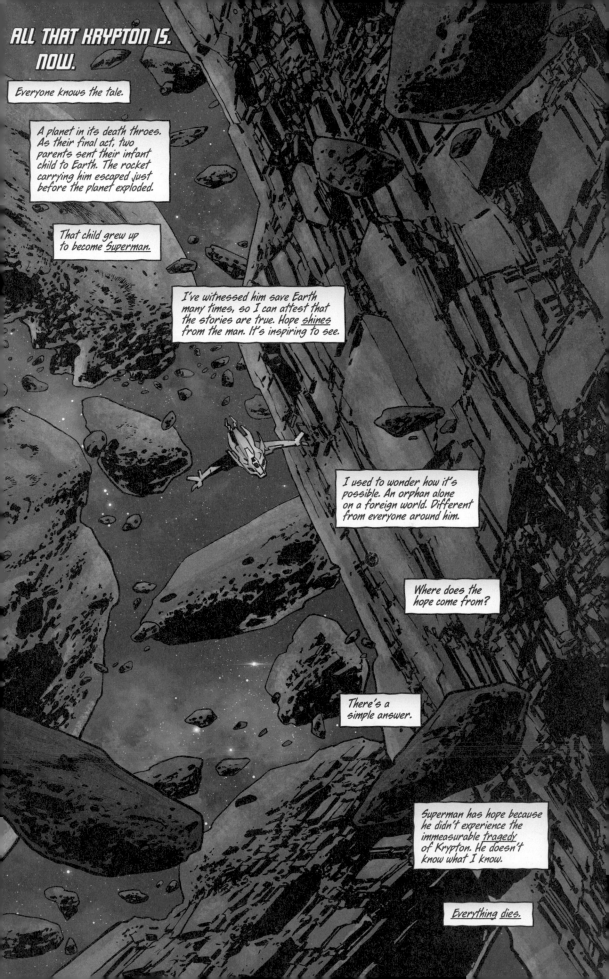

ALL THAT KRYPTON IS.
NOW.

Everyone knows the tale.

A planet in its death throes.
As their final act, two
parents sent their infant
child to Earth. The rocket
carrying him escaped just
before the planet exploded.

That child grew up
to become Superman.

I've witnessed him save Earth
many times, so I can attest that
the stories are true. Hope shines
from the man. It's inspiring to see.

I used to wonder how it's
possible. An orphan alone
on a foreign world. Different
from everyone around him.

Where does the
hope come from?

There's a
simple answer.

Superman has hope because
he didn't experience the
immeasurable tragedy
of Krypton. He doesn't
know what I know.

Everything dies.

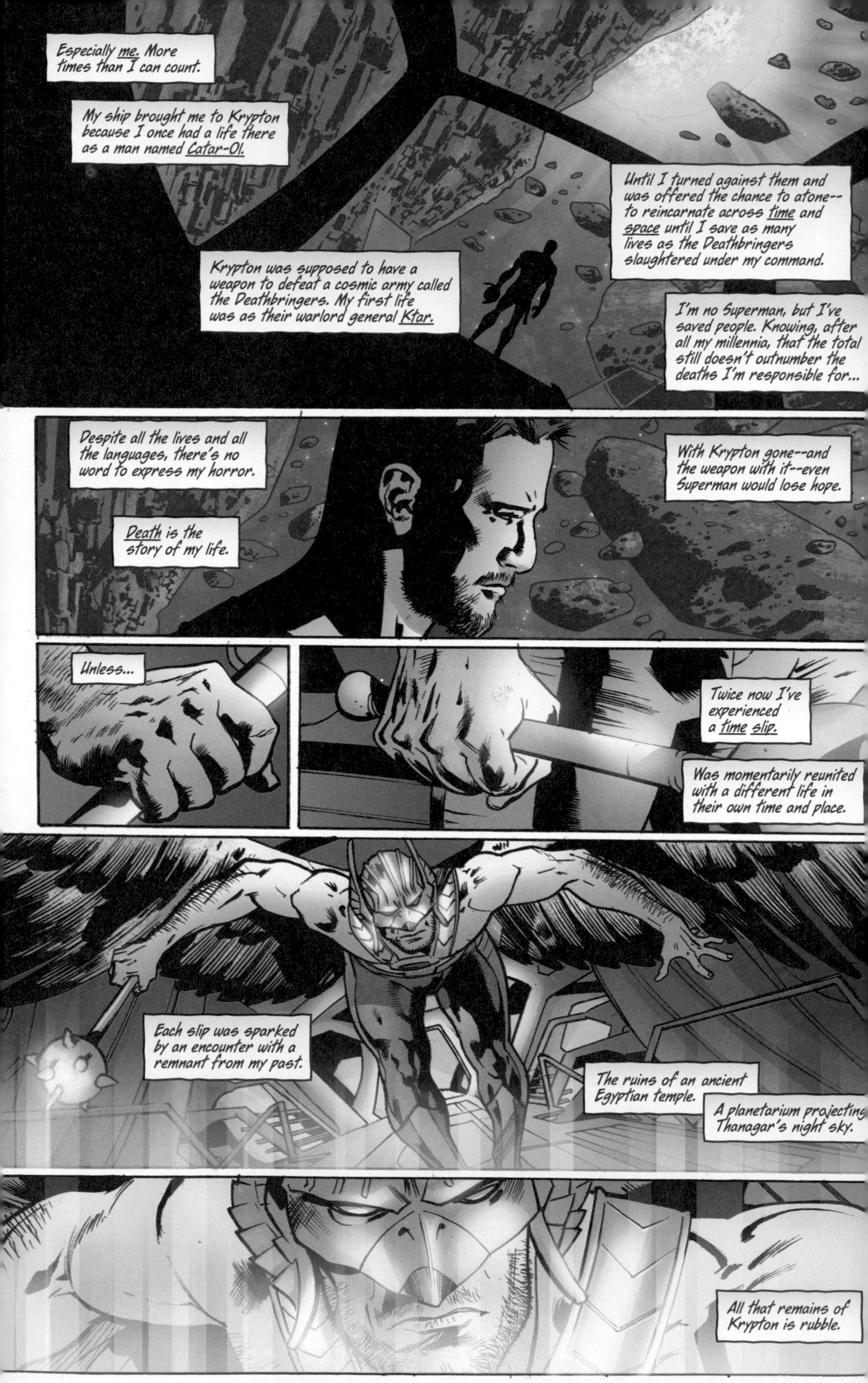
Especially me. More times than I can count.
My ship brought me to Krypton because I once had a life there as a man named Catar-Ol.
Krypton was supposed to have a weapon to defeat a cosmic army called the Deathbringers. My first life was as their warlord general Ktar.
Until I turned against them and was offered the chance to atone--to reincarnate across time and space until I save as many lives as the Deathbringers slaughtered under my command.
I'm no Superman, but I've saved people. Knowing, after all my millennia, that the total still doesn't outnumber the deaths I'm responsible for...
Despite all the lives and all the languages, there's no word to express my horror.
Death is the story of my life.
With Krypton gone--and the weapon with it--even Superman would lose hope.
Unless...
Twice now I've experienced a time slip.
Was momentarily reunited with a different life in their own time and place.
Each slip was sparked by an encounter with a remnant from my past.
The ruins of an ancient Egyptian temple.
A planetarium projecting Thanagar's night sky.
All that remains of Krypton is rubble.

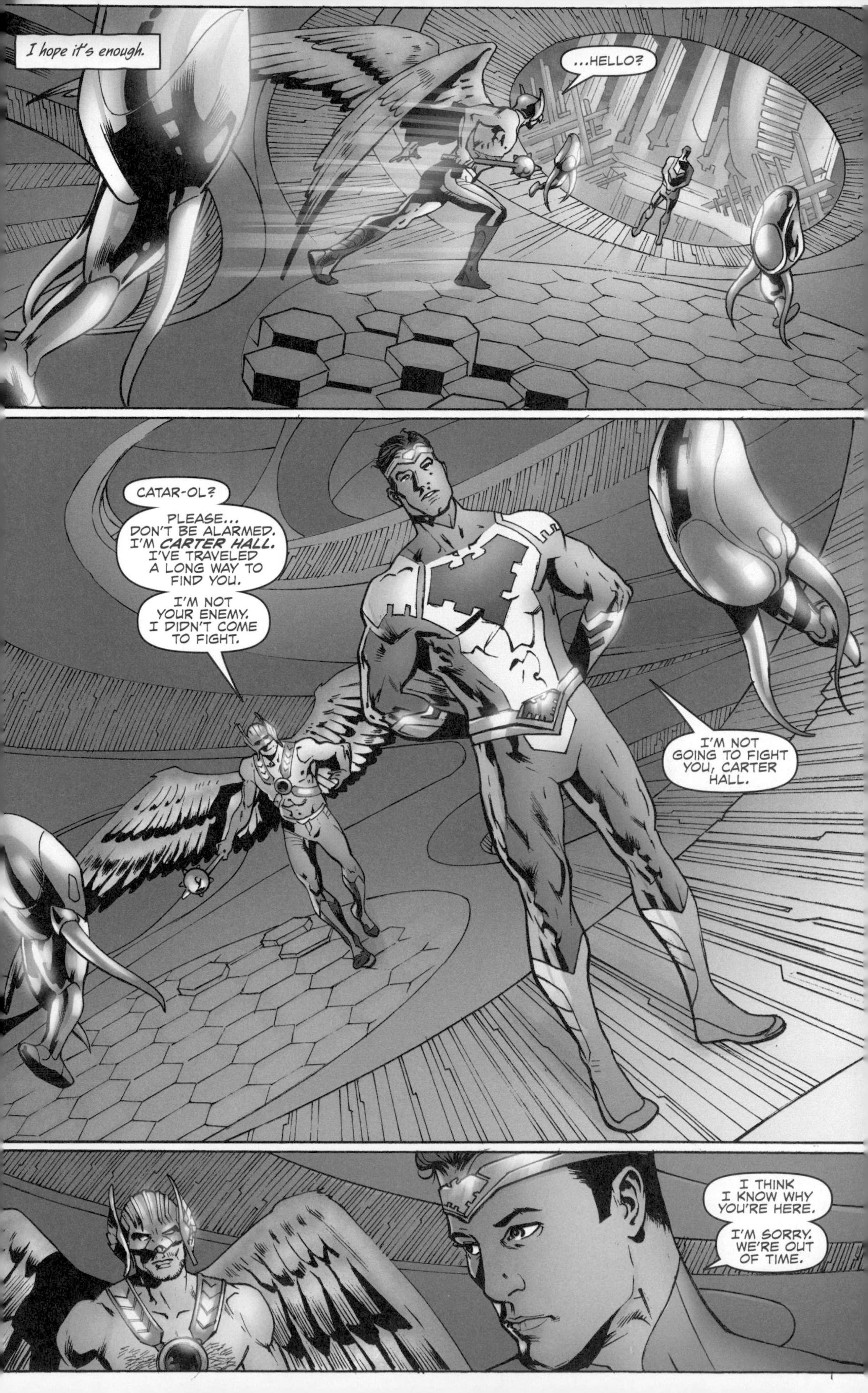

I hope it's enough.
...HELLO?
CATAR-OL?
PLEASE... DON'T BE ALARMED. I'M CARTER HALL. I'VE TRAVELED A LONG WAY TO FIND YOU.
I'M NOT YOUR ENEMY. I DIDN'T COME TO FIGHT.
I'M NOT GOING TO FIGHT YOU, CARTER HALL.
I THINK I KNOW WHY YOU'RE HERE.
I'M SORRY. WE'RE OUT OF TIME.

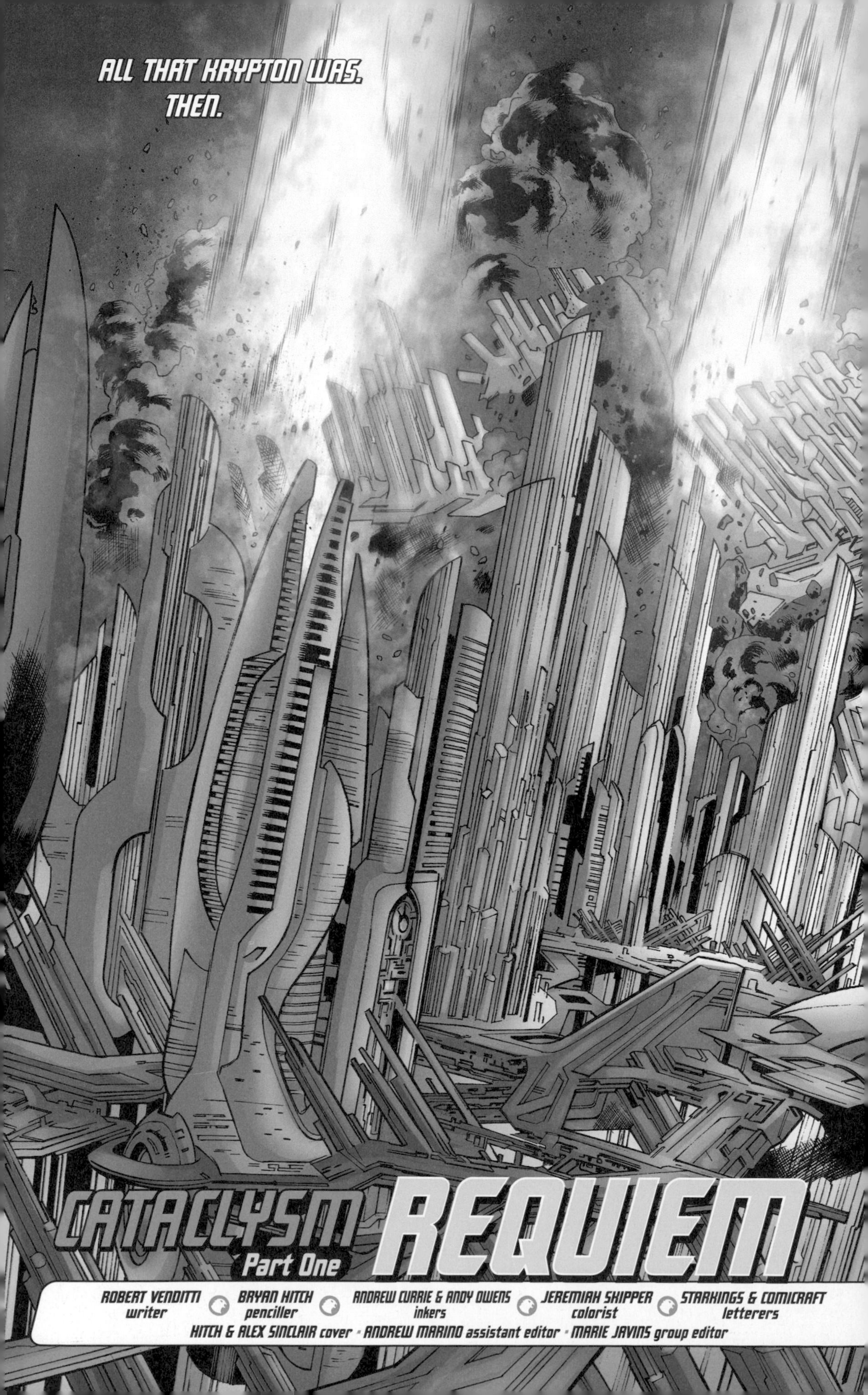
ALL THAT KRYPTON WAS.
THEN.
CATACLYSM Part One
REQUIEM
ROBERT VENDITTI writer
BRYAN HITCH penciller
ANDREW CURRIE & ANDY OWENS inkers
JEREMIAH SKIPPER colorist
STARKINGS & COMICRAFT letterers
HITCH & ALEX SINCLAIR cover - ANDREW MARINO assistant editor - MARIE JAVINS group editor

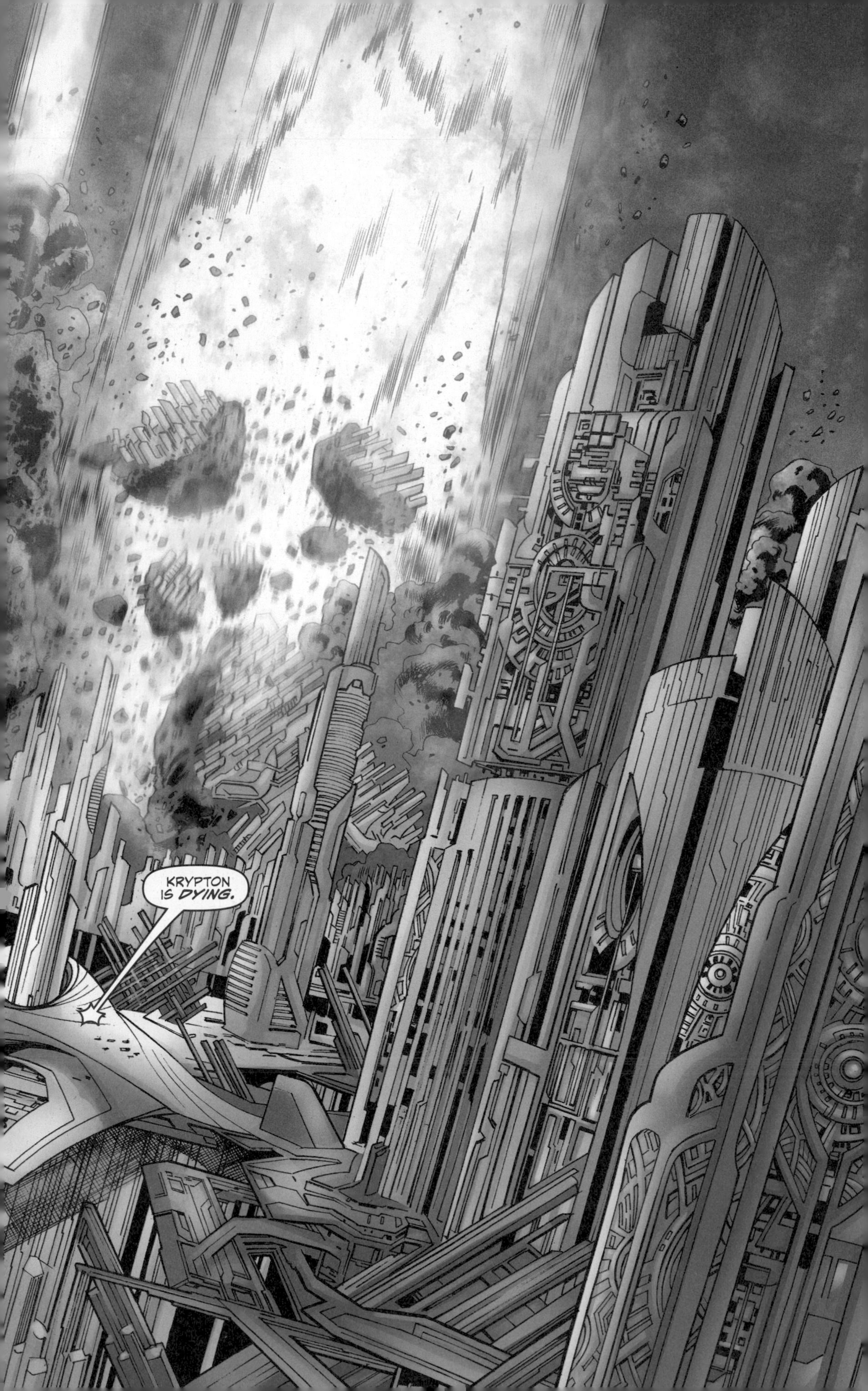
KRYPTON IS *DYING.*

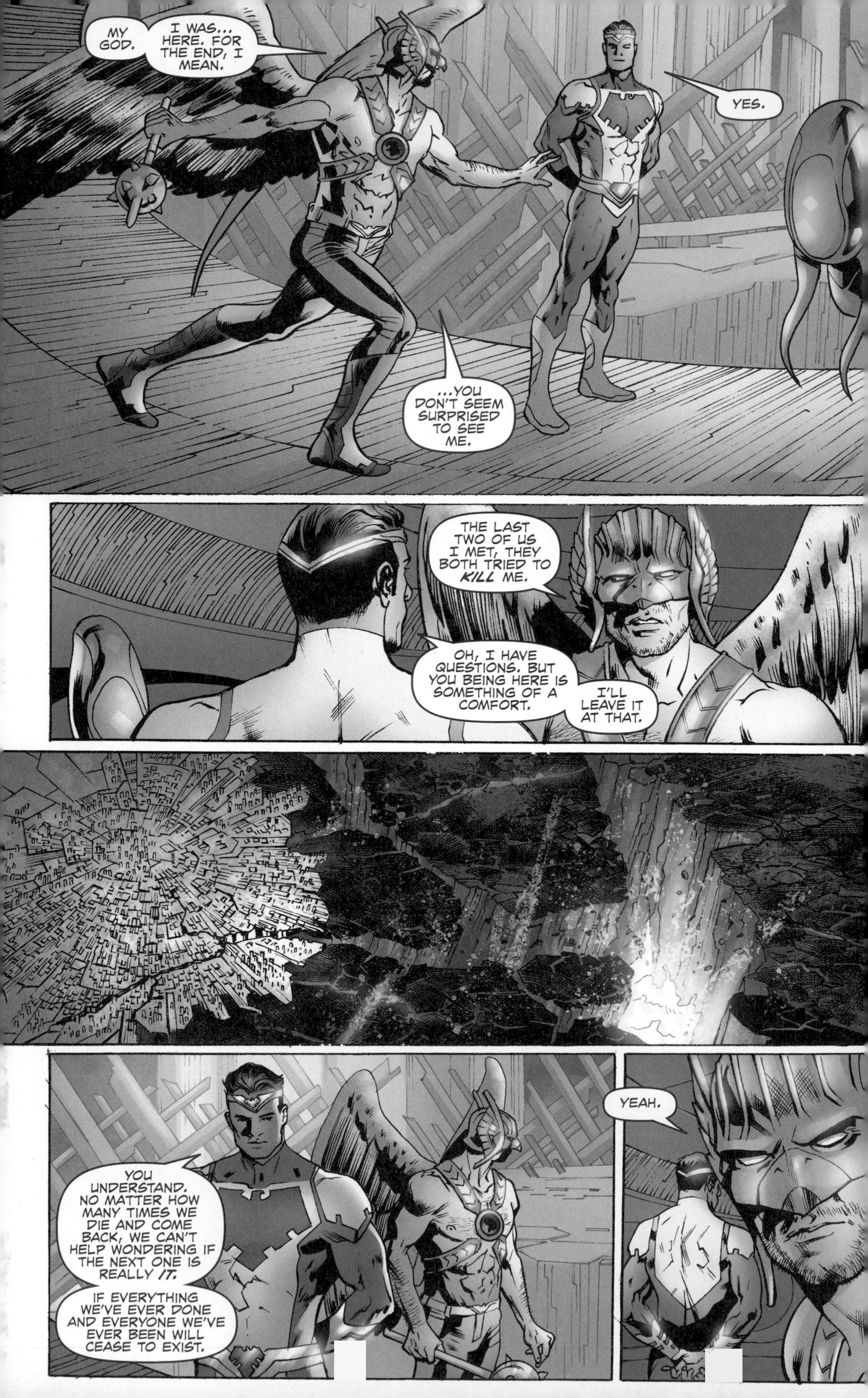
MY GOD.
I WAS... HERE. FOR THE END, I MEAN.
YES.
...YOU DON'T SEEM SURPRISED TO SEE ME.
THE LAST TWO OF US I MET, THEY BOTH TRIED TO KILL ME.
OH, I HAVE QUESTIONS. BUT YOU BEING HERE IS SOMETHING OF A COMFORT.
I'LL LEAVE IT AT THAT.
YOU UNDERSTAND. NO MATTER HOW MANY TIMES WE DIE AND COME BACK, WE CAN'T HELP WONDERING IF THE NEXT ONE IS REALLY IT.
IF EVERYTHING WE'VE EVER DONE AND EVERYONE WE'VE EVER BEEN WILL CEASE TO EXIST.
YEAH.

THIS MUSEUM HOUSES KRYPTON'S MOST PRECIOUS ARTIFACTS.

I INSTALLED STABILIZERS TO SAFEGUARD THE STRUCTURE FROM THE WORSENING SEISMIC TREMORS. N^TH METAL, THE SAME AS MY BELT. AND, I SUSPECT, YOUR FLIGHT HARNESS.

WE'RE MADE TO SOAR.

WELL PUT.

SUCH A WASTE. THE MUSEUM WILL COLLAPSE. *EVERYTHING* WILL BE LOST.

THOUGH I SUPPOSE AT LEAST IT WON'T BE A BUMPY RIDE.

WHERE ARE YOU GOING?

WE HAVE TO--

DO SOMETHING? SAVE SOMEONE?

WHO? WHERE WOULD WE TAKE THEM? THERE'S NOWHERE TO GO. NO SAFE HAVEN FROM *PLANETARY EXPIRATION*.

THIS IS THE FINAL PAGE OF THE FINAL CHAPTER OF KRYPTON'S STORY.

IF IT HELPS... THERE ARE SURVIVORS. ONE IS A FRIEND OF MINE. ON EARTH WE CALL HIM *SUPERMAN*.

HERE, HIS NAME WOULD BE *KAL-EL*.

JOR-EL'S BOY?

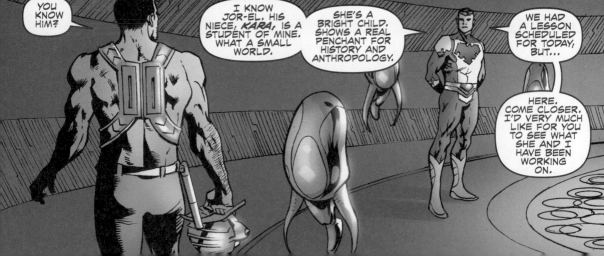

YOU KNOW HIM?

I KNOW JOR-EL. HIS NIECE, *KARA*, IS A STUDENT OF MINE. WHAT A SMALL WORLD.

SHE'S A BRIGHT CHILD. SHOWS A REAL PENCHANT FOR HISTORY AND ANTHROPOLOGY.

WE HAD A LESSON SCHEDULED FOR TODAY, BUT...

HERE. COME CLOSER. I'D VERY MUCH LIKE FOR YOU TO SEE WHAT SHE AND I HAVE BEEN WORKING ON.

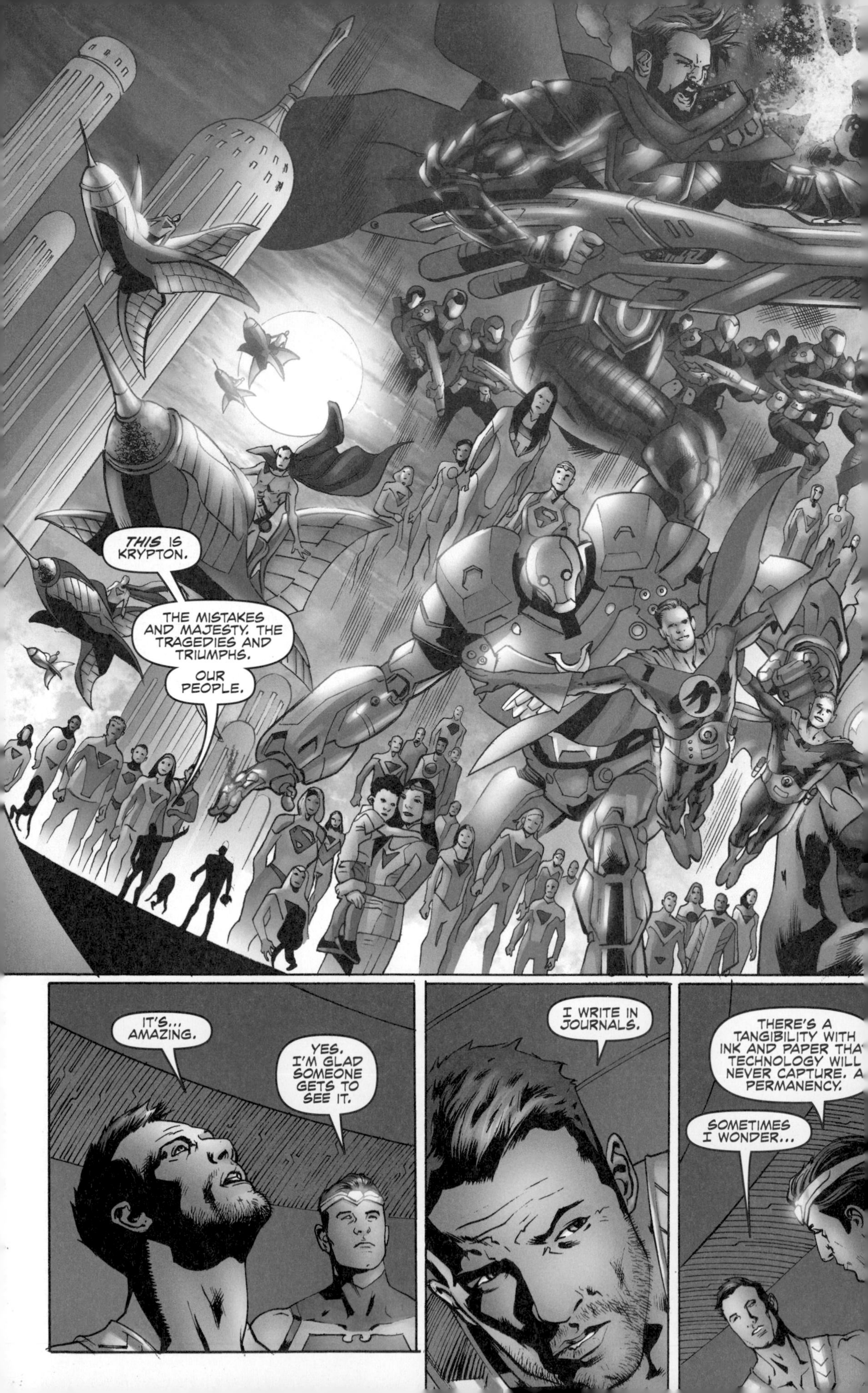

THIS IS KRYPTON.
THE MISTAKES AND MAJESTY. THE TRAGEDIES AND TRIUMPHS.
OUR PEOPLE.
IT'S... AMAZING.
YES. I'M GLAD SOMEONE GETS TO SEE IT.
I WRITE IN JOURNALS.
THERE'S A TANGIBILITY WITH INK AND PAPER THA TECHNOLOGY WILL NEVER CAPTURE. A PERMANENCY.
SOMETIMES I WONDER...

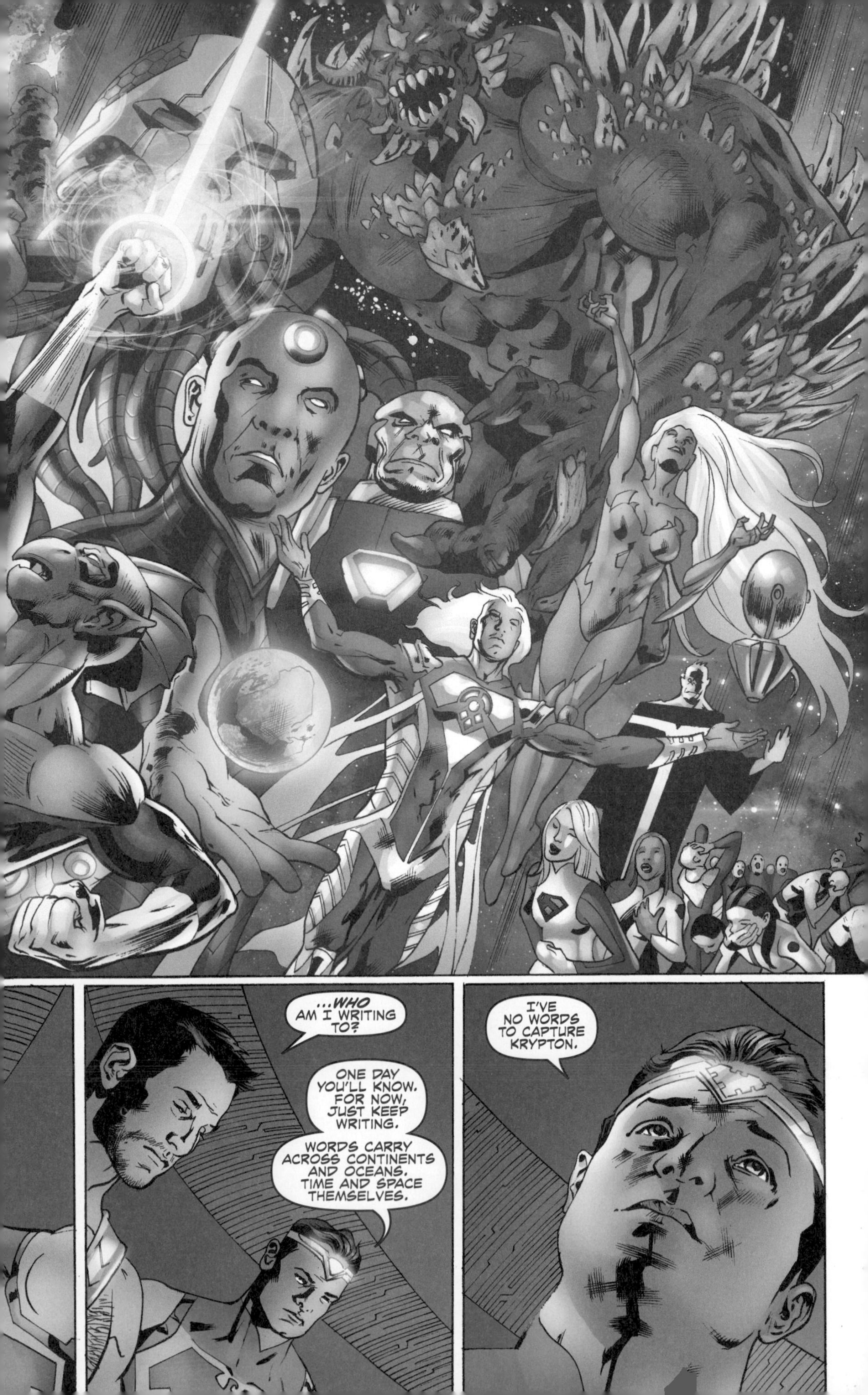
...WHO AM I WRITING TO?
ONE DAY YOU'LL KNOW. FOR NOW, JUST KEEP WRITING.
WORDS CARRY ACROSS CONTINENTS AND OCEANS. TIME AND SPACE THEMSELVES.
I'VE NO WORDS TO CAPTURE KRYPTON.

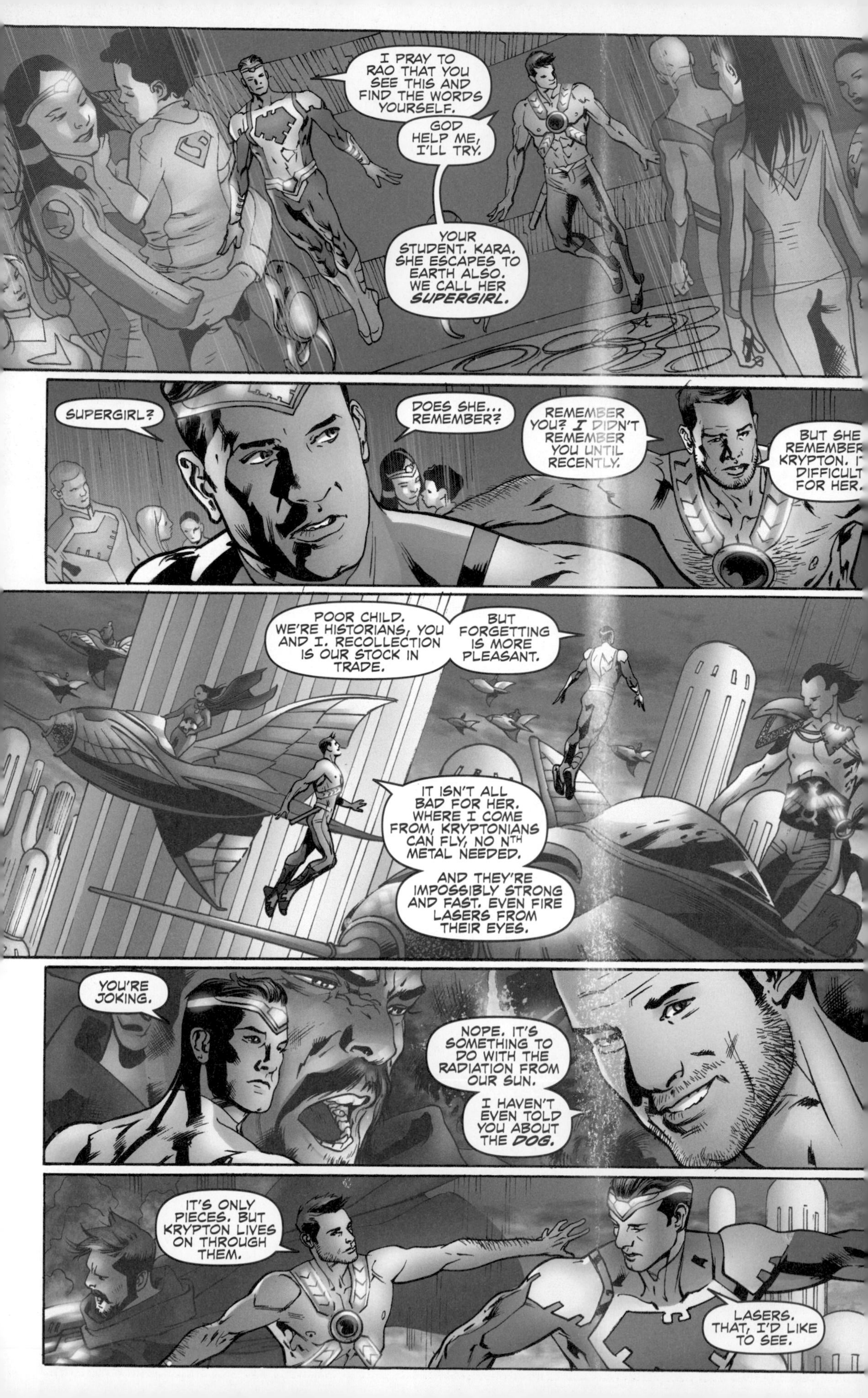

I PRAY TO RAO THAT YOU SEE THIS AND FIND THE WORDS YOURSELF.
GOD HELP ME, I'LL TRY.
YOUR STUDENT. KARA. SHE ESCAPES TO EARTH ALSO. WE CALL HER *SUPERGIRL.*
SUPERGIRL?
DOES SHE... REMEMBER?
REMEMBER YOU? *I* DIDN'T REMEMBER YOU UNTIL RECENTLY.
BUT SHE REMEMBER KRYPTON. I DIFFICULT FOR HER.
POOR CHILD. WE'RE HISTORIANS, YOU AND I. RECOLLECTION IS OUR STOCK IN TRADE.
BUT FORGETTING IS MORE PLEASANT.
IT ISN'T ALL BAD FOR HER. WHERE I COME FROM, KRYPTONIANS CAN FLY, NO N^{TH} METAL NEEDED.
AND THEY'RE IMPOSSIBLY STRONG AND FAST. EVEN FIRE LASERS FROM THEIR EYES.
YOU'RE JOKING.
NOPE. IT'S SOMETHING TO DO WITH THE RADIATION FROM OUR SUN.
I HAVEN'T EVEN TOLD YOU ABOUT THE *DOG.*
IT'S ONLY PIECES. BUT KRYPTON LIVES ON THROUGH THEM.
LASERS. THAT, I'D LIKE TO SEE.

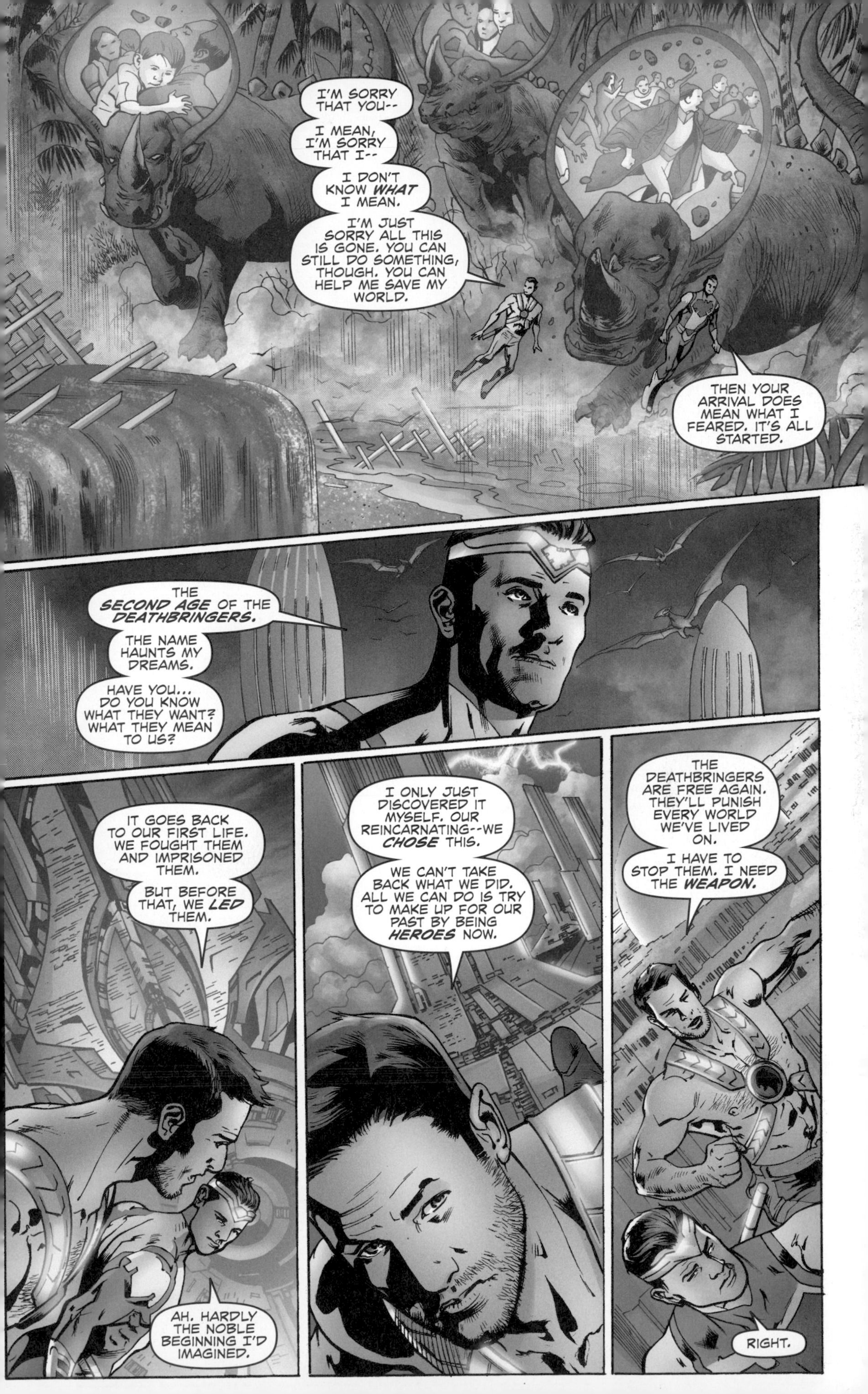
I'M SORRY THAT YOU--
I MEAN, I'M SORRY THAT I--
I DON'T KNOW *WHAT* I MEAN.
I'M JUST SORRY ALL THIS IS GONE. YOU CAN STILL DO SOMETHING, THOUGH. YOU CAN HELP ME SAVE MY WORLD.
THEN YOUR ARRIVAL DOES MEAN WHAT I FEARED. IT'S ALL STARTED.
THE *SECOND AGE* OF THE *DEATHBRINGERS.*
THE NAME HAUNTS MY DREAMS.
HAVE YOU... DO YOU KNOW WHAT THEY WANT? WHAT THEY MEAN TO US?
IT GOES BACK TO OUR FIRST LIFE. WE FOUGHT THEM AND IMPRISONED THEM.
BUT BEFORE THAT, WE *LED* THEM.
AH. HARDLY THE NOBLE BEGINNING I'D IMAGINED.
I ONLY JUST DISCOVERED IT MYSELF. OUR REINCARNATING--WE *CHOSE* THIS.
WE CAN'T TAKE BACK WHAT WE DID. ALL WE CAN DO IS TRY TO MAKE UP FOR OUR PAST BY BEING *HEROES* NOW.
THE DEATHBRINGERS ARE FREE AGAIN. THEY'LL PUNISH EVERY WORLD WE'VE LIVED ON.
I HAVE TO STOP THEM. I NEED THE *WEAPON.*
RIGHT.

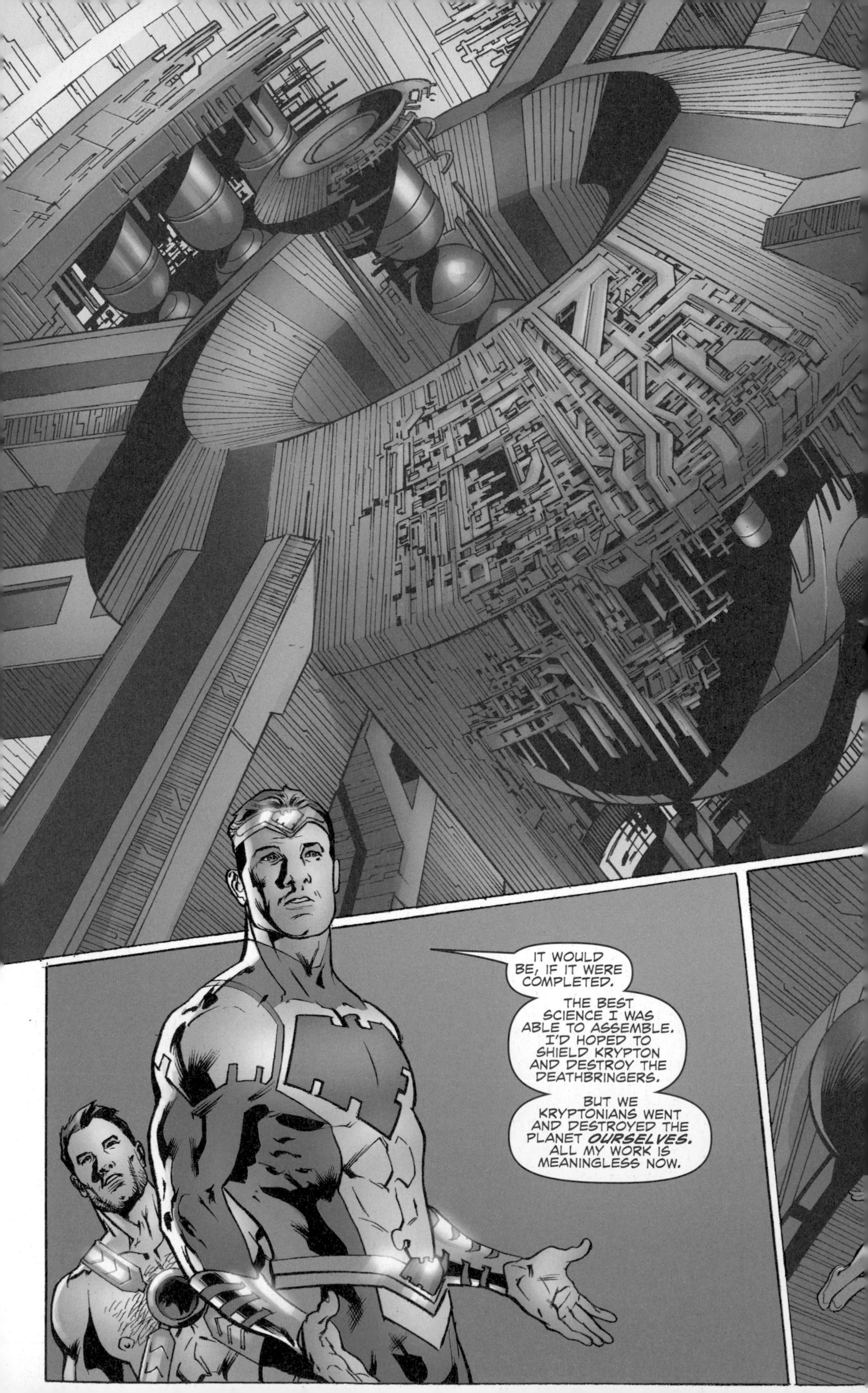
IT WOULD BE, IF IT WERE COMPLETED.
THE BEST SCIENCE I WAS ABLE TO ASSEMBLE. I'D HOPED TO SHIELD KRYPTON AND DESTROY THE DEATHBRINGERS.
BUT WE KRYPTONIANS WENT AND DESTROYED THE PLANET *OURSELVES.* ALL MY WORK IS MEANINGLESS NOW.

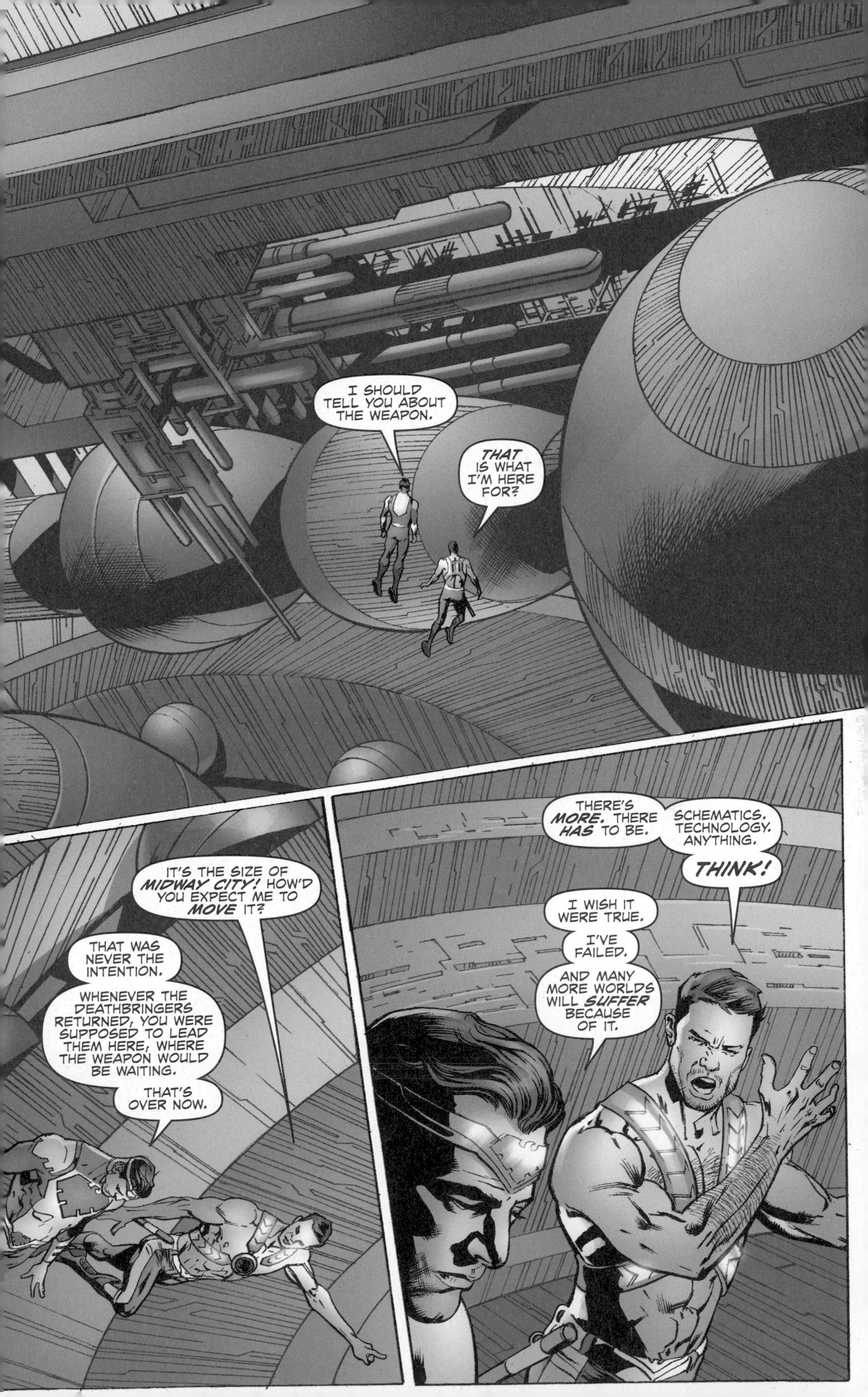
I SHOULD TELL YOU ABOUT THE WEAPON.
THAT IS WHAT I'M HERE FOR?
IT'S THE SIZE OF MIDWAY CITY! HOW'D YOU EXPECT ME TO MOVE IT?
THAT WAS NEVER THE INTENTION.
WHENEVER THE DEATHBRINGERS RETURNED, YOU WERE SUPPOSED TO LEAD THEM HERE, WHERE THE WEAPON WOULD BE WAITING.
THAT'S OVER NOW.
THERE'S MORE. THERE HAS TO BE.
SCHEMATICS. TECHNOLOGY. ANYTHING.
THINK!
I WISH IT WERE TRUE.
I'VE FAILED.
AND MANY MORE WORLDS WILL SUFFER BECAUSE OF IT.

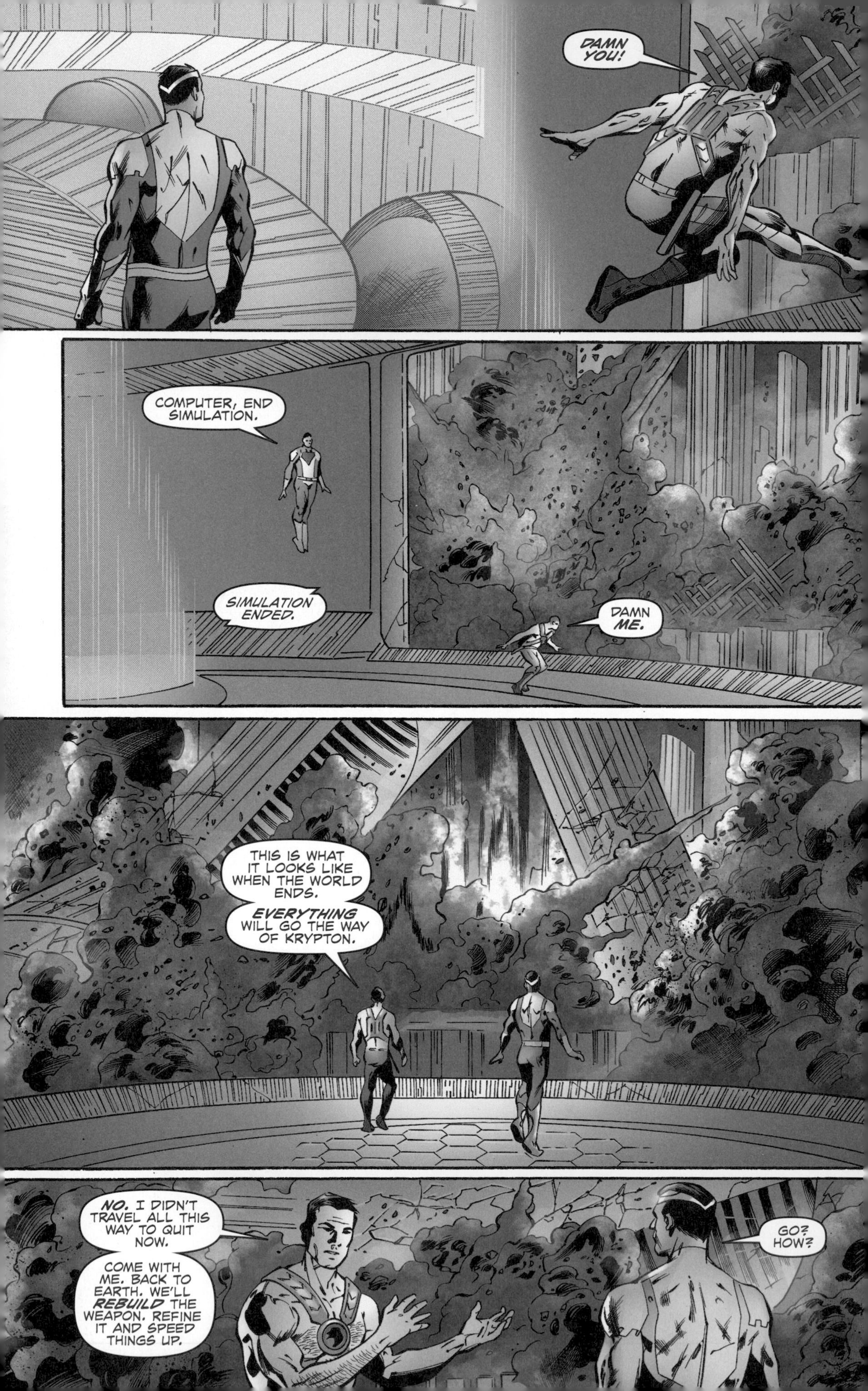

DAMN YOU!
COMPUTER, END SIMULATION.
SIMULATION ENDED.
DAMN ME.
THIS IS WHAT IT LOOKS LIKE WHEN THE WORLD ENDS.
EVERYTHING WILL GO THE WAY OF KRYPTON.
NO. I DIDN'T TRAVEL ALL THIS WAY TO QUIT NOW.
COME WITH ME. BACK TO EARTH. WE'LL REBUILD THE WEAPON. REFINE IT AND SPEED THINGS UP.
GO? HOW?

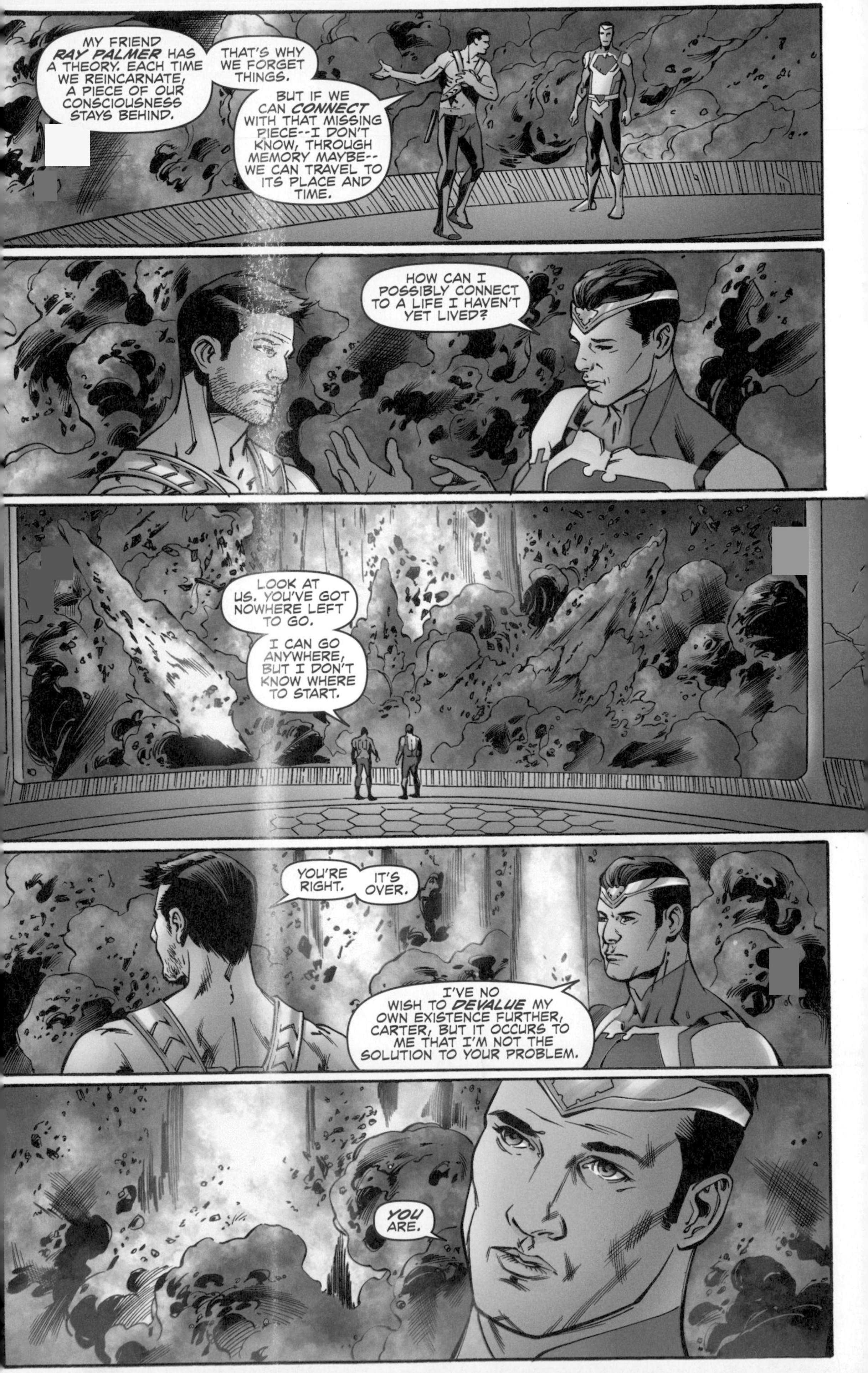
MY FRIEND RAY PALMER HAS A THEORY. EACH TIME WE REINCARNATE, A PIECE OF OUR CONSCIOUSNESS STAYS BEHIND.
THAT'S WHY WE FORGET THINGS.
BUT IF WE CAN CONNECT WITH THAT MISSING PIECE--I DON'T KNOW, THROUGH MEMORY MAYBE--WE CAN TRAVEL TO ITS PLACE AND TIME.
HOW CAN I POSSIBLY CONNECT TO A LIFE I HAVEN'T YET LIVED?
LOOK AT US. YOU'VE GOT NOWHERE LEFT TO GO.
I CAN GO ANYWHERE, BUT I DON'T KNOW WHERE TO START.
YOU'RE RIGHT.
IT'S OVER.
I'VE NO WISH TO DEVALUE MY OWN EXISTENCE FURTHER, CARTER, BUT IT OCCURS TO ME THAT I'M NOT THE SOLUTION TO YOUR PROBLEM.
YOU ARE.

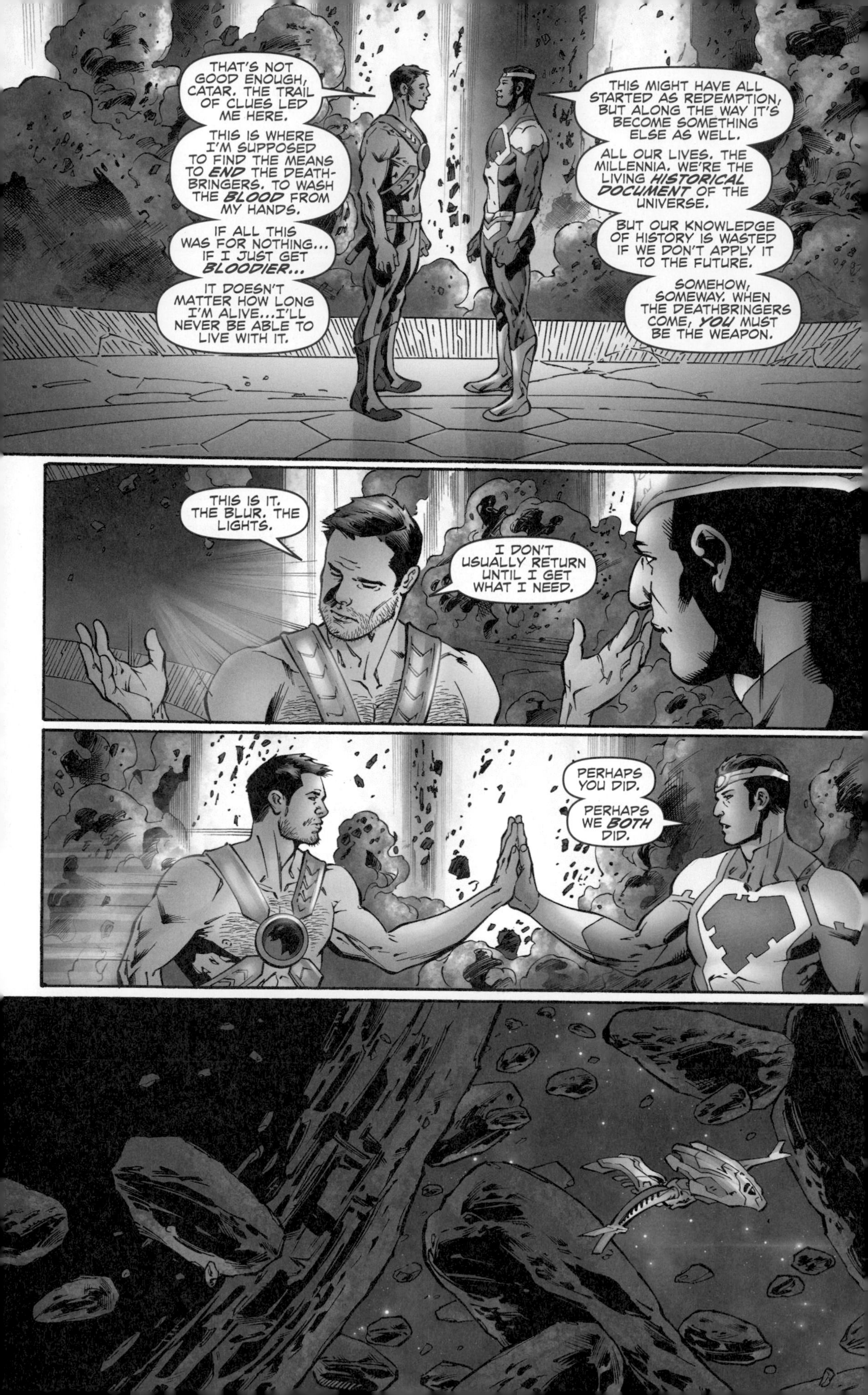
THAT'S NOT GOOD ENOUGH, CATAR. THE TRAIL OF CLUES LED ME HERE.
THIS IS WHERE I'M SUPPOSED TO FIND THE MEANS TO END THE DEATH-BRINGERS. TO WASH THE BLOOD FROM MY HANDS.
IF ALL THIS WAS FOR NOTHING... IF I JUST GET BLOODIER...
IT DOESN'T MATTER HOW LONG I'M ALIVE...I'LL NEVER BE ABLE TO LIVE WITH IT.
THIS MIGHT HAVE ALL STARTED AS REDEMPTION, BUT ALONG THE WAY IT'S BECOME SOMETHING ELSE AS WELL.
ALL OUR LIVES. THE MILLENNIA. WE'RE THE LIVING HISTORICAL DOCUMENT OF THE UNIVERSE.
BUT OUR KNOWLEDGE OF HISTORY IS WASTED IF WE DON'T APPLY IT TO THE FUTURE.
SOMEHOW, SOMEWAY. WHEN THE DEATHBRINGERS COME, YOU MUST BE THE WEAPON.
THIS IS IT. THE BLUR. THE LIGHTS.
I DON'T USUALLY RETURN UNTIL I GET WHAT I NEED.
PERHAPS YOU DID.
PERHAPS WE BOTH DID.

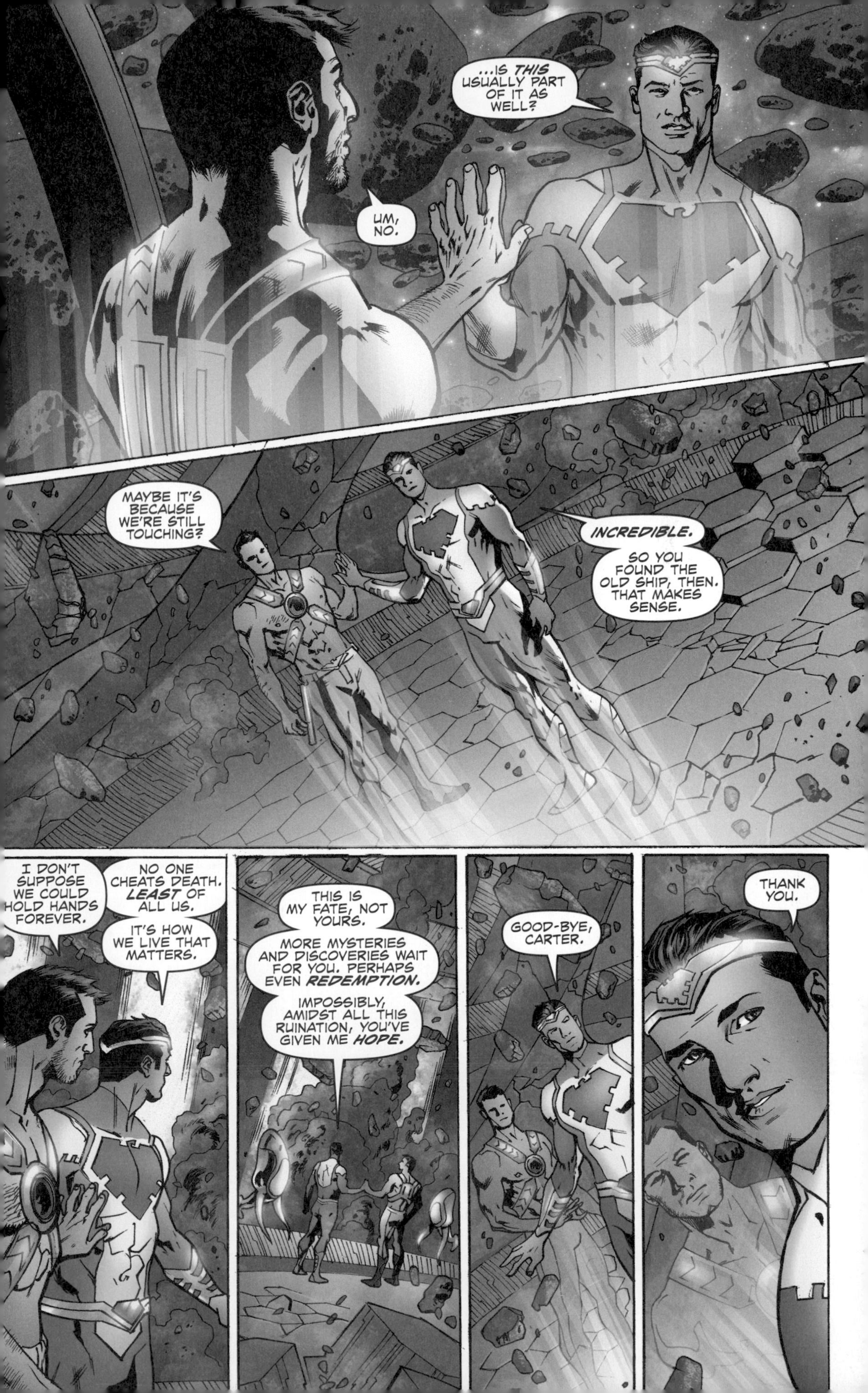
...IS THIS USUALLY PART OF IT AS WELL?
UM, NO.
MAYBE IT'S BECAUSE WE'RE STILL TOUCHING?
INCREDIBLE.
SO YOU FOUND THE OLD SHIP, THEN. THAT MAKES SENSE.
I DON'T SUPPOSE WE COULD HOLD HANDS FOREVER.
NO ONE CHEATS DEATH. LEAST OF ALL US.
IT'S HOW WE LIVE THAT MATTERS.
THIS IS MY FATE, NOT YOURS.
MORE MYSTERIES AND DISCOVERIES WAIT FOR YOU. PERHAPS EVEN REDEMPTION.
IMPOSSIBLY, AMIDST ALL THIS RUINATION, YOU'VE GIVEN ME HOPE.
GOOD-BYE, CARTER.
THANK YOU.

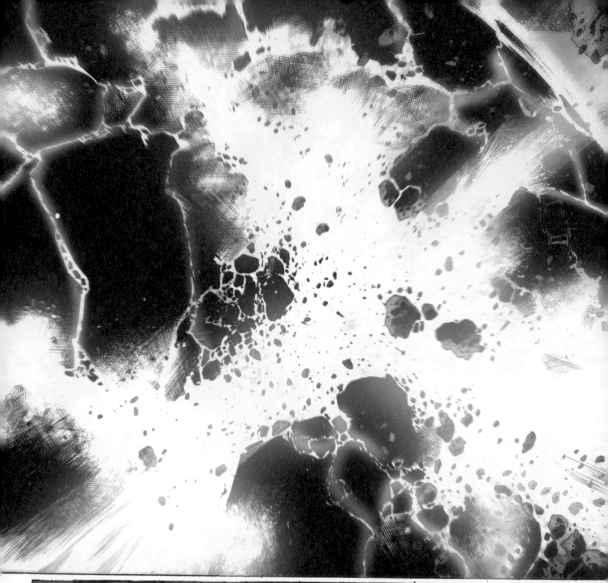

NO!

A world of life and beauty and discoveries yet to be made.

Obliterated.

I feel the *loss* all over again.

The memory is too painful to bear. Too important to let go.

Krypton's rubble isn't the remnant.

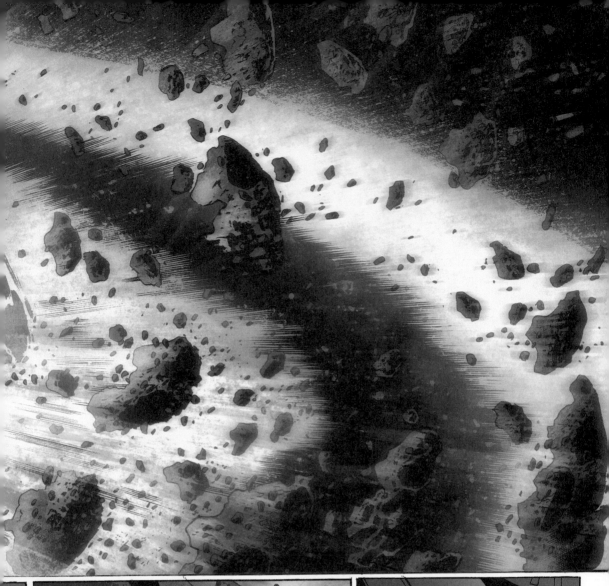

I am.

I won't be a remnant again. Krypton's fate won't be Earth's.

Earth is *my* world. Its lives and beauty and discoveries are *mine* to protect.

Catar-Ol said I must be the weapon.

I don't know how, but I have to find a way.

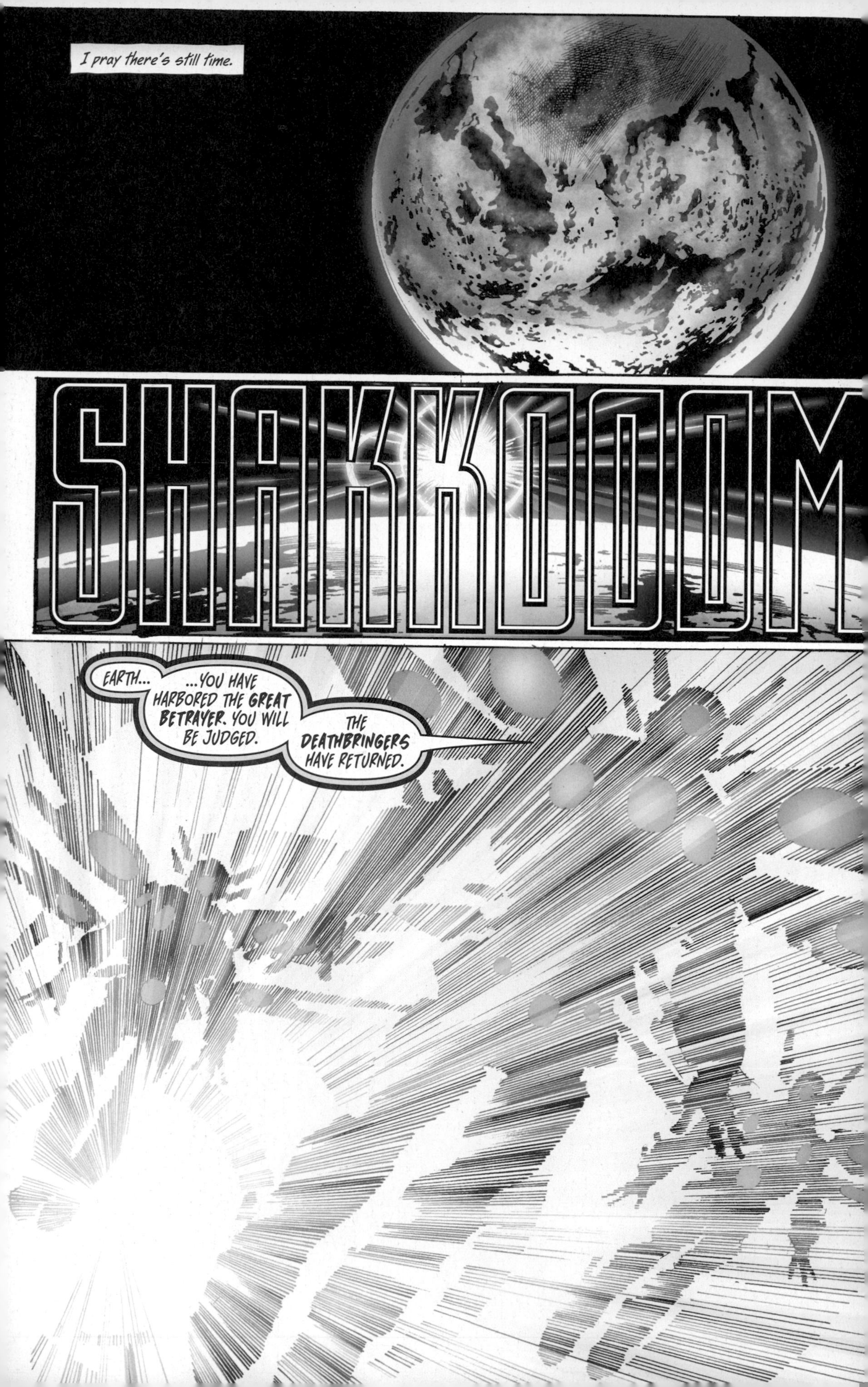
I pray there's still time.
SHAKOOOM
EARTH...
...YOU HAVE HARBORED THE GREAT BETRAYER. YOU WILL BE JUDGED.
THE DEATHBRINGERS HAVE RETURNED.

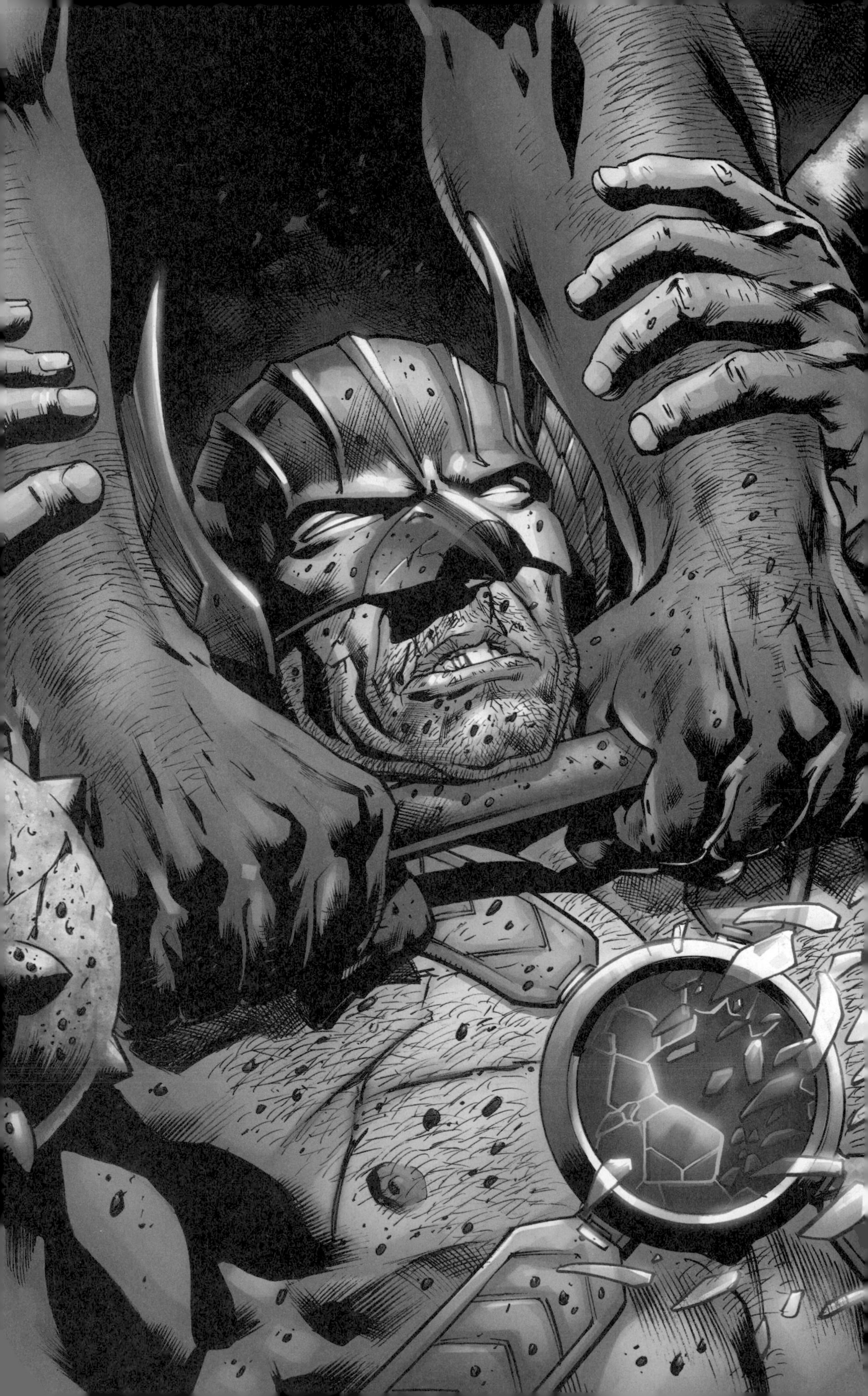

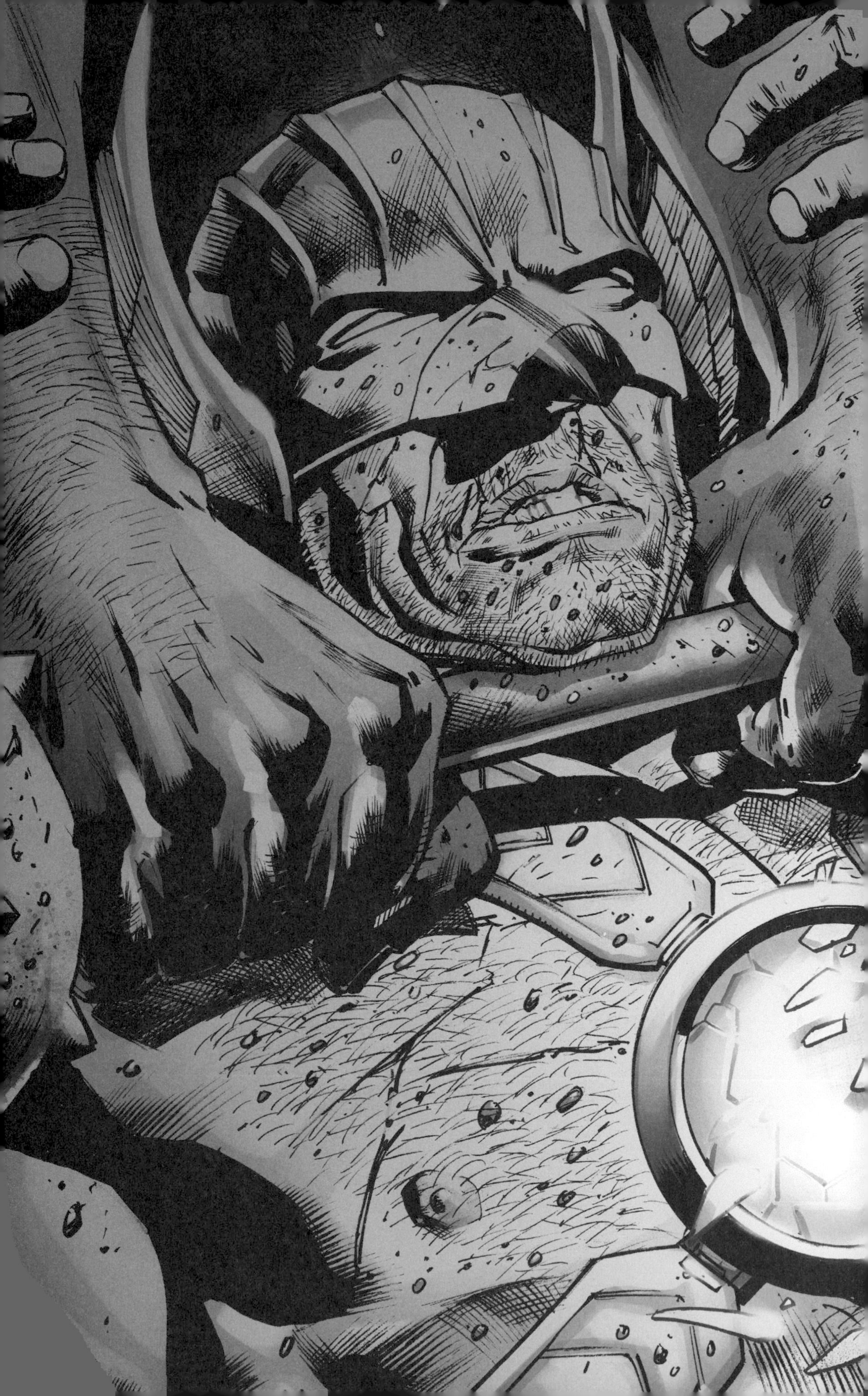

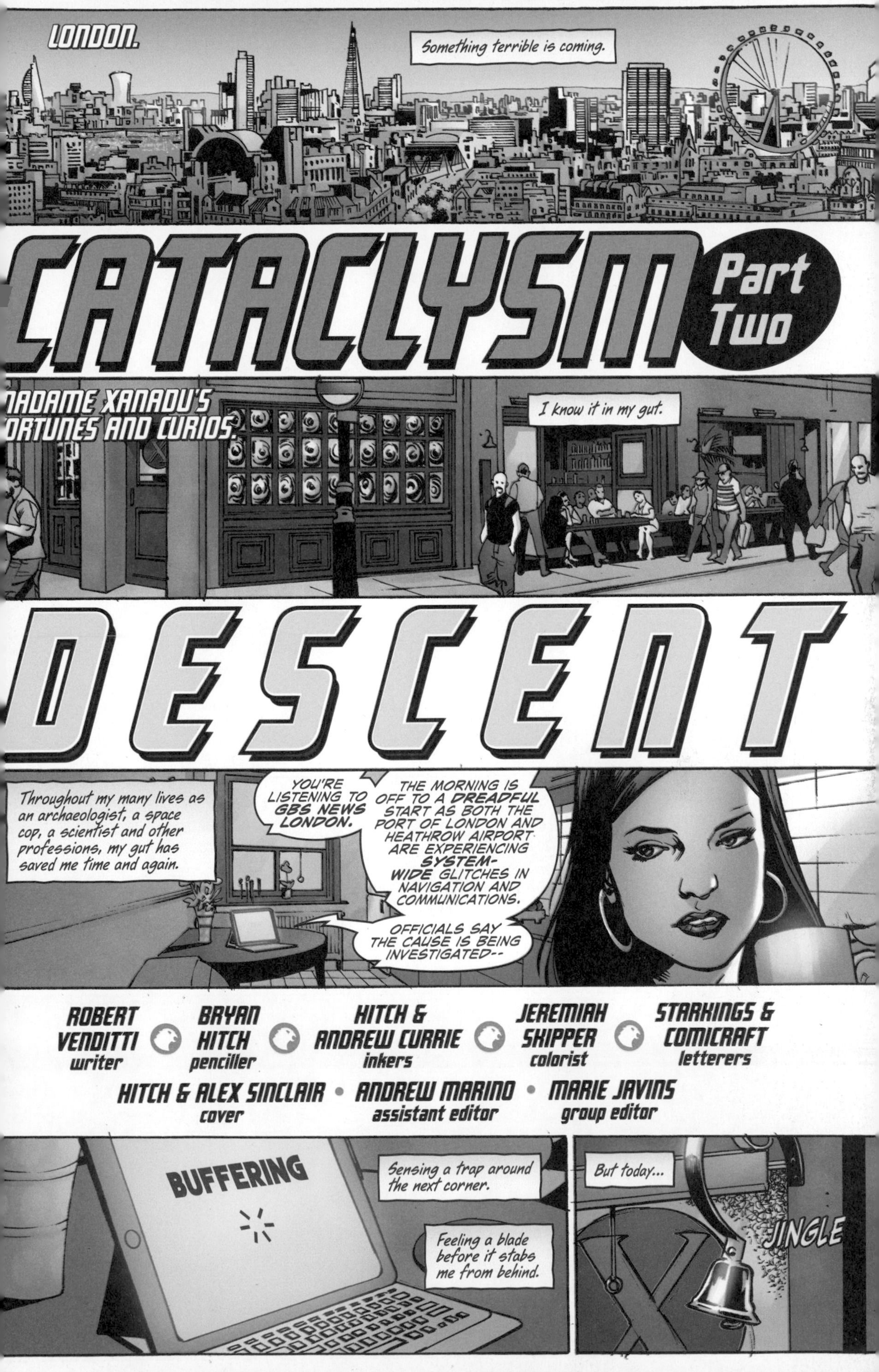
LONDON.
Something terrible is coming.
CATACLYSM
Part Two
ADAME XANADU'S
ORTUNES AND CURIOS.
I know it in my gut.
DESCENT
Throughout my many lives as an archaeologist, a space cop, a scientist and other professions, my gut has saved me time and again.
YOU'RE LISTENING TO GBS NEWS LONDON.
THE MORNING IS OFF TO A DREADFUL START AS BOTH THE PORT OF LONDON AND HEATHROW AIRPORT ARE EXPERIENCING SYSTEM-WIDE GLITCHES IN NAVIGATION AND COMMUNICATIONS.
OFFICIALS SAY THE CAUSE IS BEING INVESTIGATED--
ROBERT VENDITTI writer
BRYAN HITCH penciller
HITCH & ANDREW CURRIE inkers
JEREMIAH SKIPPER colorist
STARKINGS & COMICRAFT letterers
HITCH & ALEX SINCLAIR cover
ANDREW MARINO assistant editor
MARIE JAVINS group editor
BUFFERING
Sensing a trap around the next corner.
Feeling a blade before it stabs me from behind.
But today...
JINGLE

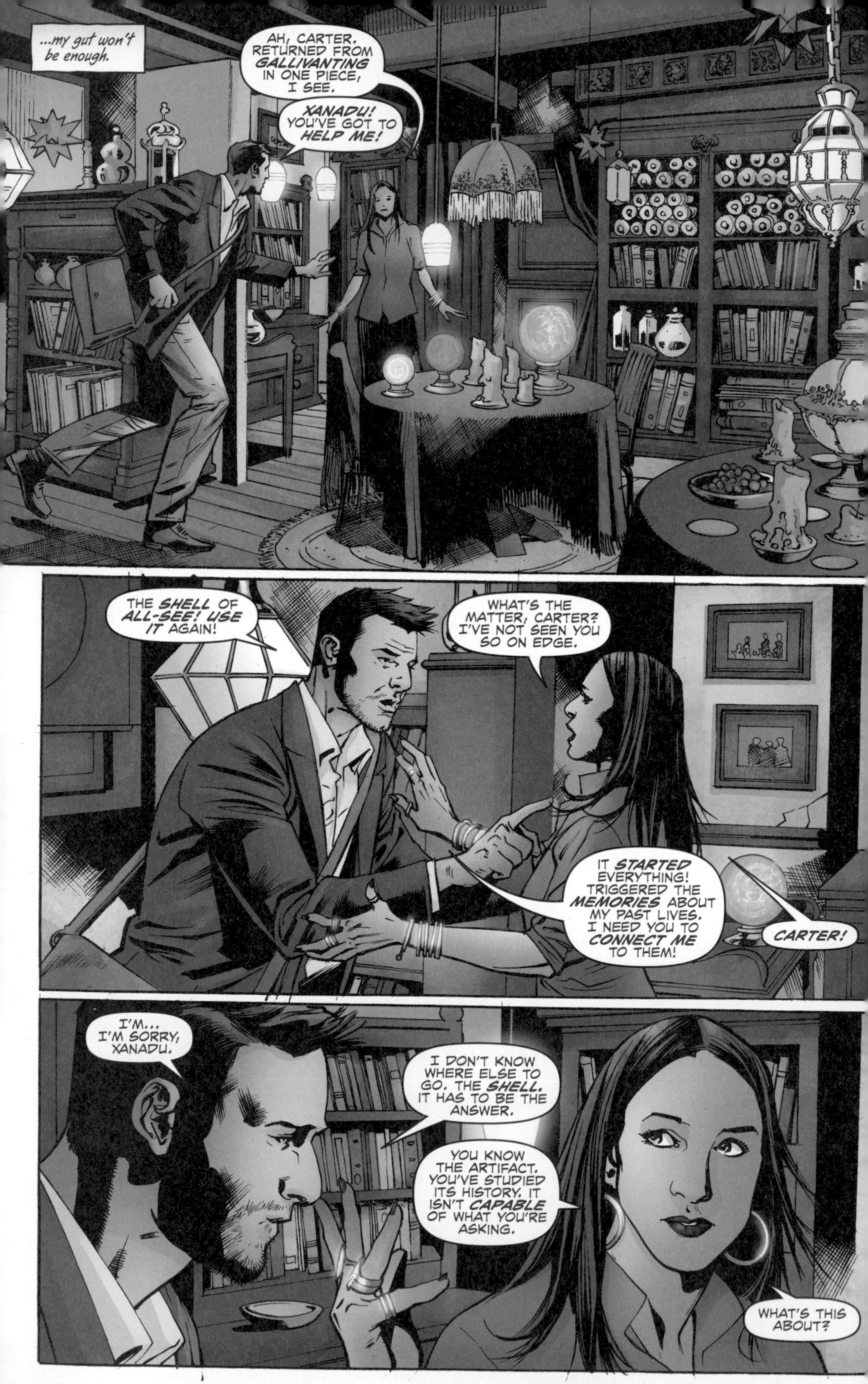
...my gut won't be enough.
AH, CARTER. RETURNED FROM GALLIVANTING IN ONE PIECE, I SEE.
XANADU! YOU'VE GOT TO HELP ME!
THE SHELL OF ALL-SEE! USE IT AGAIN!
WHAT'S THE MATTER, CARTER? I'VE NOT SEEN YOU SO ON EDGE.
IT STARTED EVERYTHING! TRIGGERED THE MEMORIES ABOUT MY PAST LIVES. I NEED YOU TO CONNECT ME TO THEM!
CARTER!
I'M... I'M SORRY, XANADU.
I DON'T KNOW WHERE ELSE TO GO. THE SHELL. IT HAS TO BE THE ANSWER.
YOU KNOW THE ARTIFACT. YOU'VE STUDIED ITS HISTORY. IT ISN'T CAPABLE OF WHAT YOU'RE ASKING.
WHAT'S THIS ABOUT?

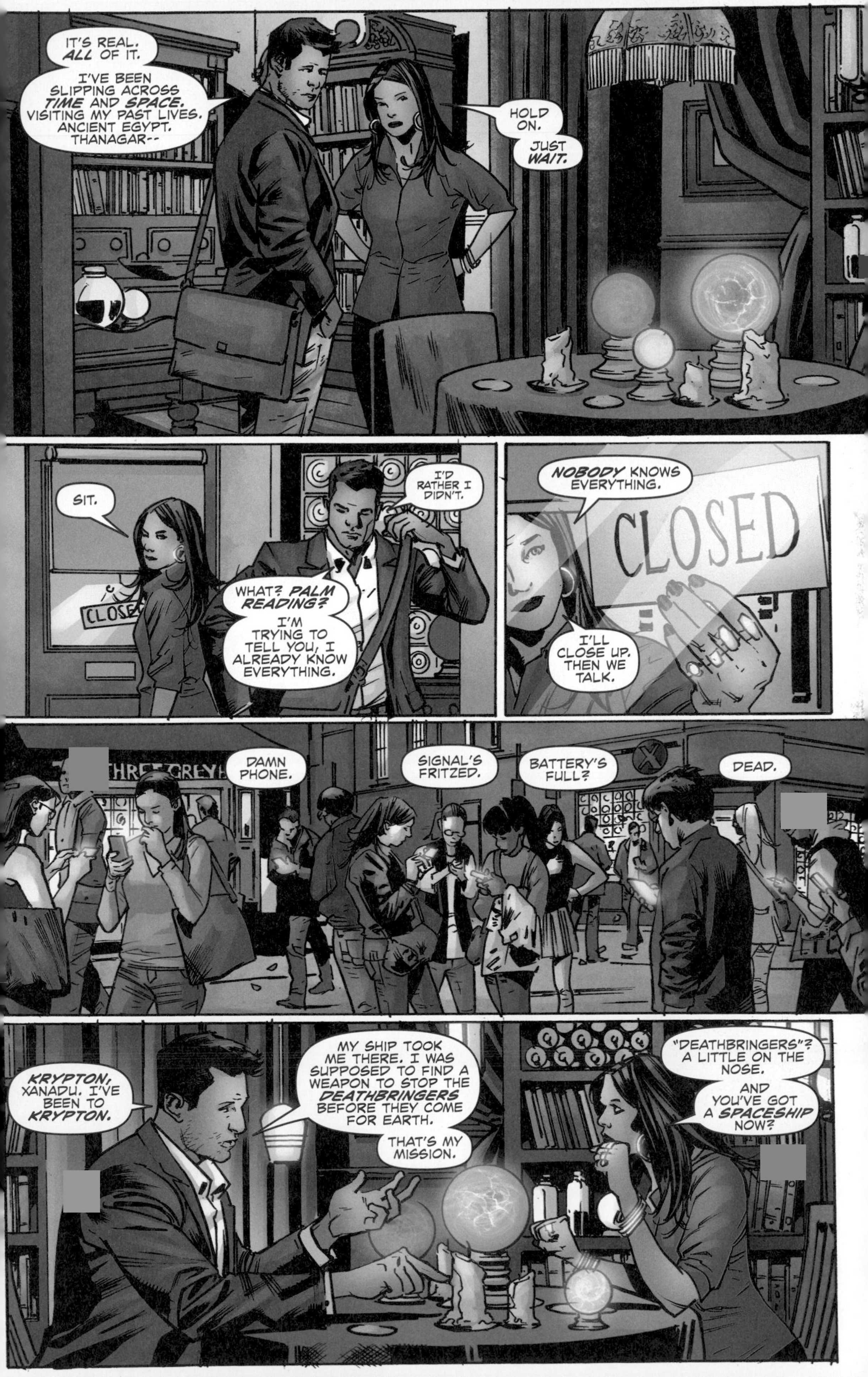

IT'S REAL. ***ALL*** OF IT.
I'VE BEEN SLIPPING ACROSS ***TIME*** AND ***SPACE.*** VISITING MY PAST LIVES. ANCIENT EGYPT. THANAGAR--
HOLD ON.
JUST ***WAIT.***
SIT.
I'D RATHER I DIDN'T.
WHAT? ***PALM READING?***
I'M TRYING TO TELL YOU, I ALREADY KNOW EVERYTHING.
NOBODY KNOWS EVERYTHING.
CLOSED
I'LL CLOSE UP. THEN WE TALK.
DAMN PHONE.
SIGNAL'S FRITZED.
BATTERY'S FULL?
DEAD.
KRYPTON, XANADU. I'VE BEEN TO ***KRYPTON.***
MY SHIP TOOK ME THERE. I WAS SUPPOSED TO FIND A WEAPON TO STOP THE ***DEATHBRINGERS*** BEFORE THEY COME FOR EARTH.
THAT'S MY MISSION.
"DEATHBRINGERS"? A LITTLE ON THE NOSE.
AND YOU'VE GOT A ***SPACESHIP*** NOW?

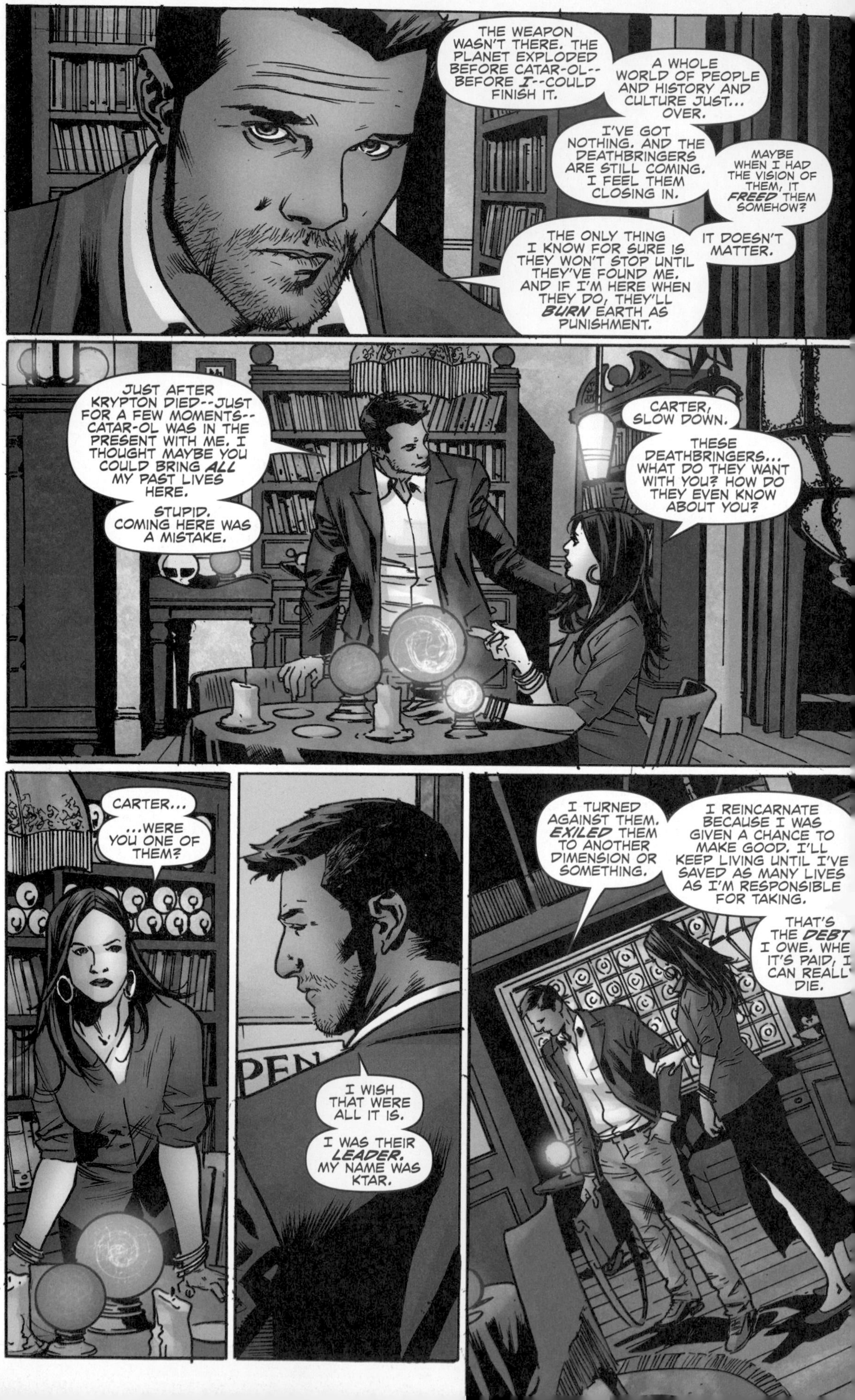
THE WEAPON WASN'T THERE. THE PLANET EXPLODED BEFORE CATAR-OL-- BEFORE *I*--COULD FINISH IT.
A WHOLE WORLD OF PEOPLE AND HISTORY AND CULTURE JUST... OVER.
I'VE GOT NOTHING. AND THE DEATHBRINGERS ARE STILL COMING. I FEEL THEM CLOSING IN.
MAYBE WHEN I HAD THE VISION OF THEM, IT *FREED* THEM SOMEHOW?
THE ONLY THING I KNOW FOR SURE IS THEY WON'T STOP UNTIL THEY'VE FOUND ME. AND IF I'M HERE WHEN THEY DO, THEY'LL *BURN* EARTH AS PUNISHMENT.
IT DOESN'T MATTER.
JUST AFTER KRYPTON DIED--JUST FOR A FEW MOMENTS-- CATAR-OL WAS IN THE PRESENT WITH ME. I THOUGHT MAYBE YOU COULD BRING *ALL* MY PAST LIVES HERE.
STUPID. COMING HERE WAS A MISTAKE.
CARTER, SLOW DOWN.
THESE DEATHBRINGERS... WHAT DO THEY WANT WITH YOU? HOW DO THEY EVEN KNOW ABOUT YOU?
CARTER...
...WERE YOU ONE OF THEM?
I WISH THAT WERE ALL IT IS.
I WAS THEIR *LEADER.* MY NAME WAS KTAR.
I TURNED AGAINST THEM. *EXILED* THEM TO ANOTHER DIMENSION OR SOMETHING.
I REINCARNATE BECAUSE I WAS GIVEN A CHANCE TO MAKE GOOD. I'LL KEEP LIVING UNTIL I'VE SAVED AS MANY LIVES AS I'M RESPONSIBLE FOR TAKING.
THAT'S THE *DEBT* I OWE. WHE IT'S PAID, I CAN REALL DIE.

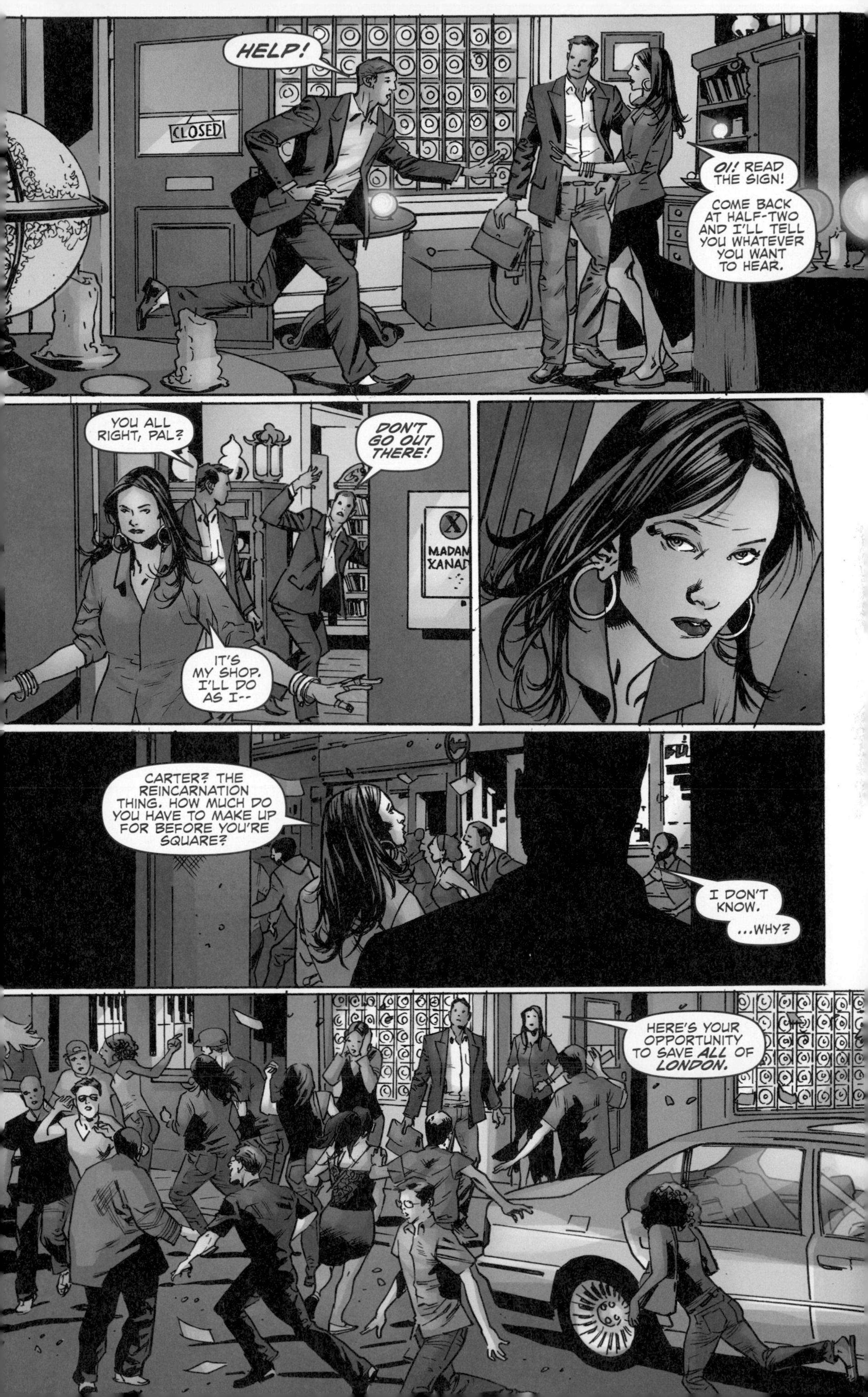
HELP!
OI! READ THE SIGN!
COME BACK AT HALF-TWO AND I'LL TELL YOU WHATEVER YOU WANT TO HEAR.
CLOSED
YOU ALL RIGHT, PAL?
DON'T GO OUT THERE!
MADAM XANAD
IT'S MY SHOP. I'LL DO AS I--
CARTER? THE REINCARNATION THING. HOW MUCH DO YOU HAVE TO MAKE UP FOR BEFORE YOU'RE SQUARE?
I DON'T KNOW.
...WHY?
HERE'S YOUR OPPORTUNITY TO SAVE ALL OF LONDON.

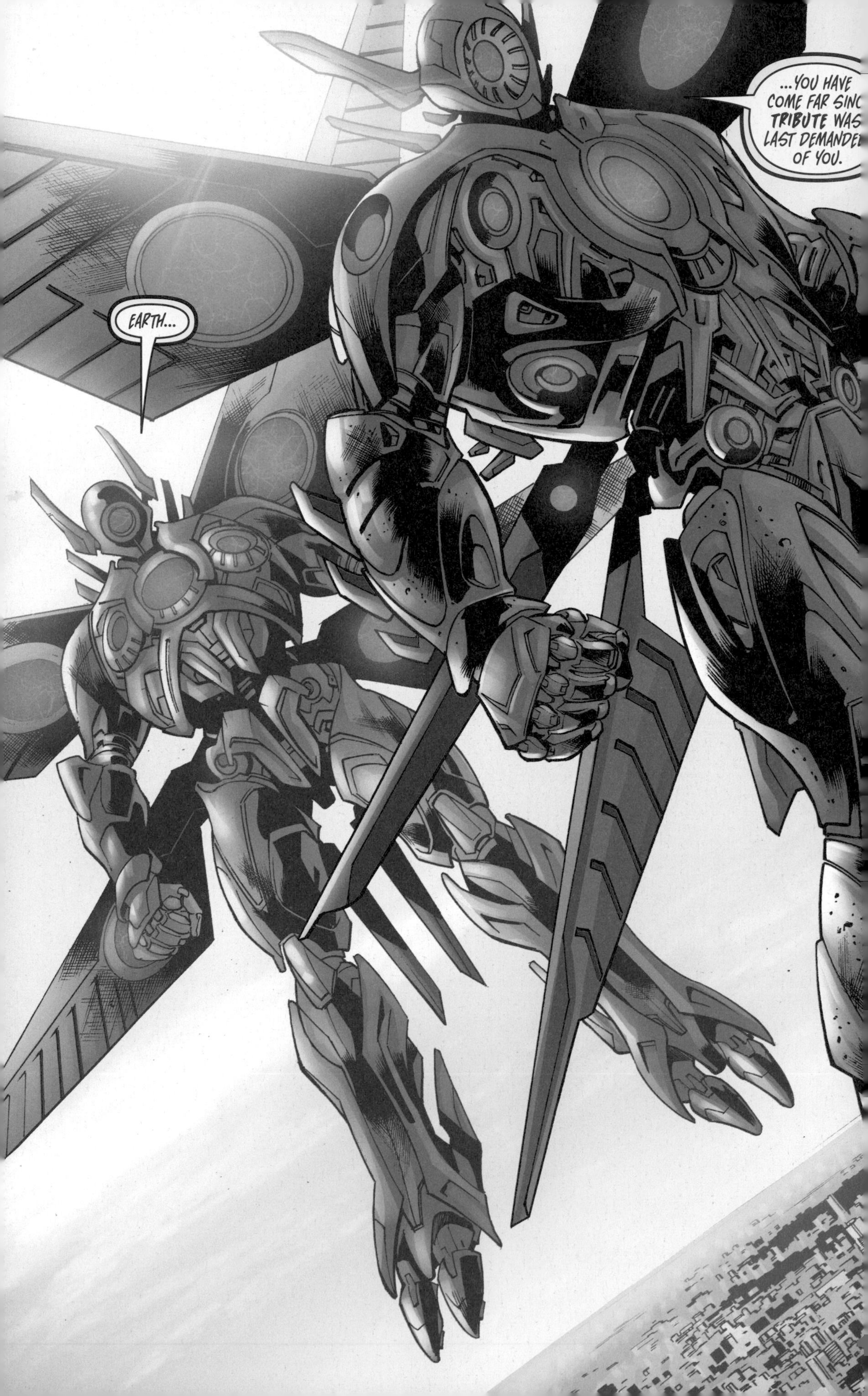
EARTH...
...YOU HAVE COME FAR SINC TRIBUTE WAS LAST DEMANDED OF YOU.

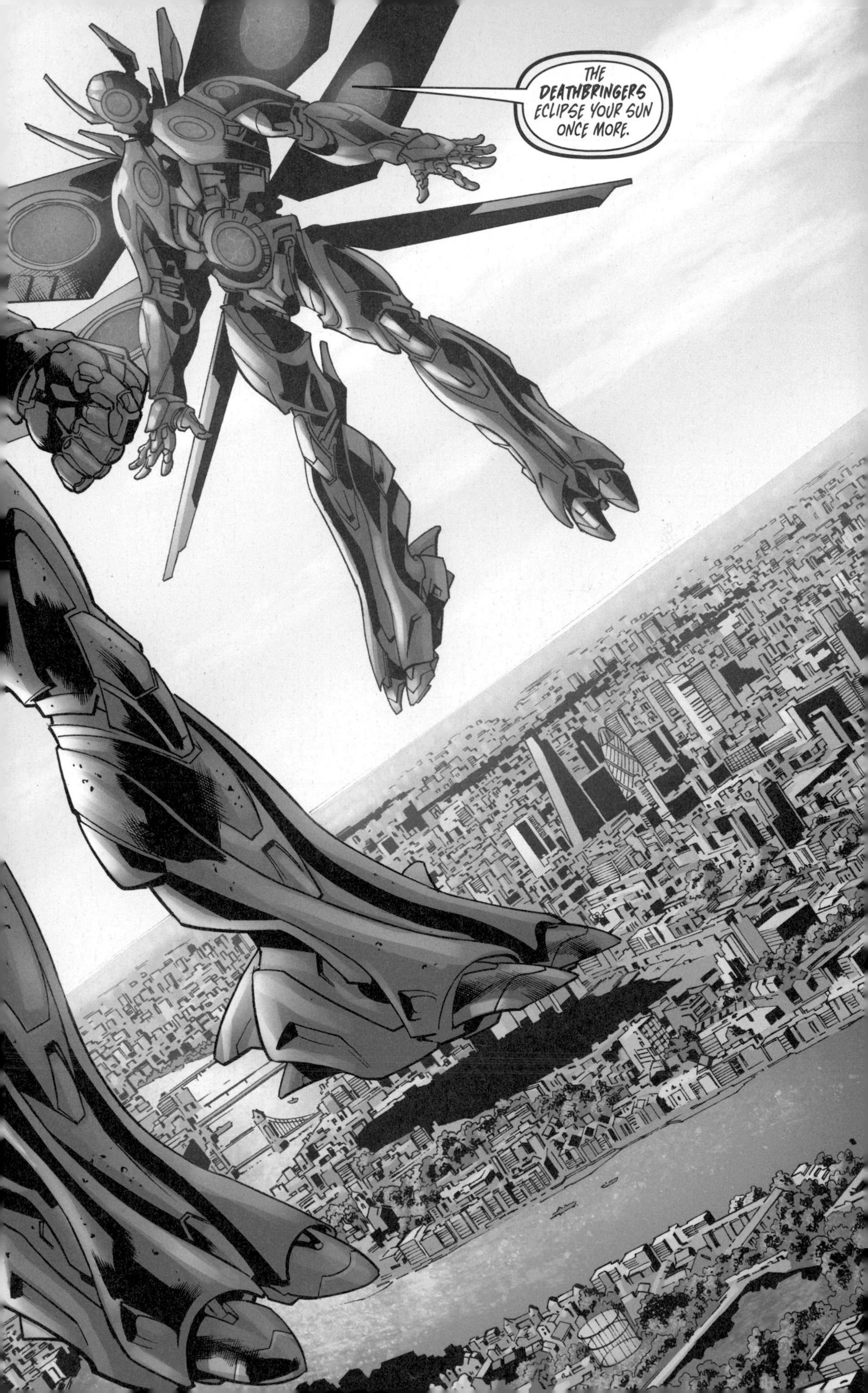
THE DEATHBRINGERS ECLIPSE YOUR SUN ONCE MORE.

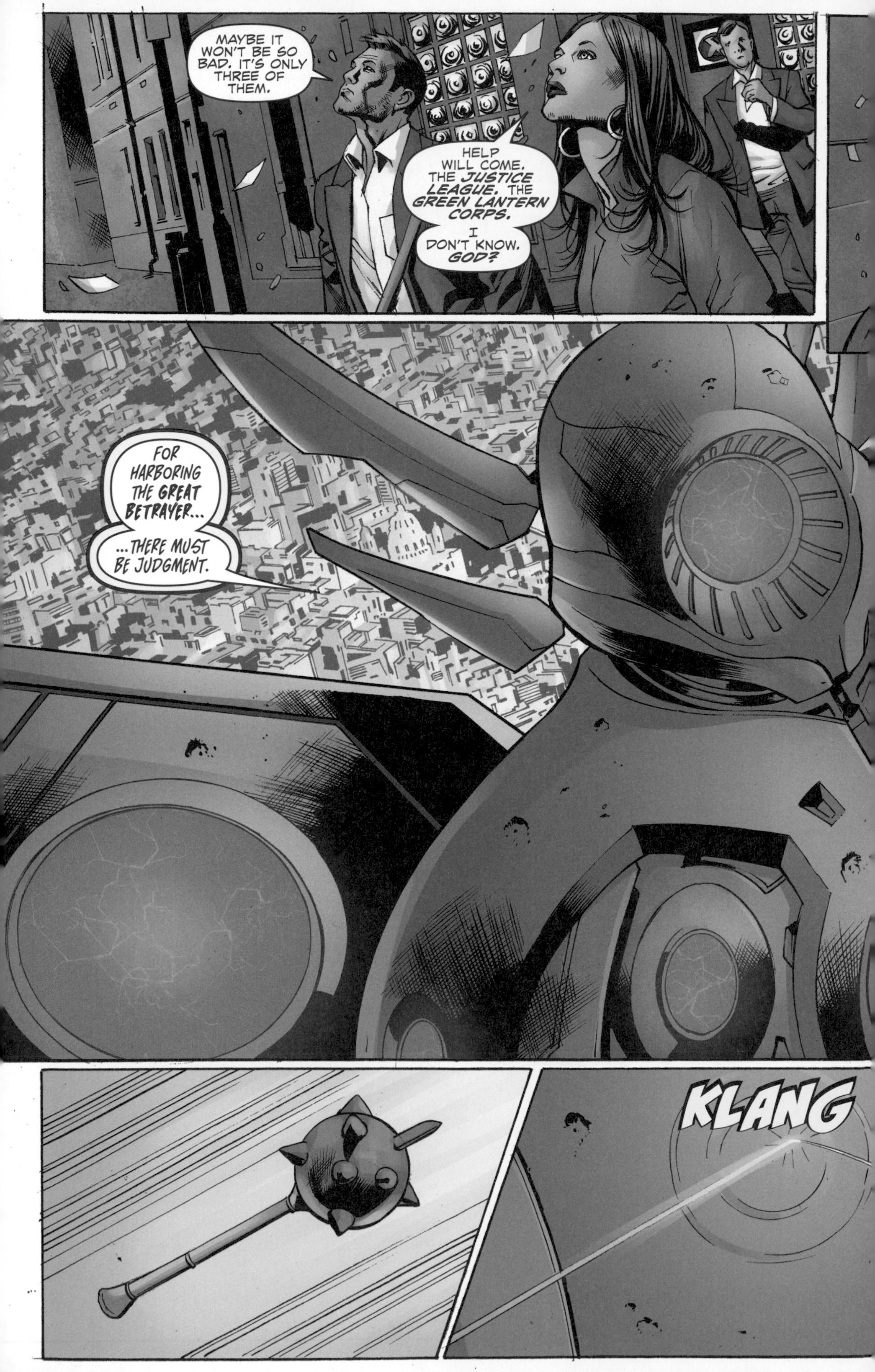
MAYBE IT WON'T BE SO BAD. IT'S ONLY THREE OF THEM.
HELP WILL COME. THE JUSTICE LEAGUE. THE GREEN LANTERN CORPS.
I DON'T KNOW. GOD?
FOR HARBORING THE GREAT BETRAYER...
...THERE MUST BE JUDGMENT.
KLANG

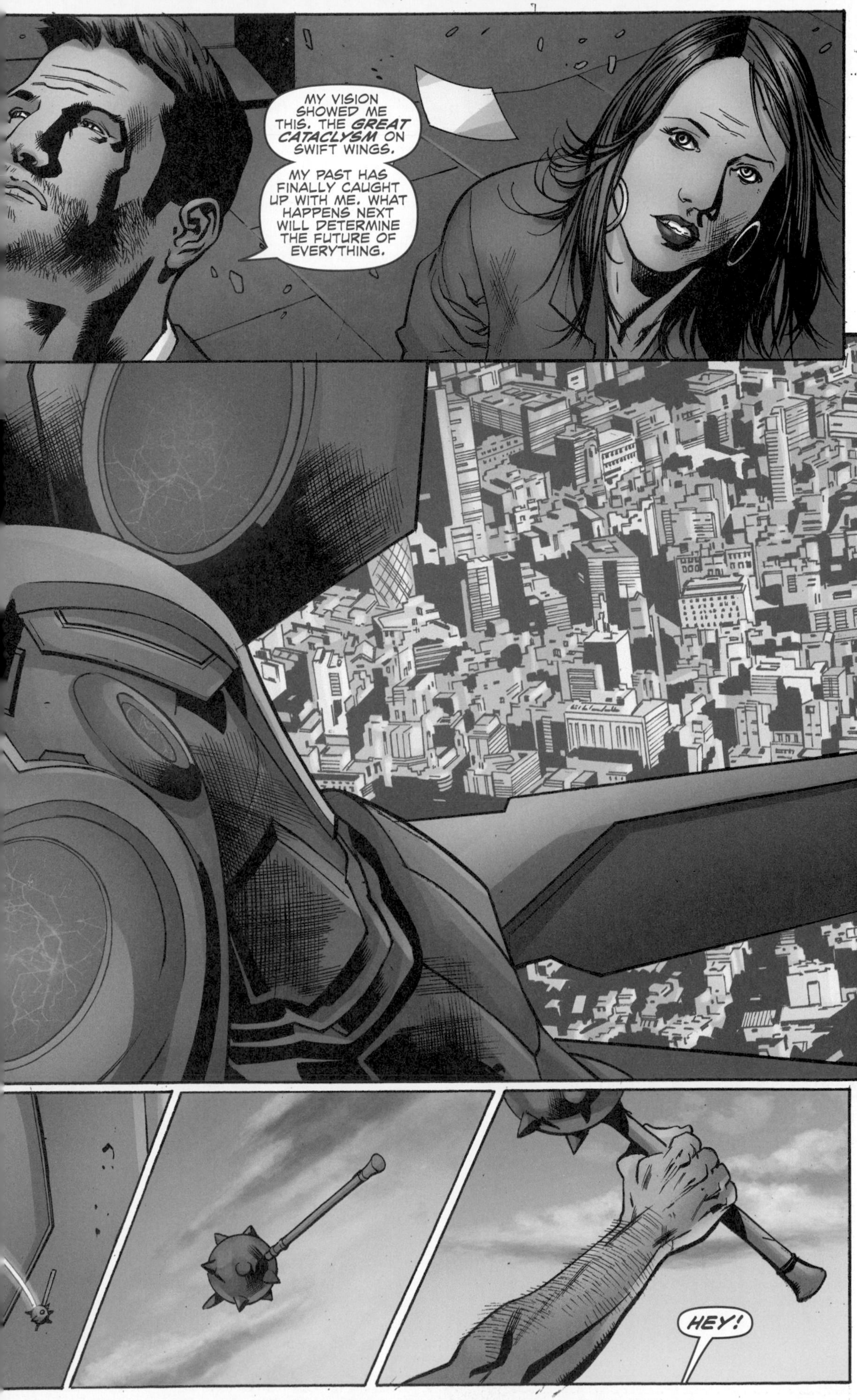
MY VISION SHOWED ME THIS. THE **GREAT CATACLYSM** ON SWIFT WINGS.
MY PAST HAS FINALLY CAUGHT UP WITH ME. WHAT HAPPENS NEXT WILL DETERMINE THE FUTURE OF EVERYTHING.
HEY!

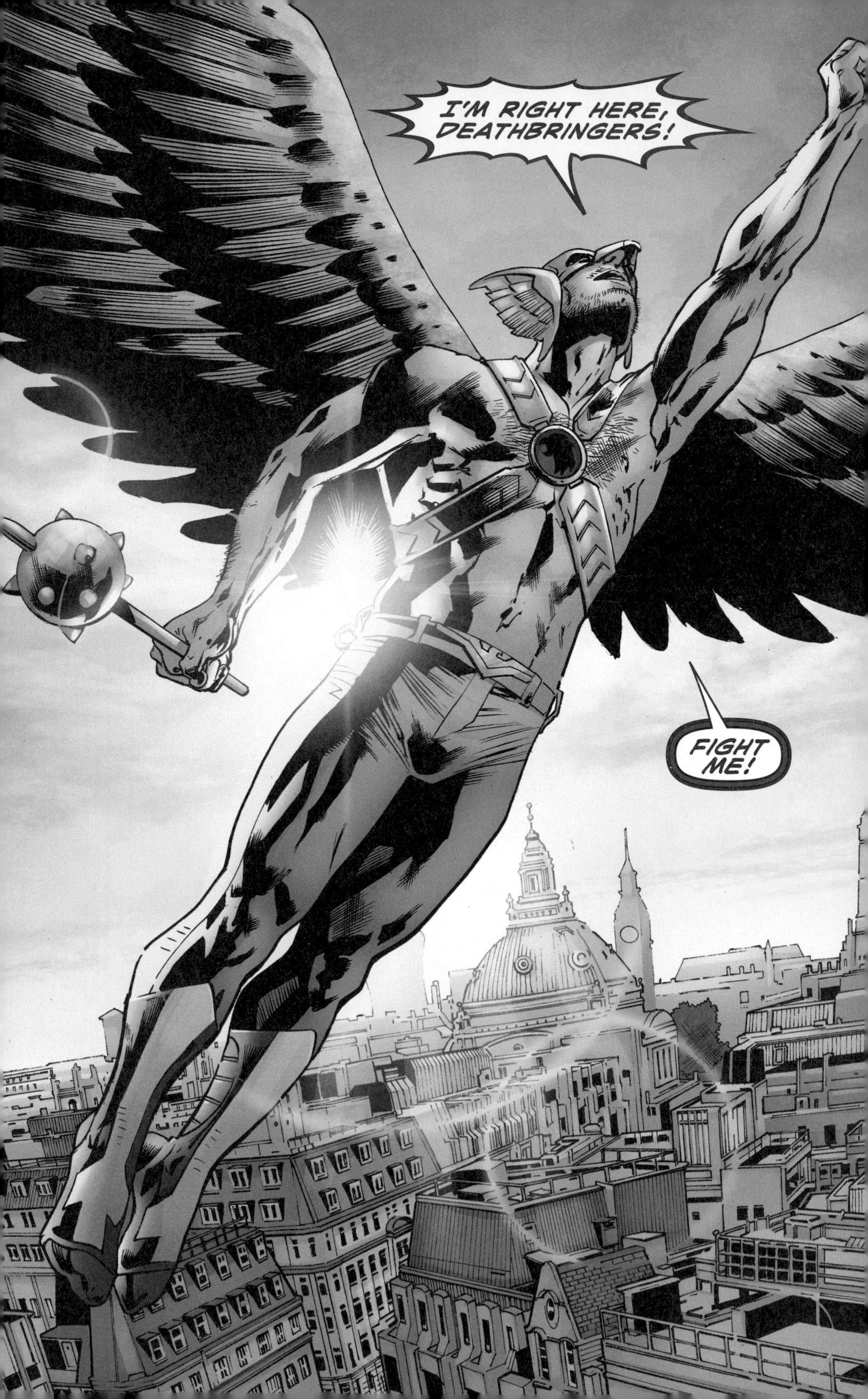
I'M RIGHT HERE, DEATHBRINGERS!
FIGHT ME!

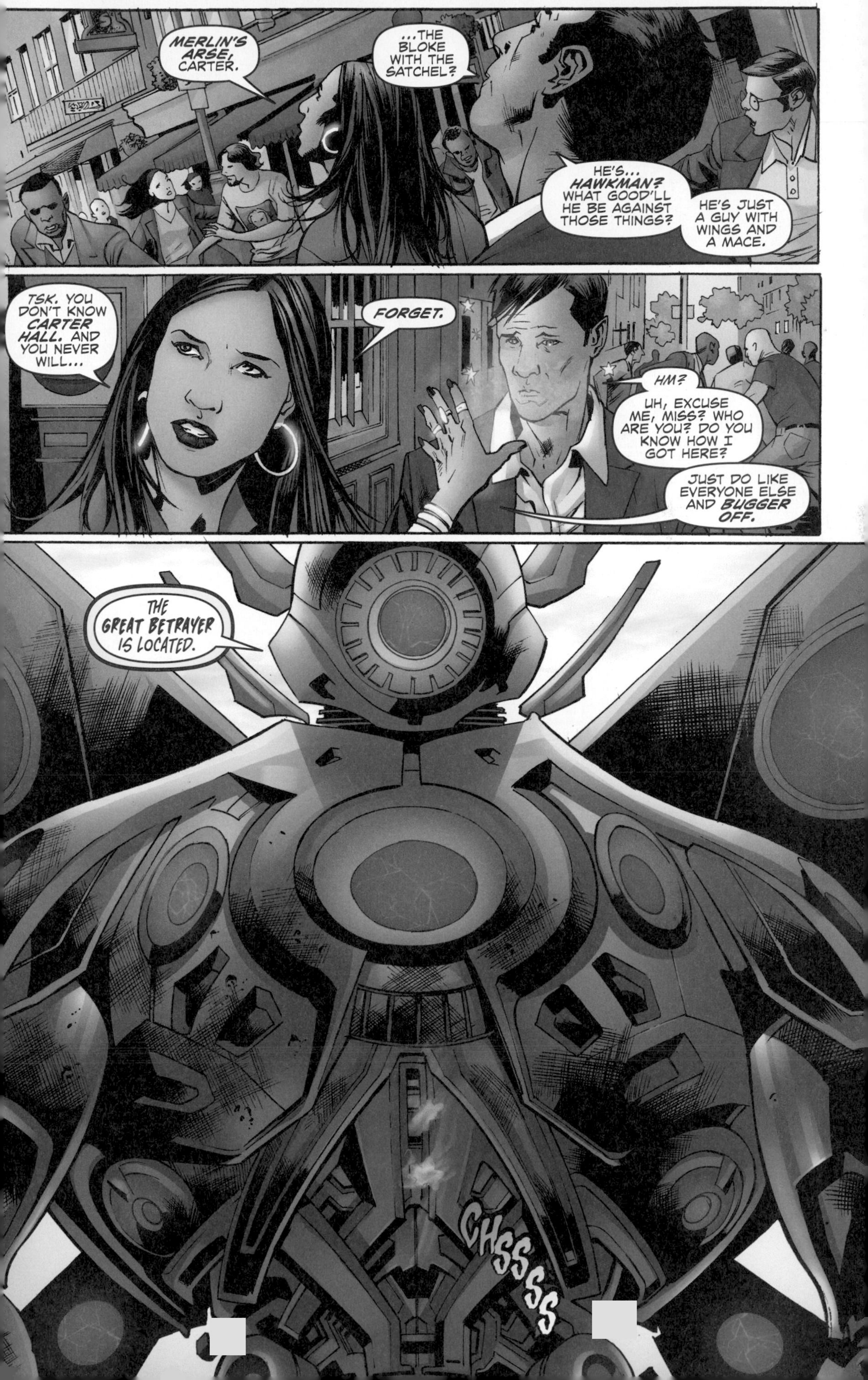
MERLIN'S ARSE, CARTER.
...THE BLOKE WITH THE SATCHEL?
HE'S... HAWKMAN? WHAT GOOD'LL HE BE AGAINST THOSE THINGS?
HE'S JUST A GUY WITH WINGS AND A MACE.
TSK. YOU DON'T KNOW CARTER HALL. AND YOU NEVER WILL...
FORGET.
HM?
UH, EXCUSE ME, MISS? WHO ARE YOU? DO YOU KNOW HOW I GOT HERE?
JUST DO LIKE EVERYONE ELSE AND BUGGER OFF.
THE GREAT BETRAYER IS LOCATED.
CHSSSSS

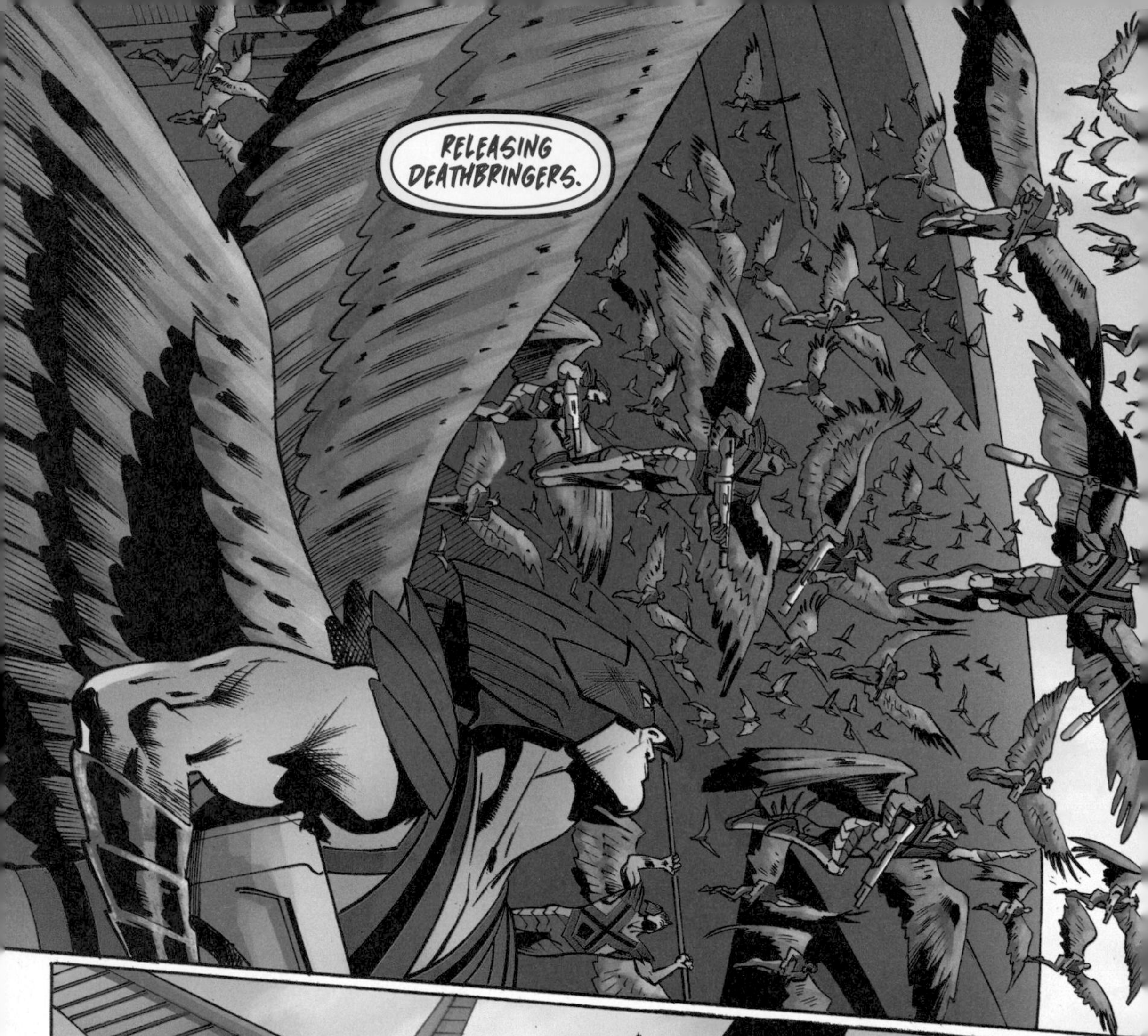
RELEASING DEATHBRINGERS.
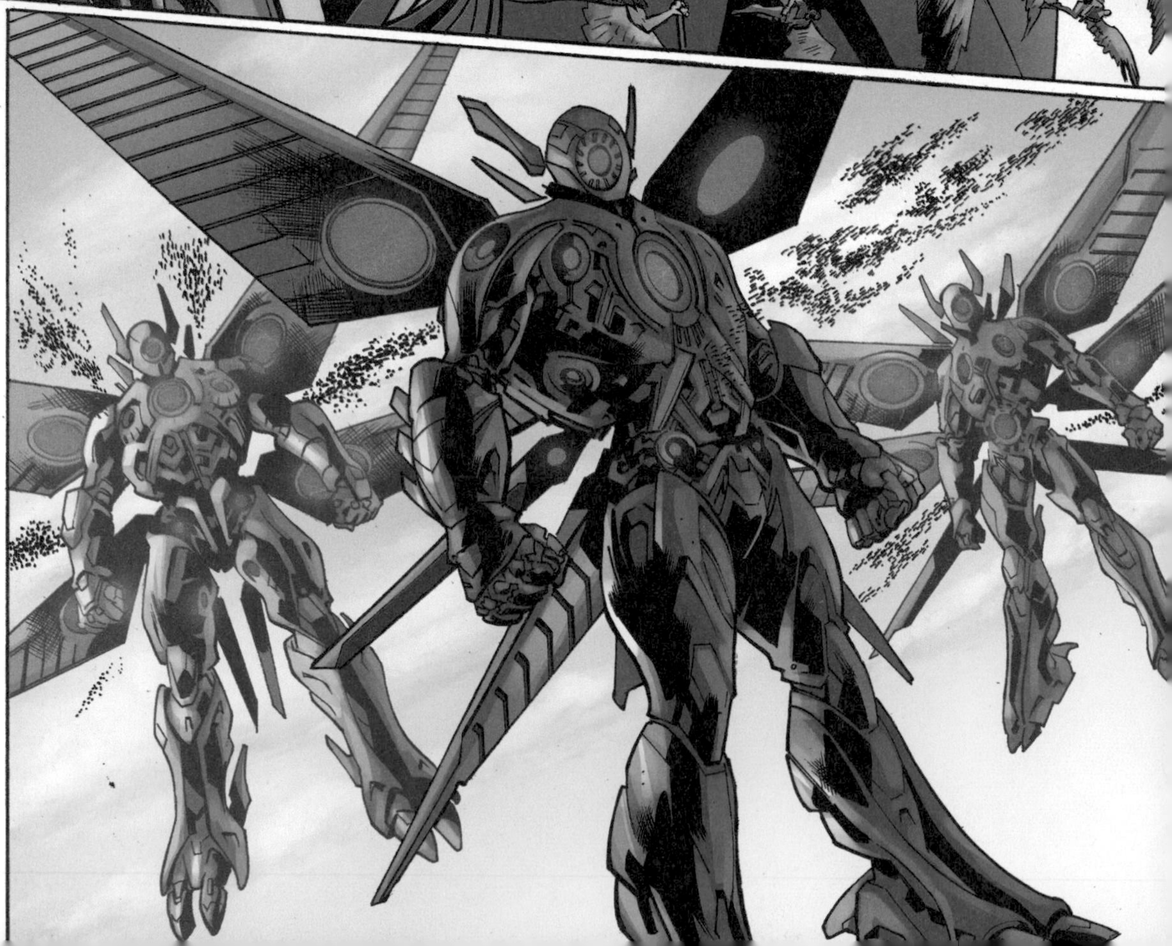

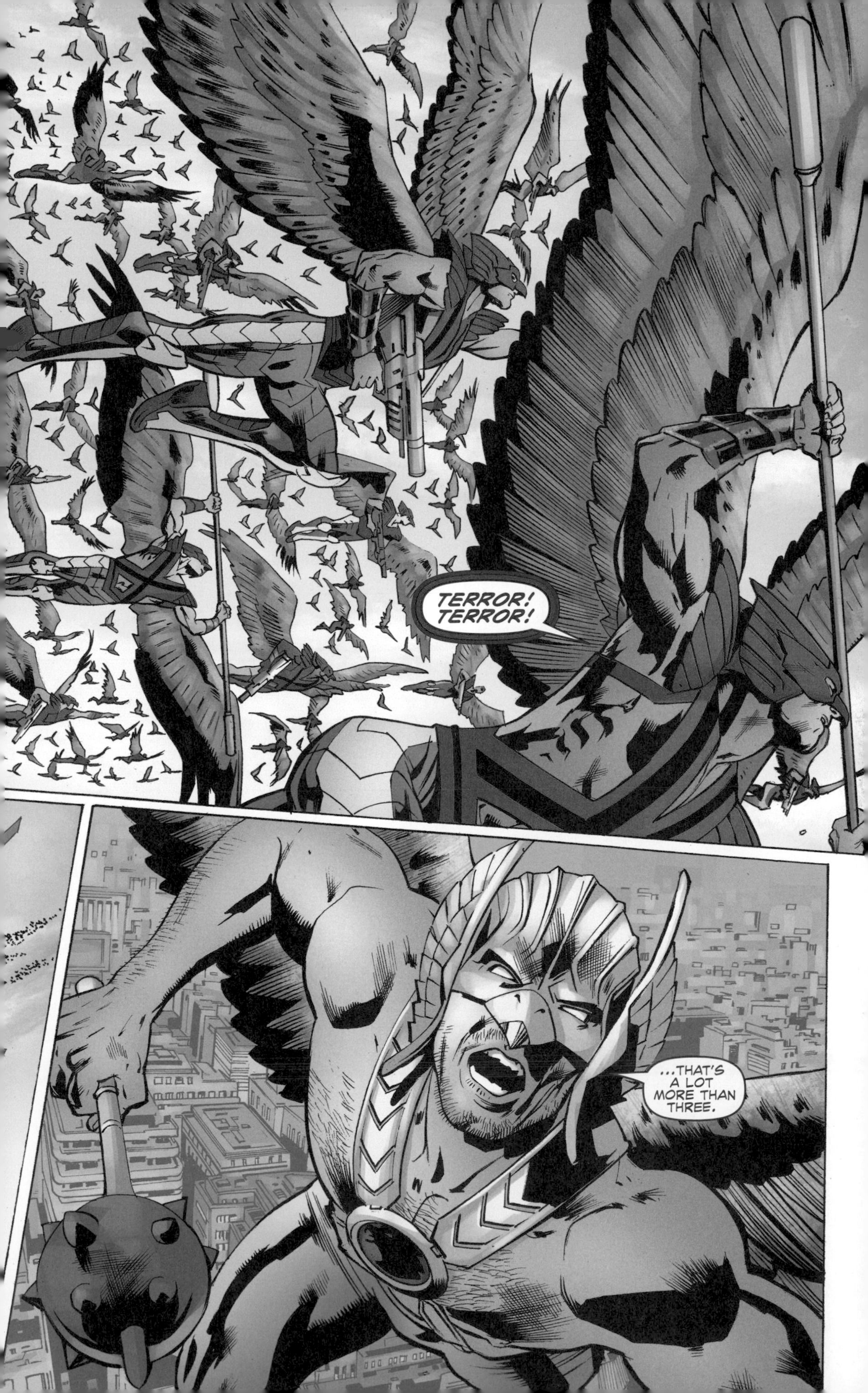
TERROR! TERROR!
...THAT'S A LOT MORE THAN THREE.

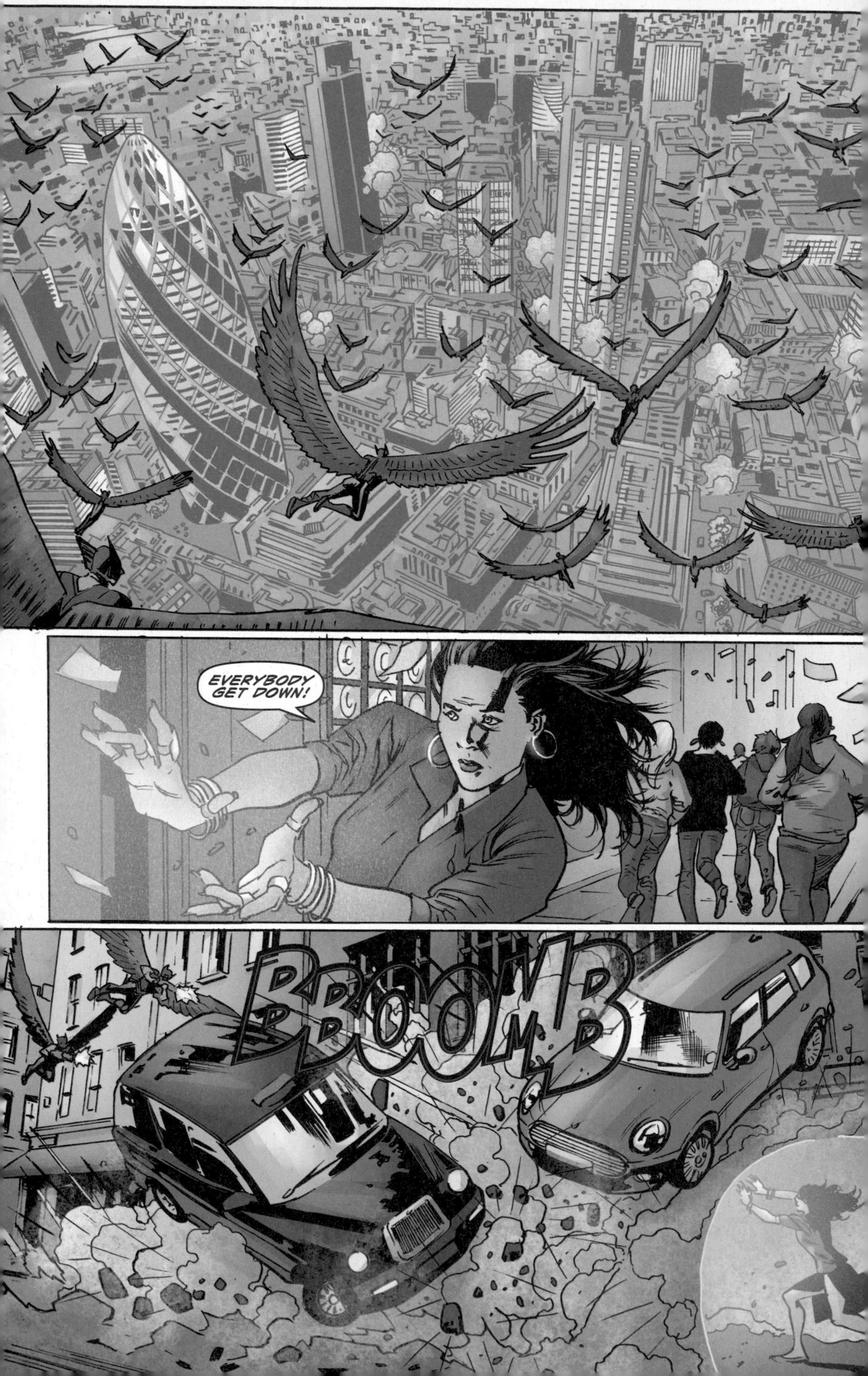
EVERYBODY GET DOWN!
BBOOOMB

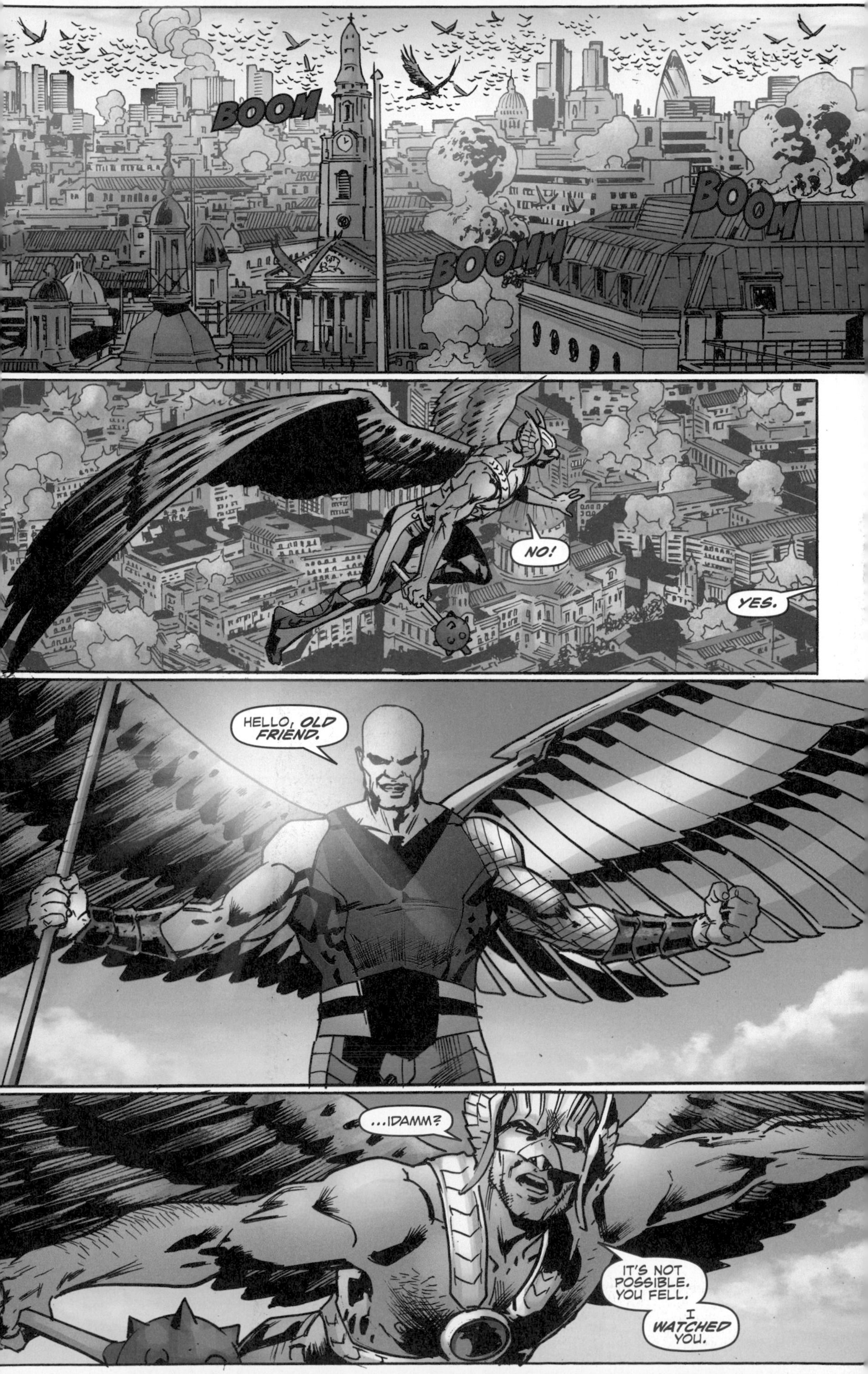
BOOM
BOOMM
BOOM
NO!
YES.
HELLO, OLD FRIEND.
...IDAMM?
IT'S NOT POSSIBLE. YOU FELL.
I WATCHED YOU.

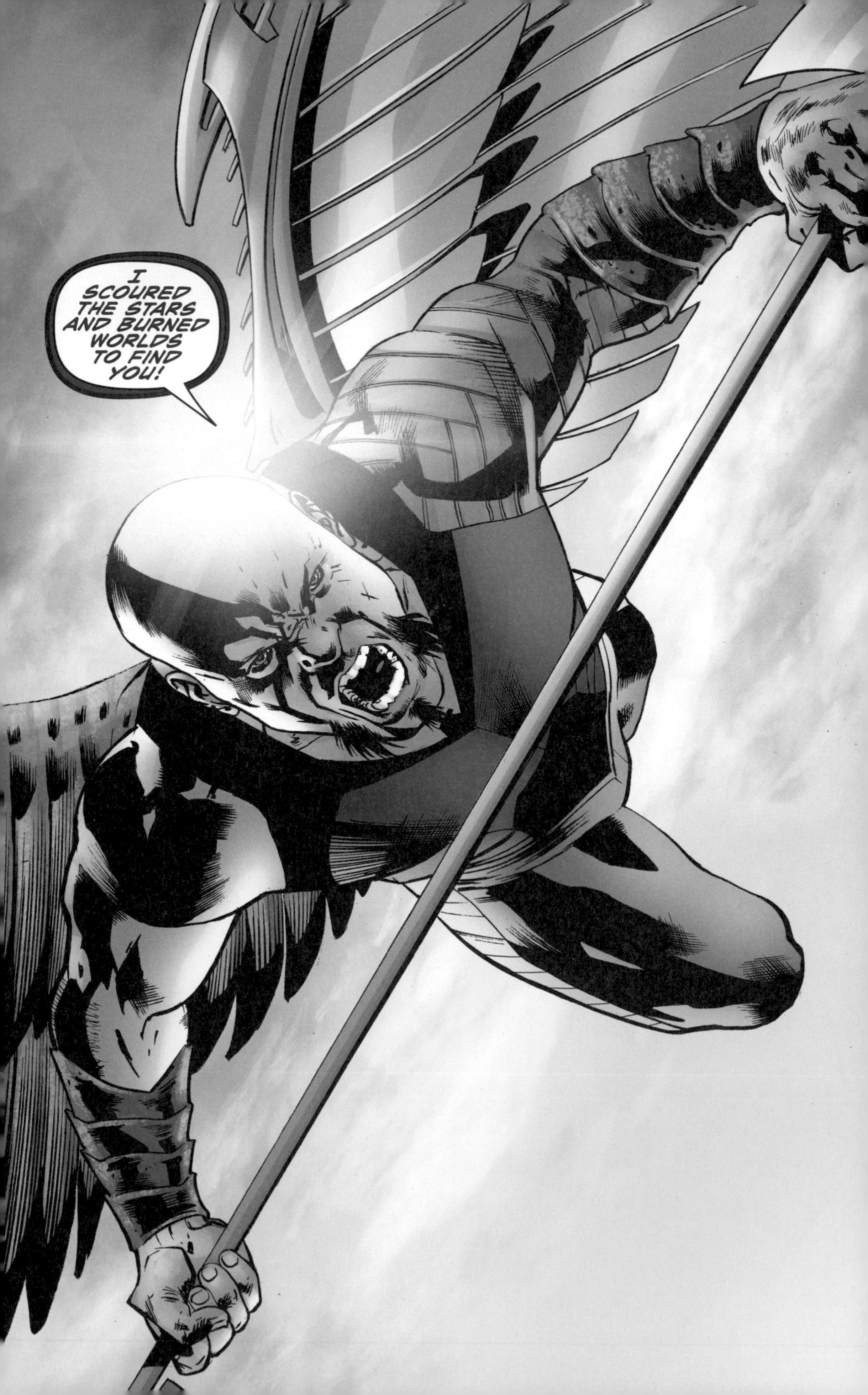
I SCOURED THE STARS AND BURNED WORLDS TO FIND YOU!

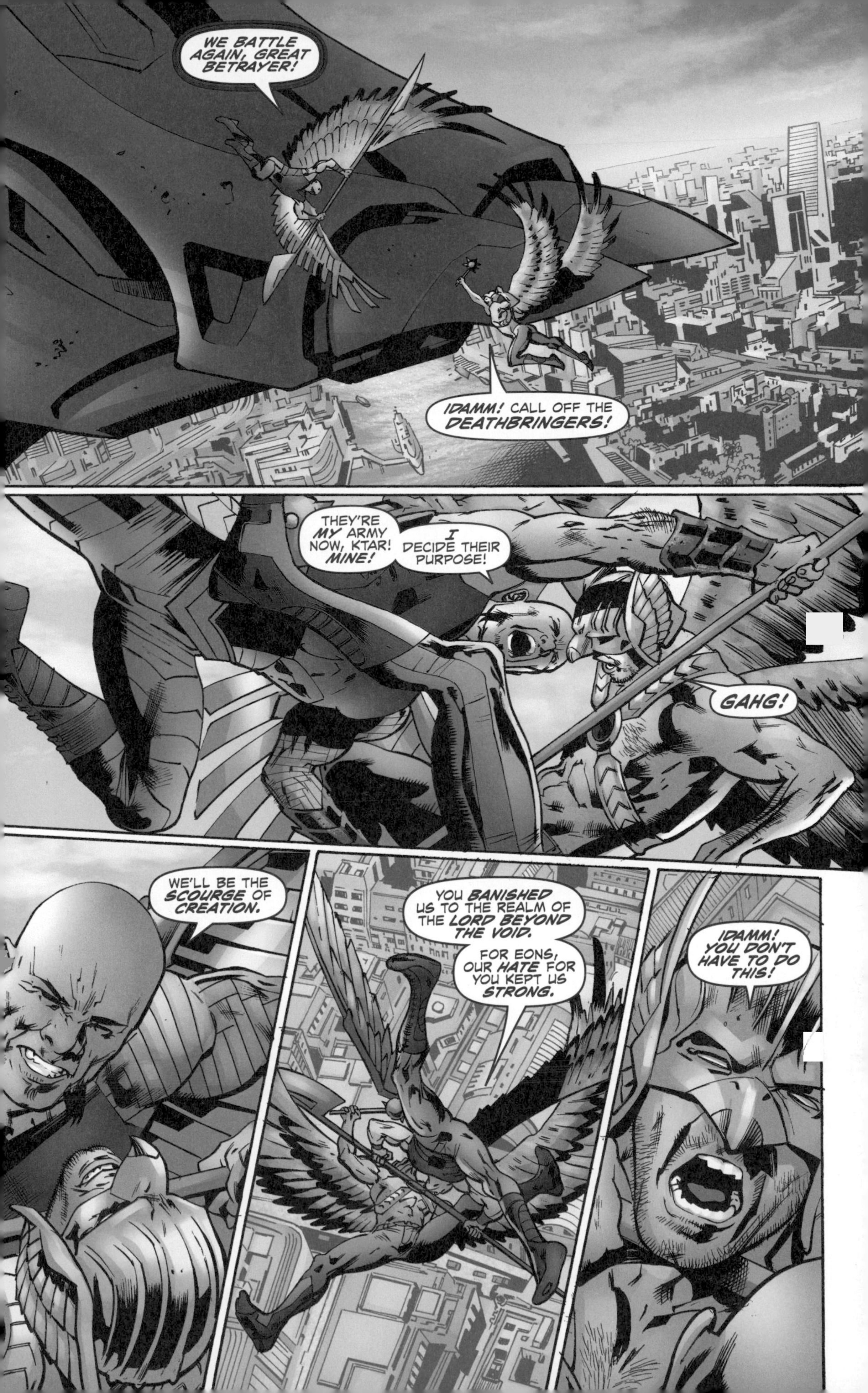
WE BATTLE AGAIN, GREAT BETRAYER!
IDAMM! CALL OFF THE DEATHBRINGERS!
THEY'RE MY ARMY NOW, KTAR! MINE!
I DECIDE THEIR PURPOSE!
GAHG!
WE'LL BE THE SCOURGE OF CREATION.
YOU BANISHED US TO THE REALM OF THE LORD BEYOND THE VOID.
FOR EONS, OUR HATE FOR YOU KEPT US STRONG.
IDAMM! YOU DON'T HAVE TO DO THIS!

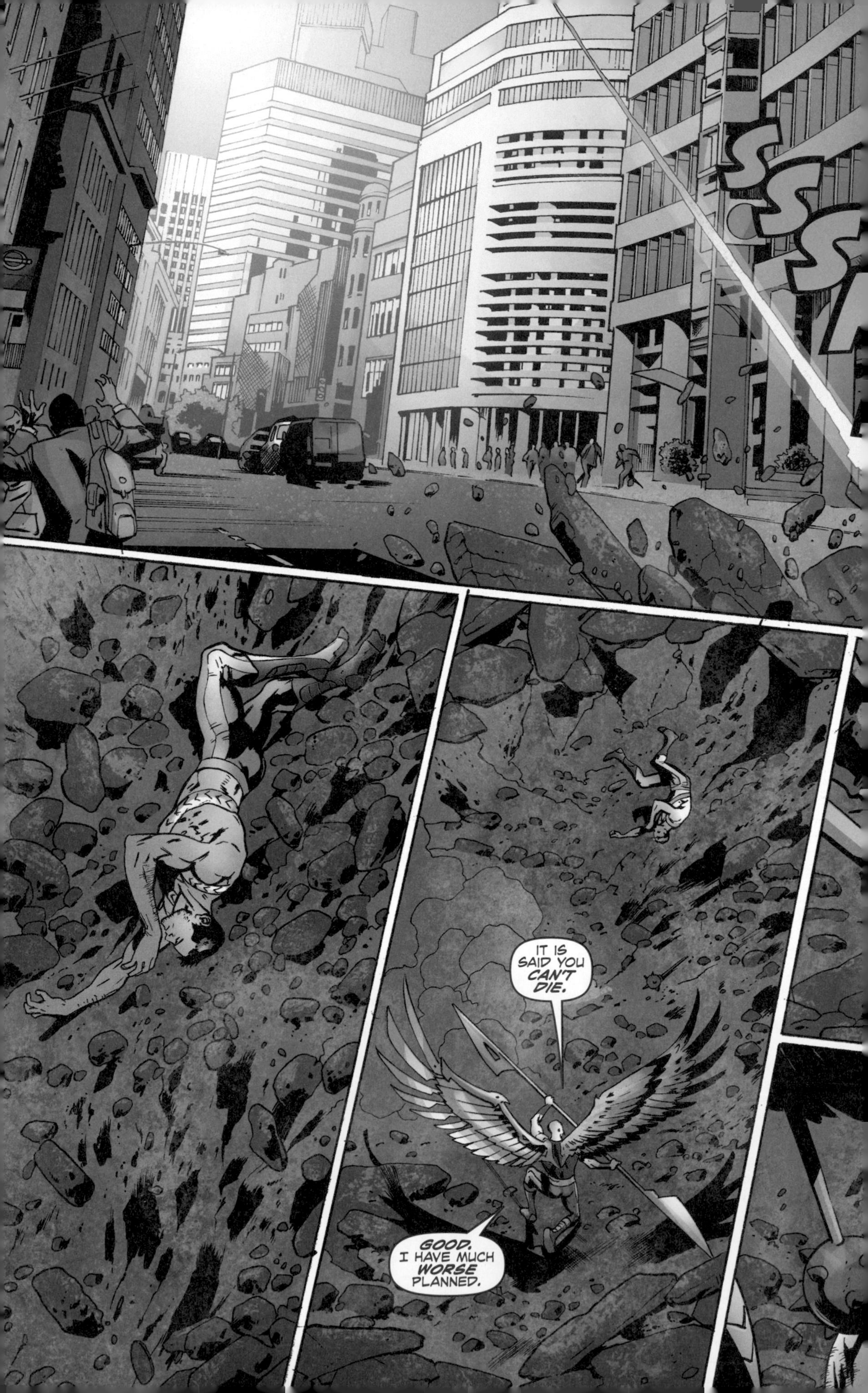
SSSH
IT IS SAID YOU CAN'T DIE.
GOOD. I HAVE MUCH WORSE PLANNED.

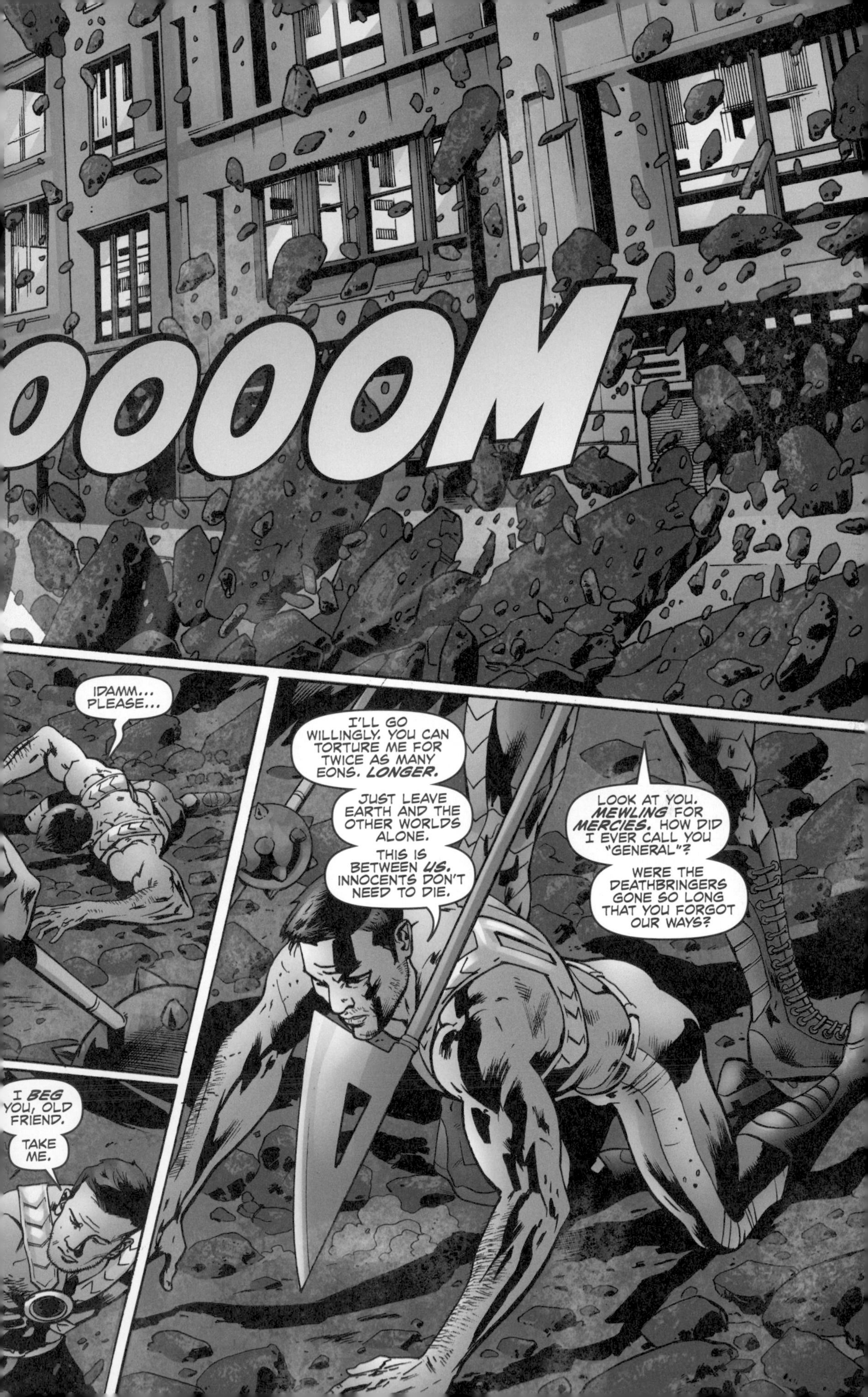
OOOOM
IDAMM... PLEASE...
I'LL GO WILLINGLY. YOU CAN TORTURE ME FOR TWICE AS MANY EONS. LONGER.
JUST LEAVE EARTH AND THE OTHER WORLDS ALONE.
THIS IS BETWEEN US. INNOCENTS DON'T NEED TO DIE.
LOOK AT YOU. MEWLING FOR MERCIES. HOW DID I EVER CALL YOU "GENERAL"?
WERE THE DEATHBRINGERS GONE SO LONG THAT YOU FORGOT OUR WAYS?
I BEG YOU, OLD FRIEND.
TAKE ME.

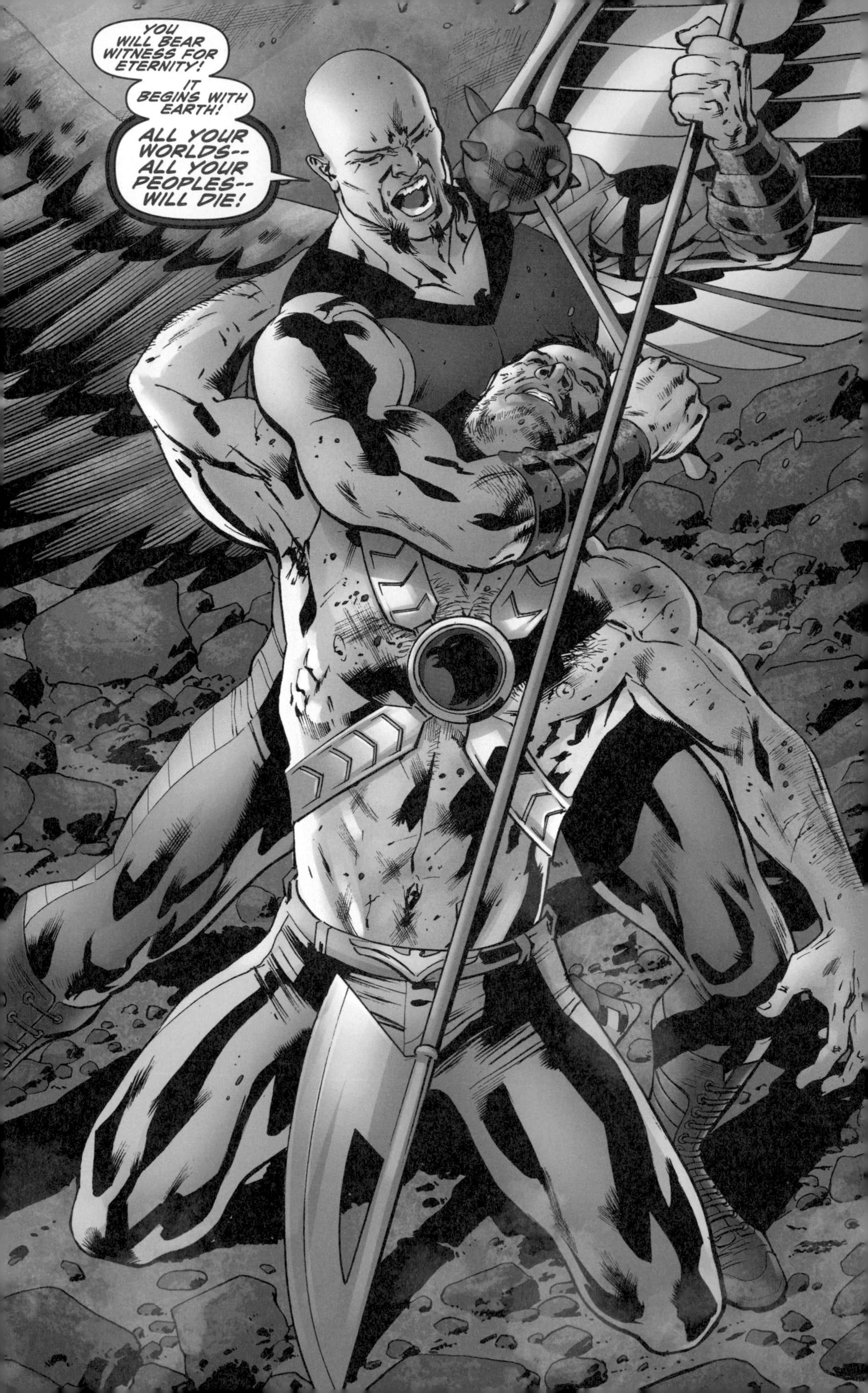
YOU WILL BEAR WITNESS FOR ETERNITY!
IT BEGINS WITH EARTH!
ALL YOUR WORLDS-- ALL YOUR PEOPLES-- WILL DIE!

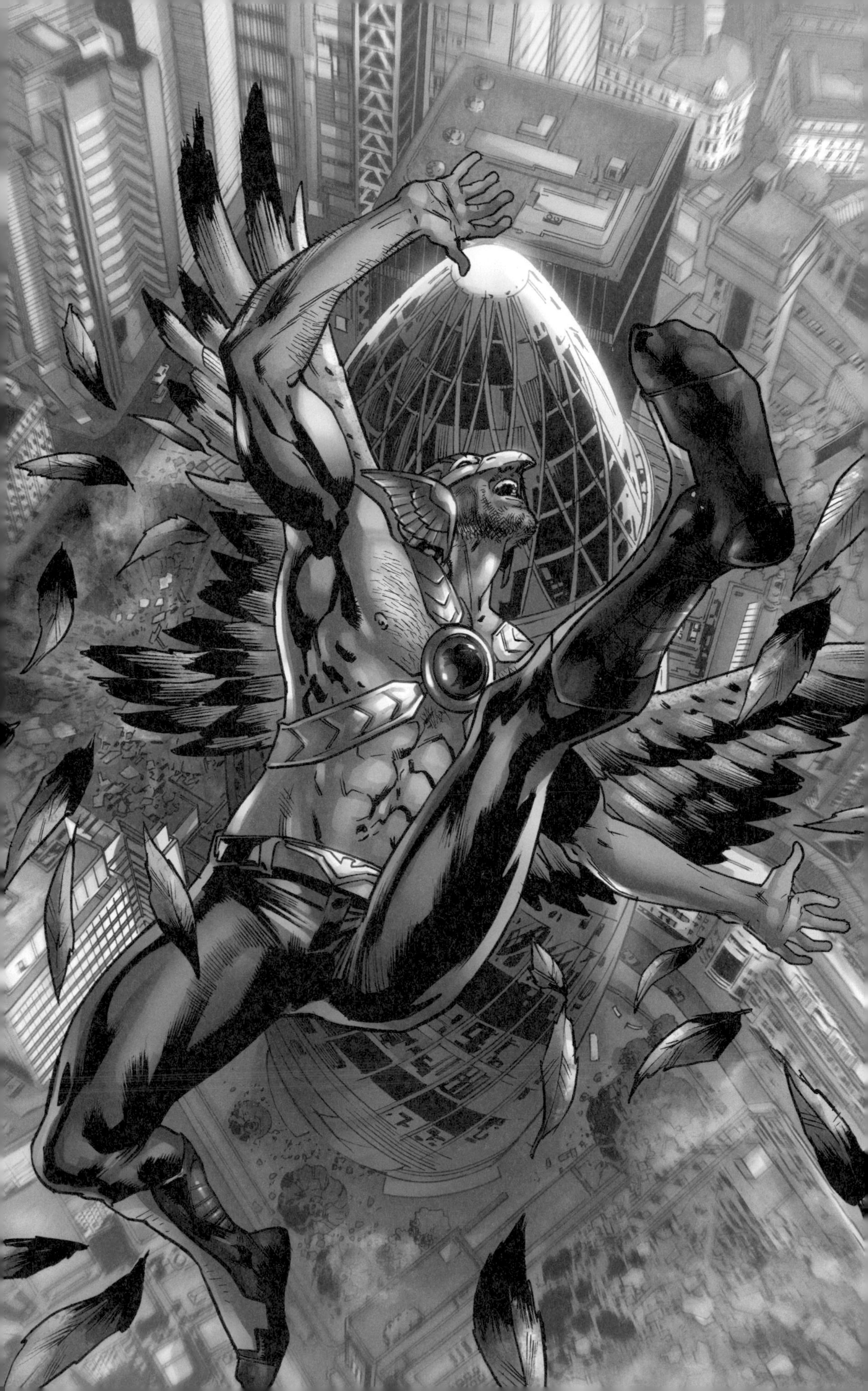

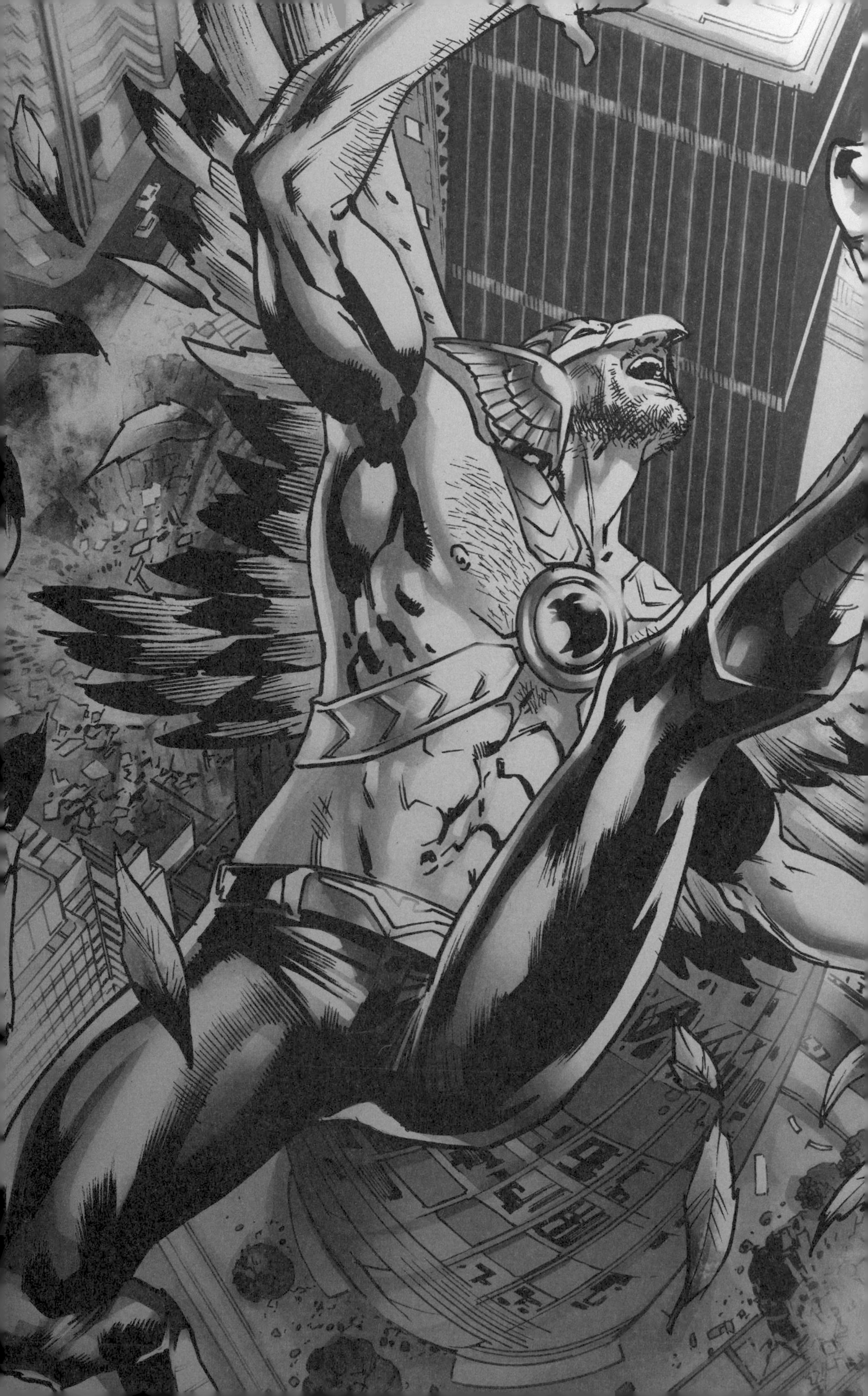

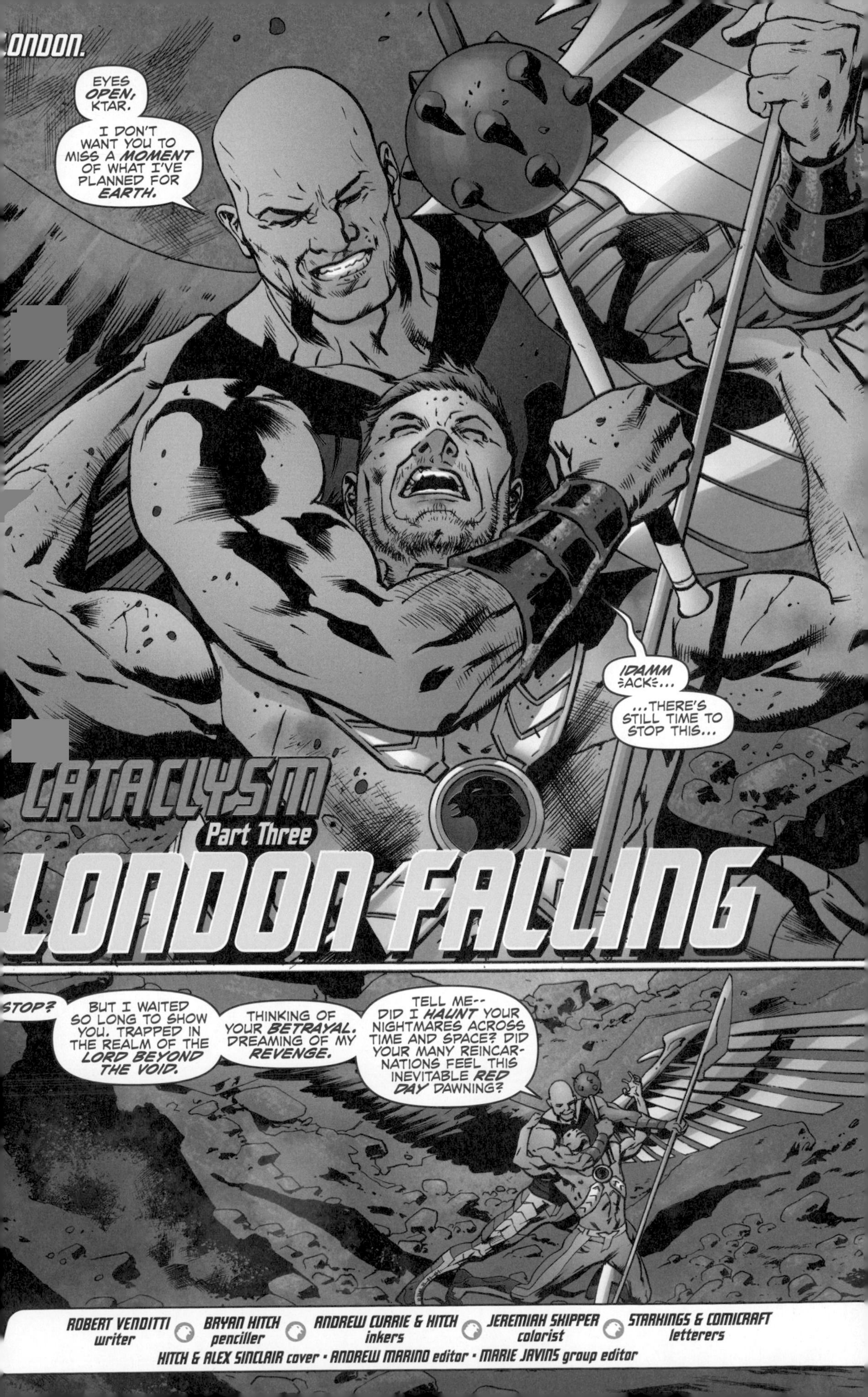
LONDON.
EYES OPEN, KTAR.
I DON'T WANT YOU TO MISS A MOMENT OF WHAT I'VE PLANNED FOR EARTH.
IDAMM ACK...
...THERE'S STILL TIME TO STOP THIS...
CATACLYSM
Part Three
LONDON FALLING
STOP?
BUT I WAITED SO LONG TO SHOW YOU. TRAPPED IN THE REALM OF THE LORD BEYOND THE VOID.
THINKING OF YOUR BETRAYAL. DREAMING OF MY REVENGE.
TELL ME-- DID I HAUNT YOUR NIGHTMARES ACROSS TIME AND SPACE? DID YOUR MANY REINCARNATIONS FEEL THIS INEVITABLE RED DAY DAWNING?
ROBERT VENDITTI writer
BRYAN HITCH penciller
ANDREW CURRIE & HITCH inkers
JEREMIAH SHIPPER colorist
STARKINGS & COMICRAFT letterers
HITCH & ALEX SINCLAIR cover • ANDREW MARINO editor • MARIE JAVINS group editor

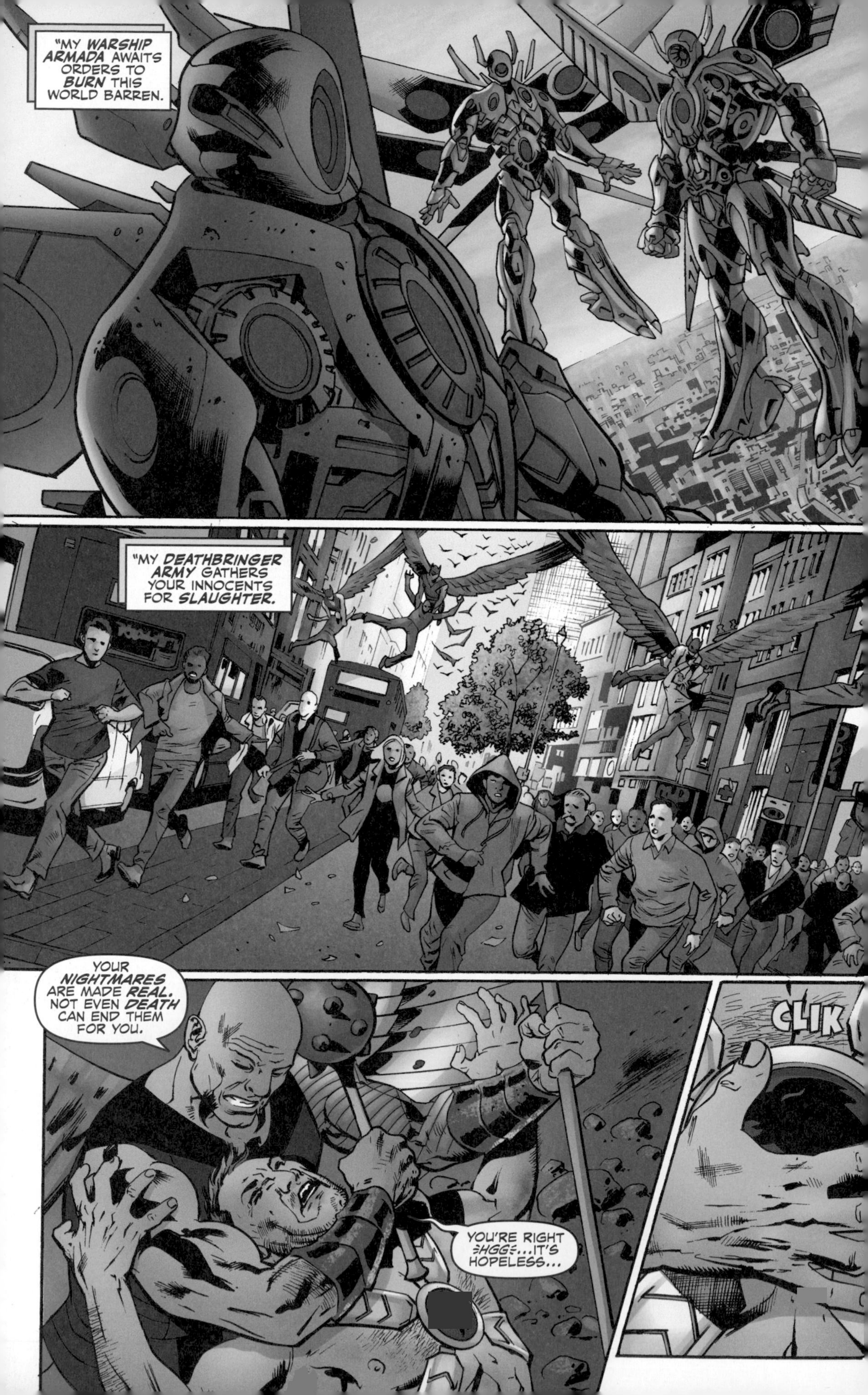
"MY WARSHIP ARMADA AWAITS ORDERS TO BURN THIS WORLD BARREN.
"MY DEATHBRINGER ARMY GATHERS YOUR INNOCENTS FOR SLAUGHTER.
YOUR NIGHTMARES ARE MADE REAL. NOT EVEN DEATH CAN END THEM FOR YOU.
YOU'RE RIGHT HGG...IT'S HOPELESS...
CLIK

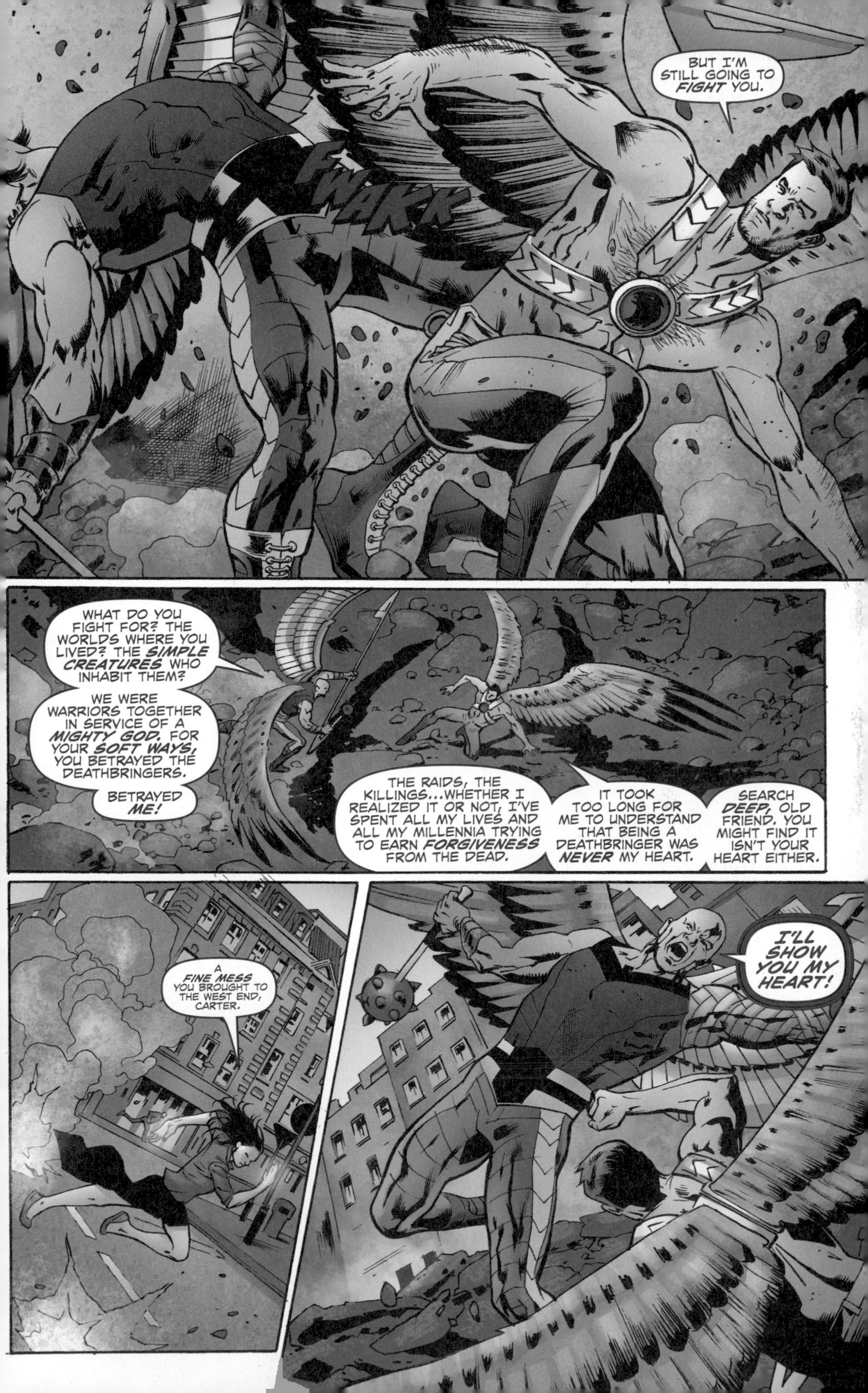
BUT I'M STILL GOING TO FIGHT YOU.
FWAKK
WHAT DO YOU FIGHT FOR? THE WORLDS WHERE YOU LIVED? THE SIMPLE CREATURES WHO INHABIT THEM?
WE WERE WARRIORS TOGETHER IN SERVICE OF A MIGHTY GOD. FOR YOUR SOFT WAYS, YOU BETRAYED THE DEATHBRINGERS.
BETRAYED ME!
THE RAIDS, THE KILLINGS...WHETHER I REALIZED IT OR NOT, I'VE SPENT ALL MY LIVES AND ALL MY MILLENNIA TRYING TO EARN FORGIVENESS FROM THE DEAD.
IT TOOK TOO LONG FOR ME TO UNDERSTAND THAT BEING A DEATHBRINGER WAS NEVER MY HEART.
SEARCH DEEP, OLD FRIEND. YOU MIGHT FIND IT ISN'T YOUR HEART EITHER.
A FINE MESS YOU BROUGHT TO THE WEST END, CARTER.
I'LL SHOW YOU MY HEART!

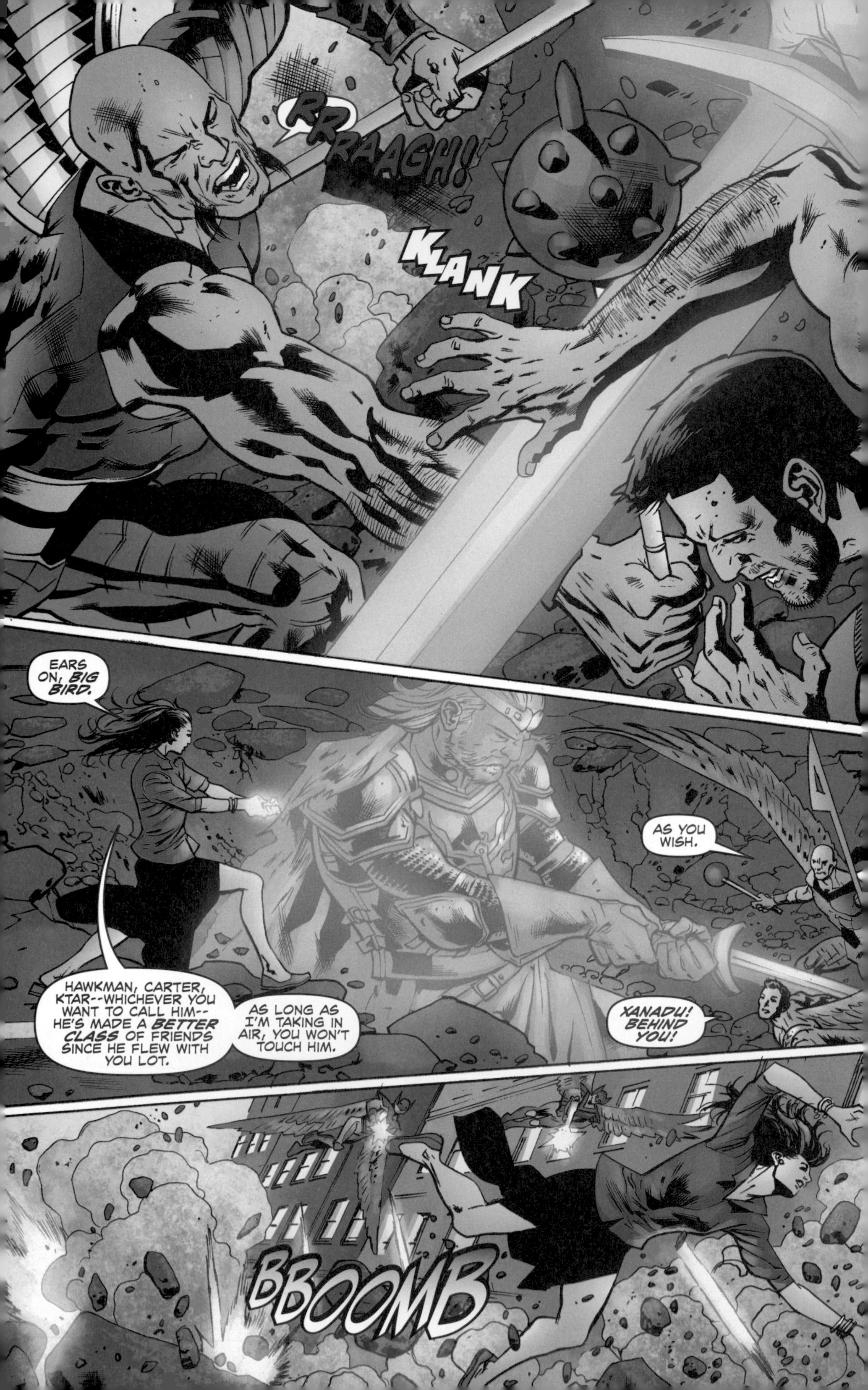
RRRAAGH!
KLANK
EARS ON, BIG BIRD.
AS YOU WISH.
HAWKMAN, CARTER, KTAR--WHICHEVER YOU WANT TO CALL HIM-- HE'S MADE A BETTER CLASS OF FRIENDS SINCE HE FLEW WITH YOU LOT.
AS LONG AS I'M TAKING IN AIR, YOU WON'T TOUCH HIM.
XANADU! BEHIND YOU!
BBOOMB

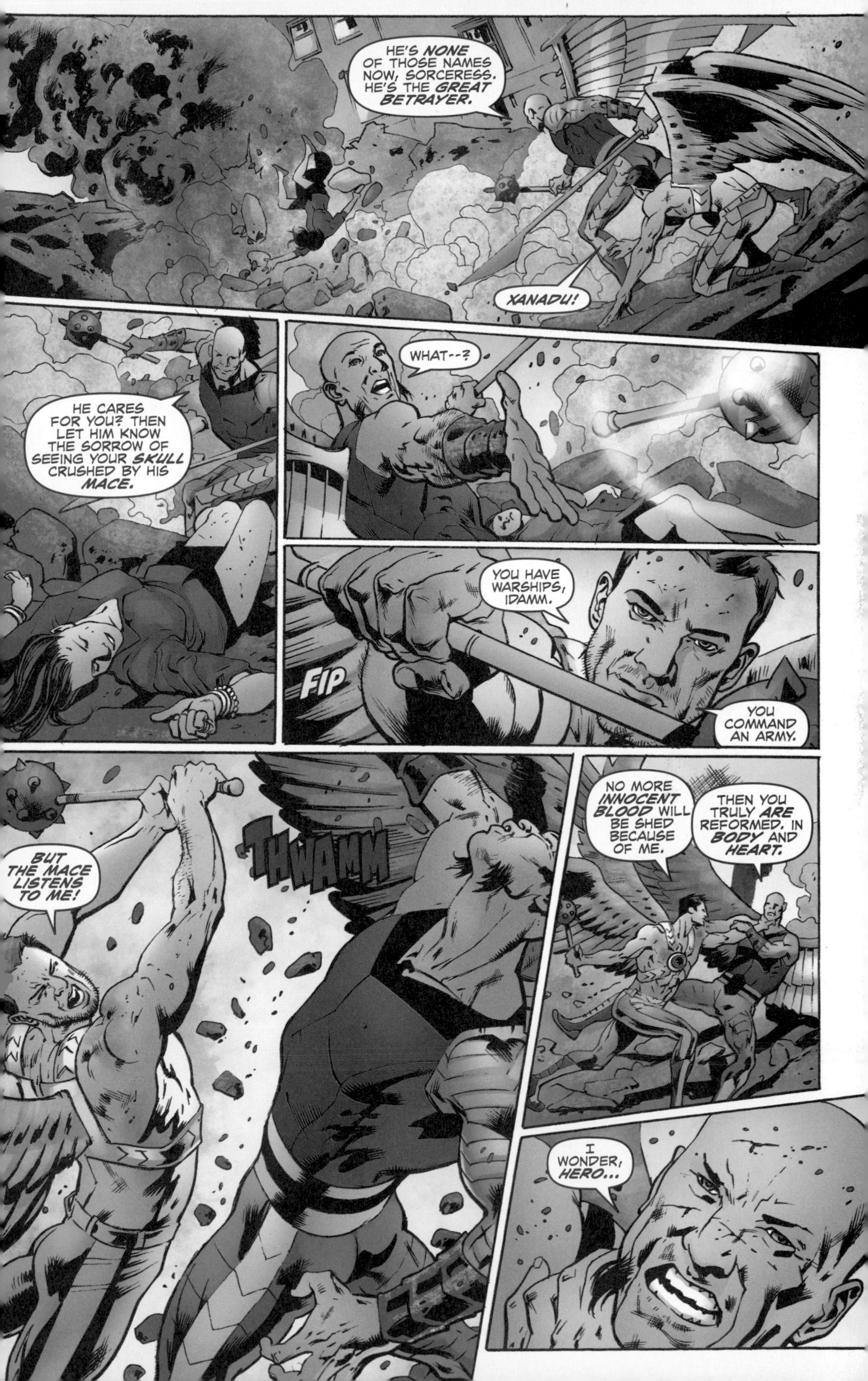
HE'S NONE OF THOSE NAMES NOW, SORCERESS. HE'S THE GREAT BETRAYER.
XANADU!
HE CARES FOR YOU? THEN LET HIM KNOW THE SORROW OF SEEING YOUR SKULL CRUSHED BY HIS MACE.
WHAT--?
YOU HAVE WARSHIPS, IDAMM.
FIP
YOU COMMAND AN ARMY.
BUT THE MACE LISTENS TO ME!
THWAMM
NO MORE INNOCENT BLOOD WILL BE SHED BECAUSE OF ME.
THEN YOU TRULY ARE REFORMED. IN BODY AND HEART.
I WONDER, HERO...

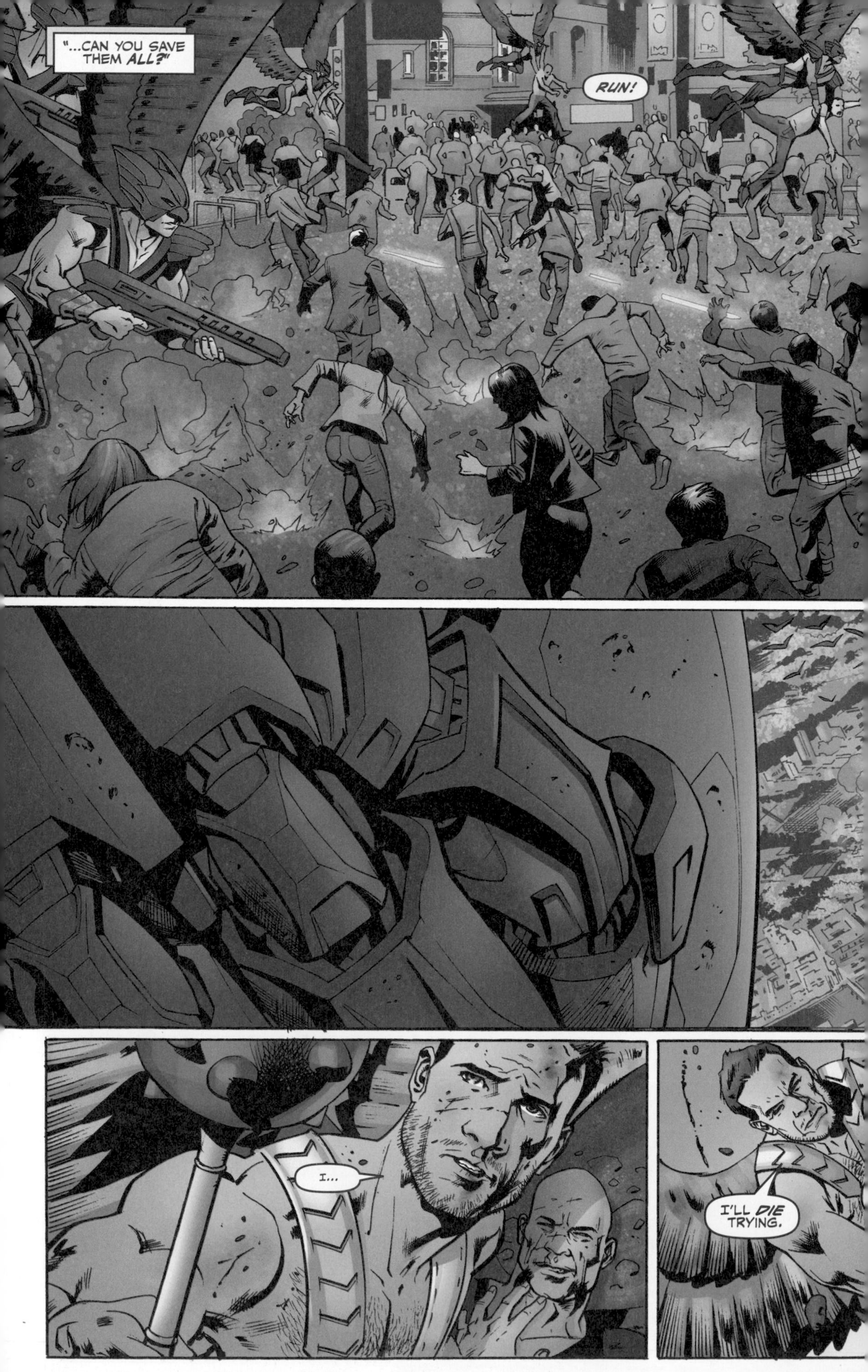
"...CAN YOU SAVE THEM ALL?"
RUN!
I...
I'LL DIE TRYING.

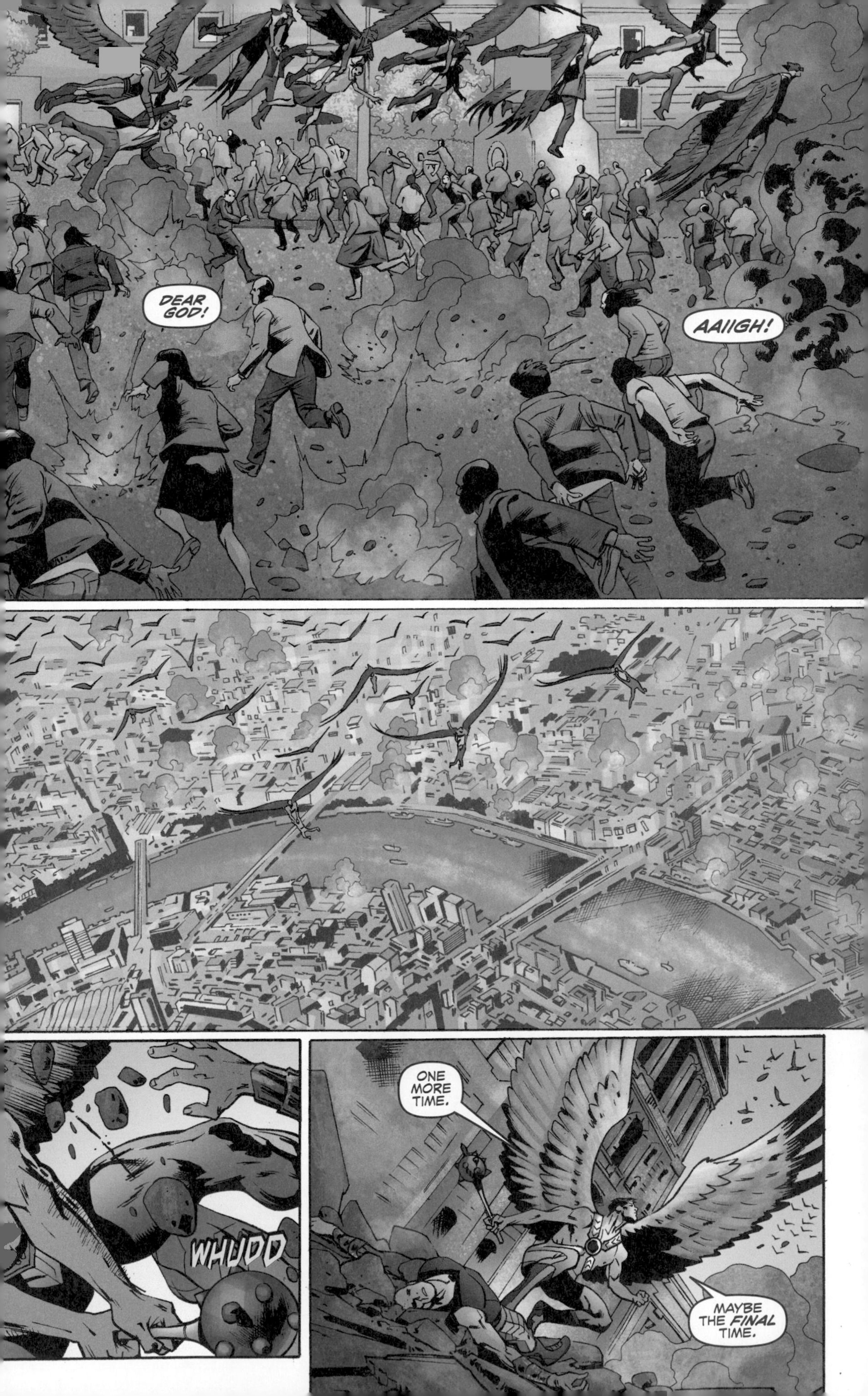
DEAR GOD!
AAIIGH!
WHUDD
ONE MORE TIME.
MAYBE THE *FINAL* TIME.

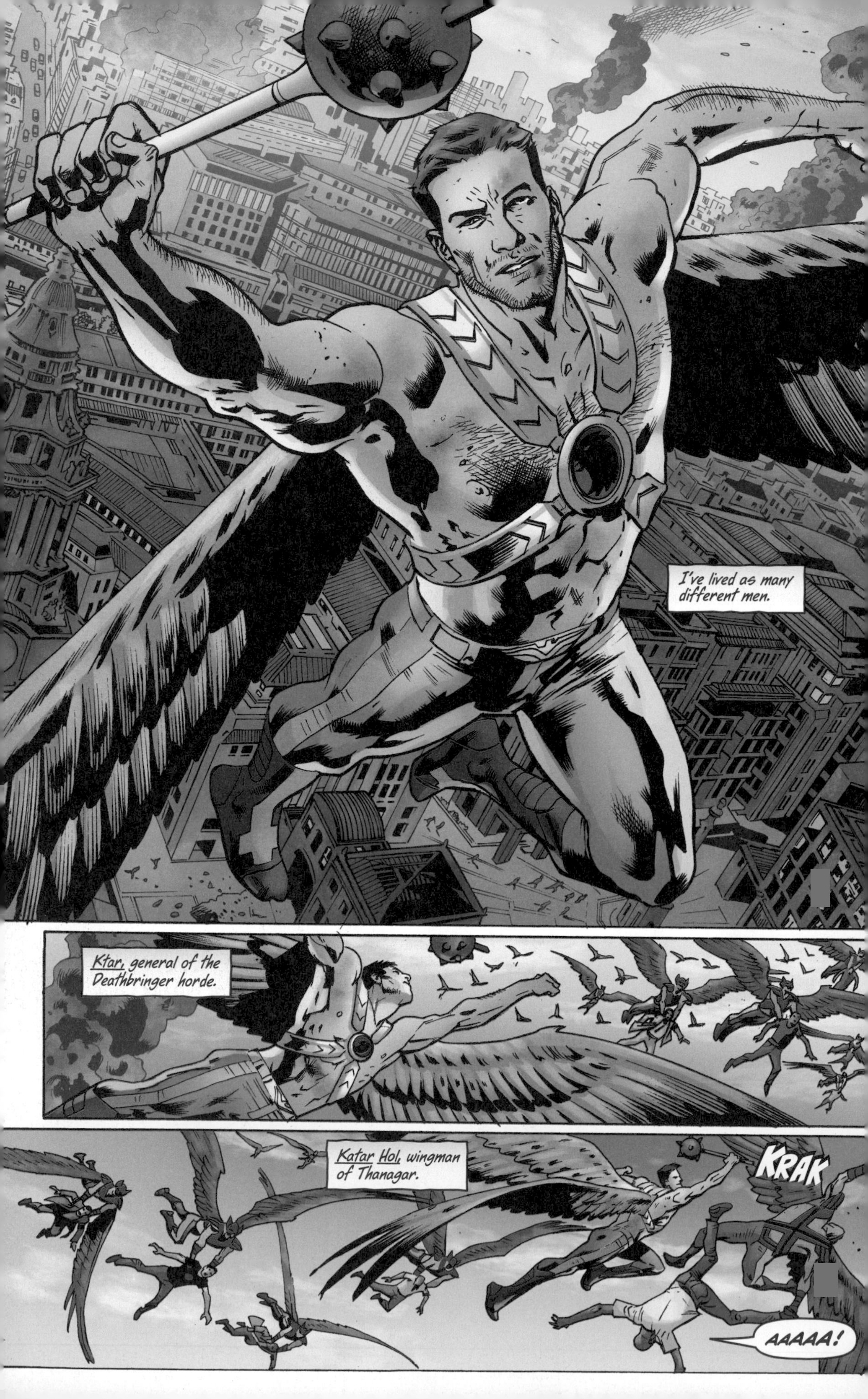
I've lived as many different men.
Ktar, general of the Deathbringer horde.
Katar Hol, wingman of Thanagar.
KRAK
AAAAA!

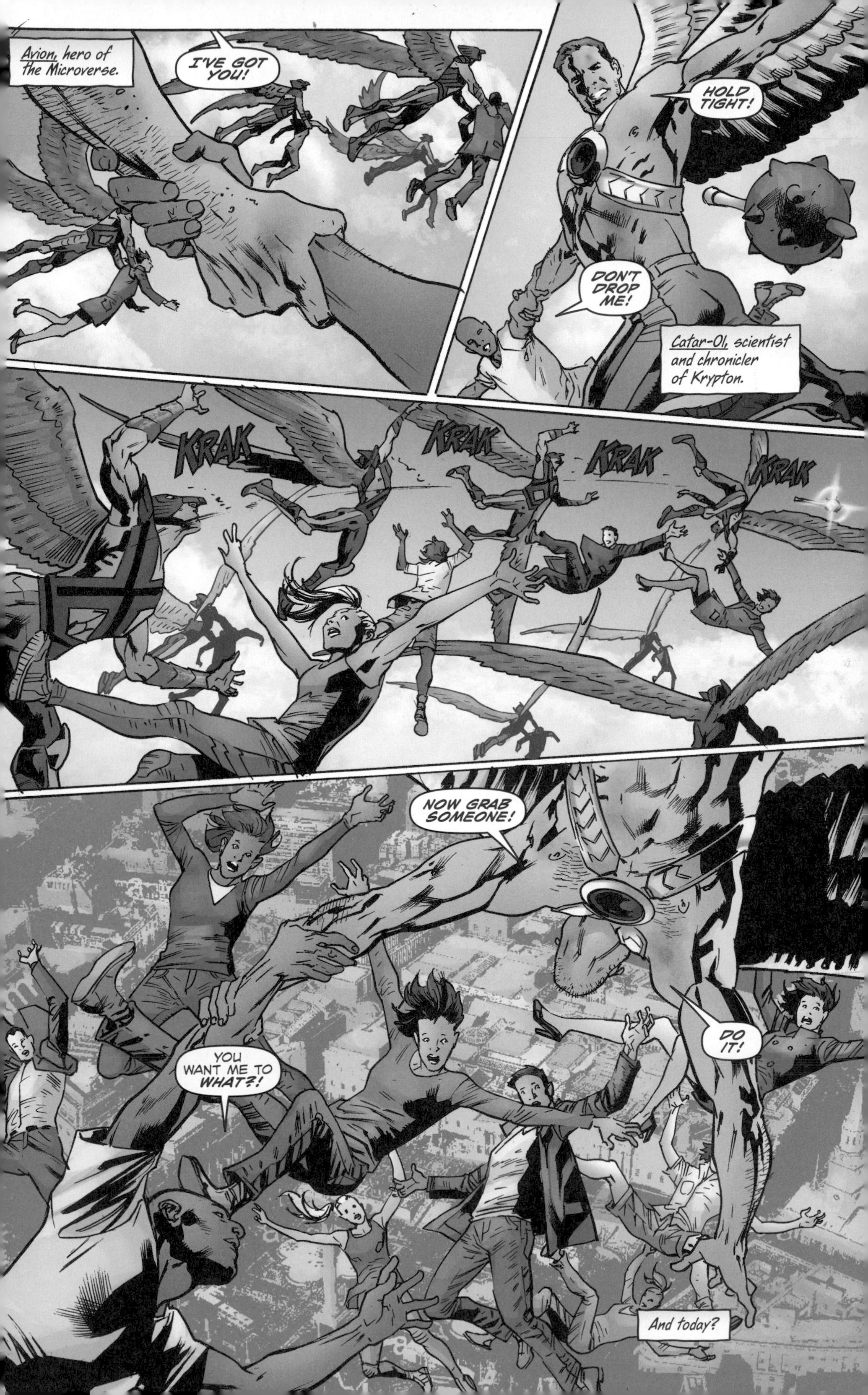
Avion, hero of the Microverse.
I'VE GOT YOU!
HOLD TIGHT!
DON'T DROP ME!
Catar-Ol, scientist and chronicler of Krypton.
KRAK
KRAK
KRAK
KRAK
NOW GRAB SOMEONE!
YOU WANT ME TO WHAT?!
DO IT!
And today?

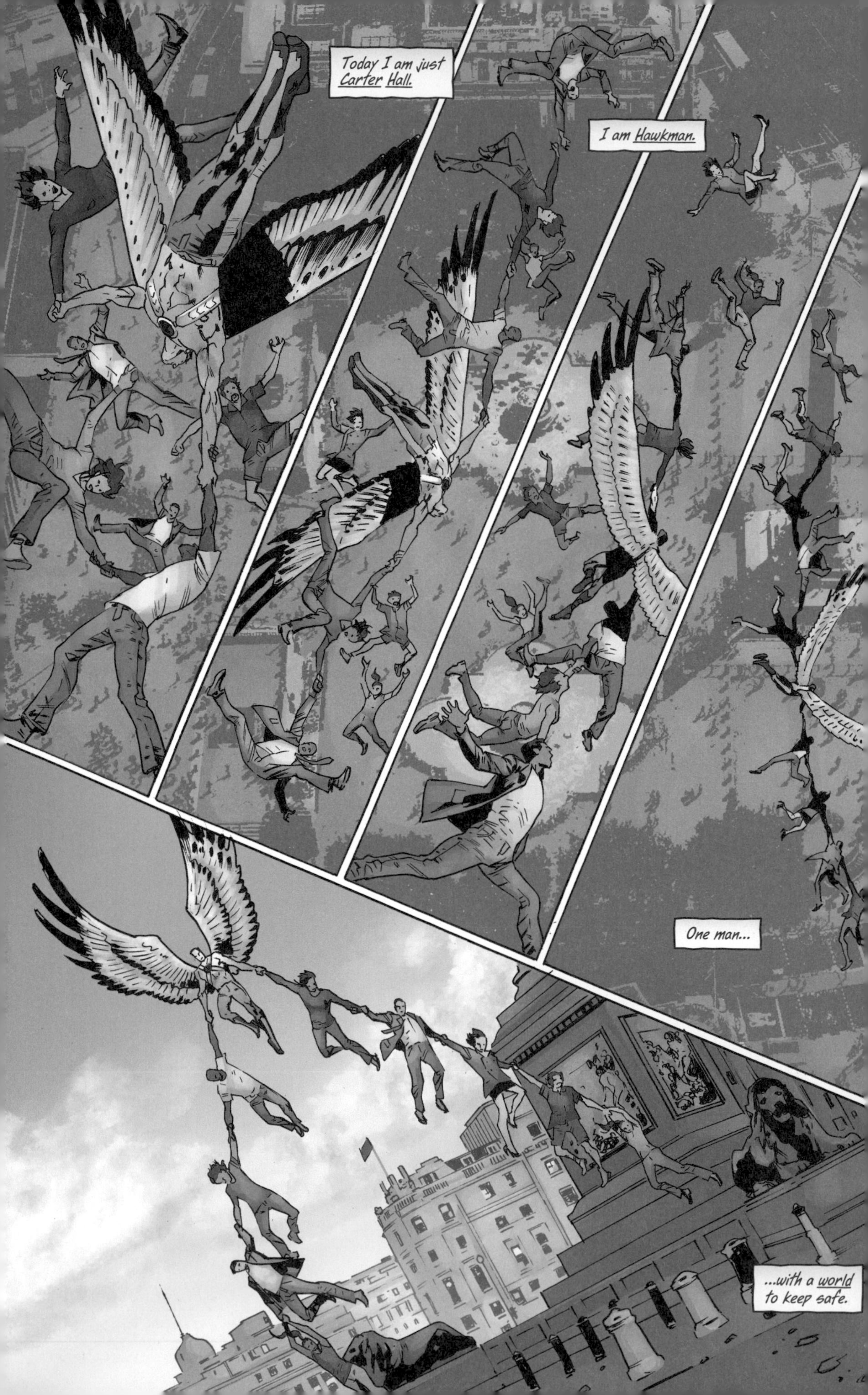
Today I am just Carter Hall.
I am Hawkman.
One man...
...with a world to keep safe.

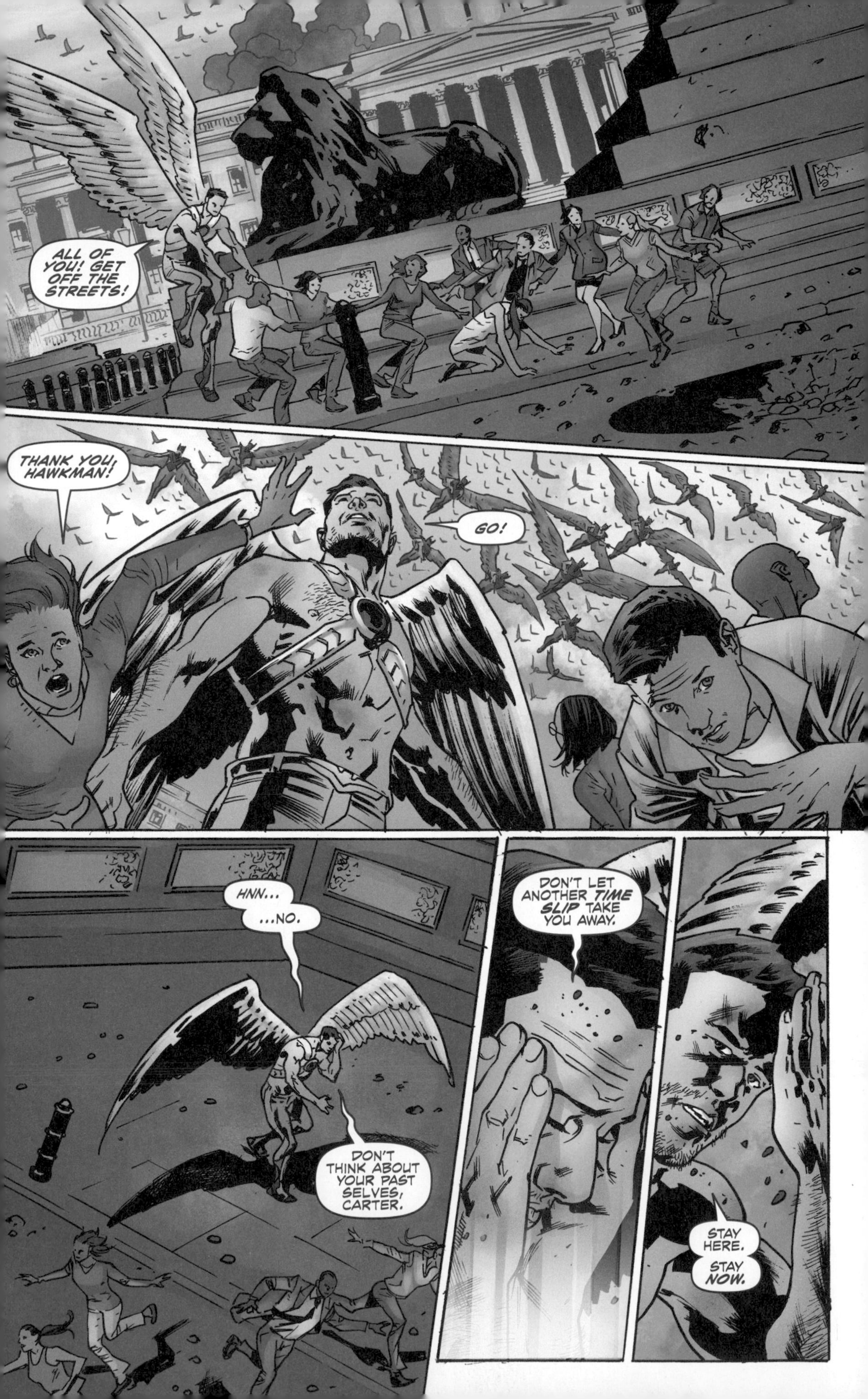
ALL OF YOU! GET OFF THE STREETS!
THANK YOU, HAWKMAN!
GO!
HNN...
...NO.
DON'T THINK ABOUT YOUR PAST SELVES, CARTER.
DON'T LET ANOTHER TIME SLIP TAKE YOU AWAY.
STAY HERE.
STAY NOW.

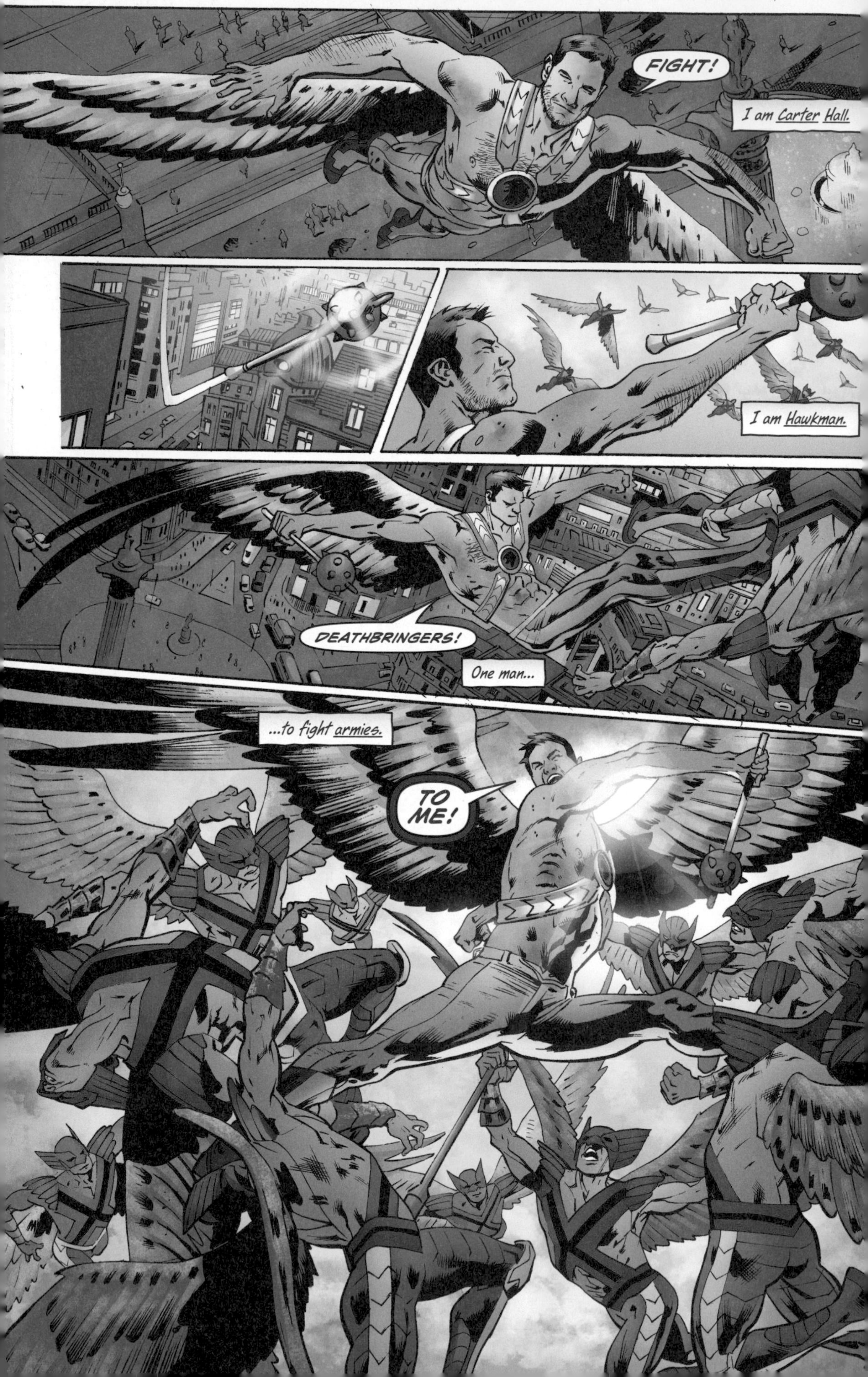
FIGHT!
I am Carter Hall.
I am Hawkman.
DEATHBRINGERS!
One man...
...to fight armies.
TO ME!

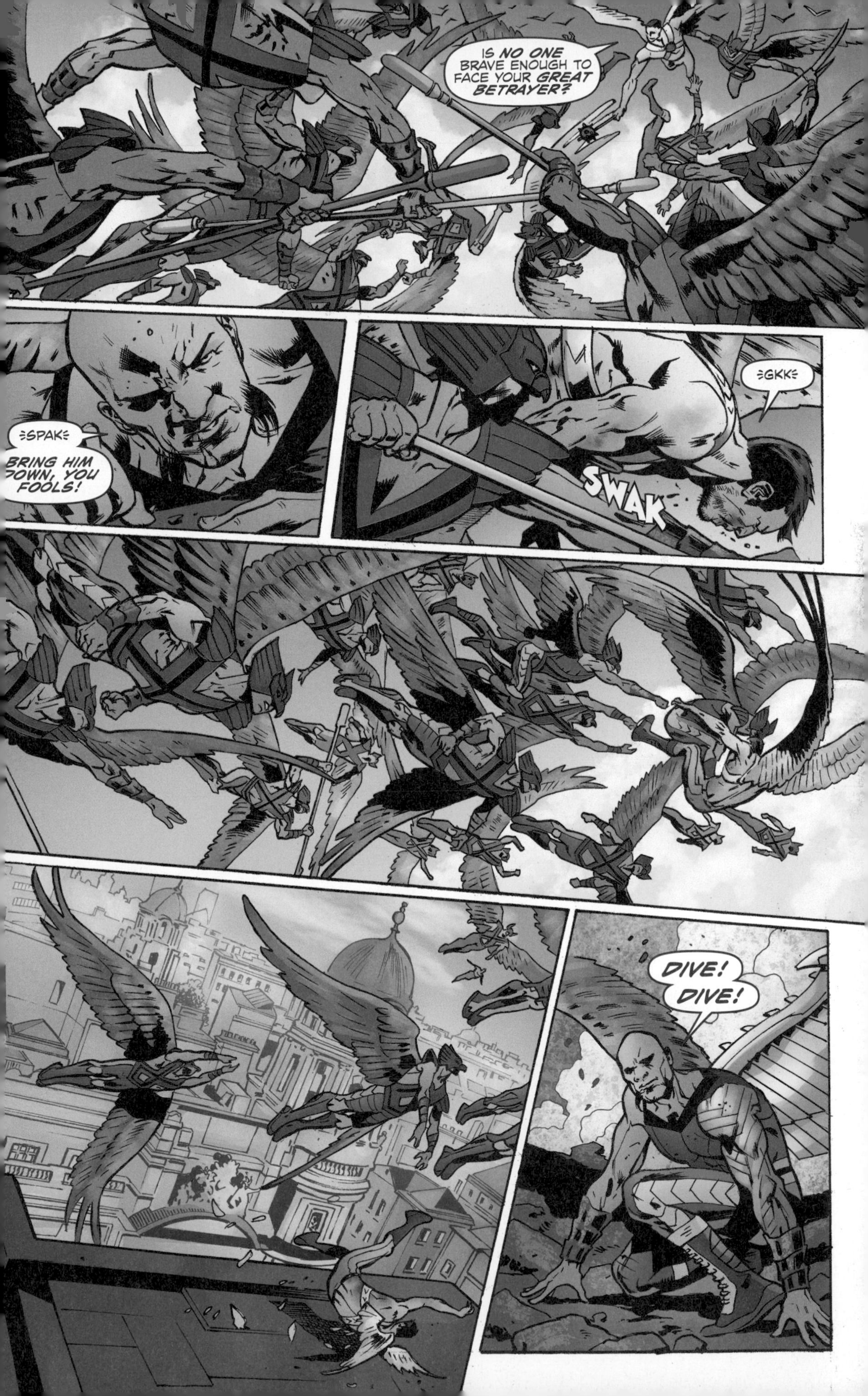

IS NO ONE BRAVE ENOUGH TO FACE YOUR GREAT BETRAYER?
SPAK
BRING HIM DOWN, YOU FOOLS!
GKK
SWAK
DIVE! DIVE!

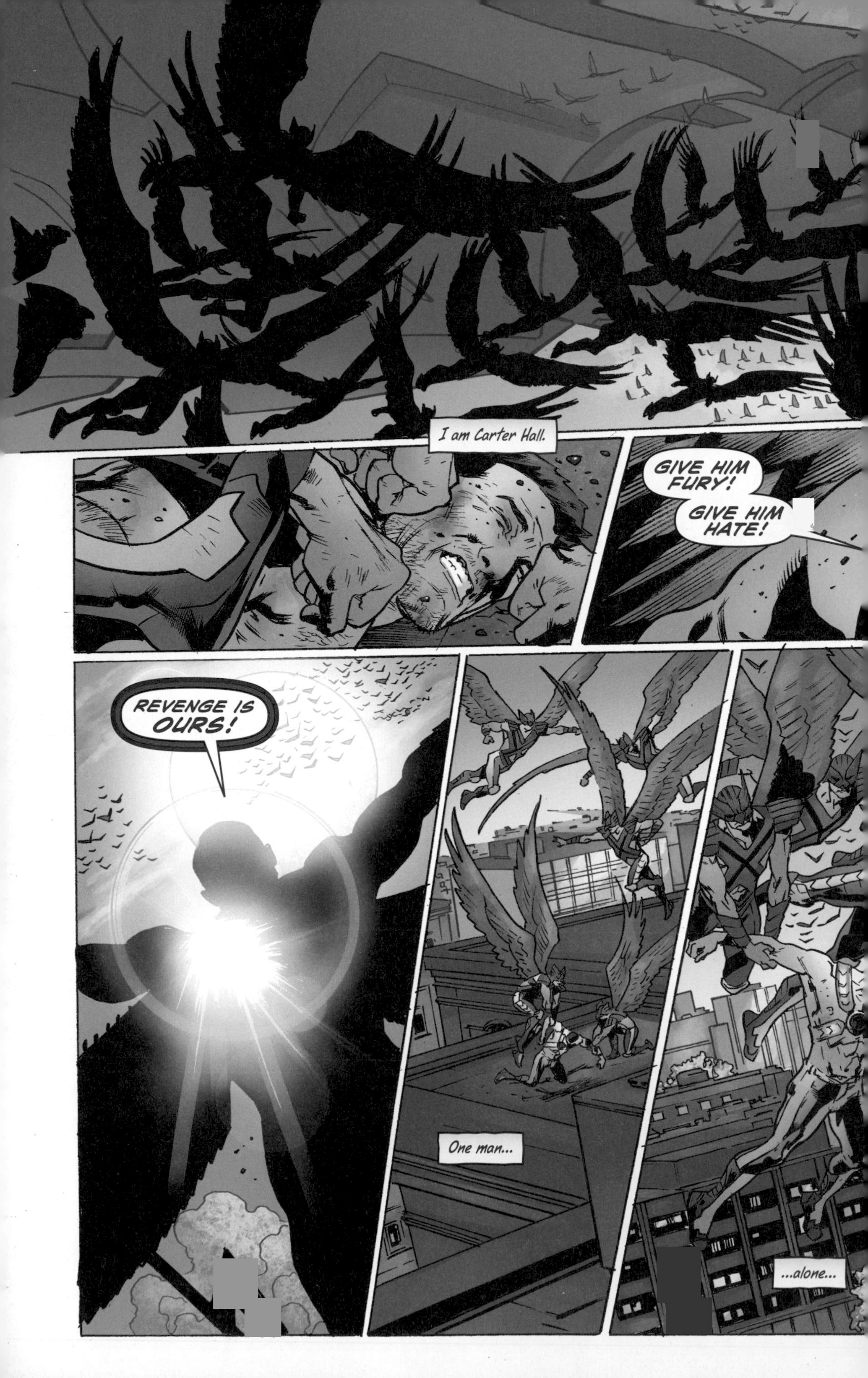
I am Carter Hall.
GIVE HIM FURY!
GIVE HIM HATE!
REVENGE IS OURS!
One man...
...alone...

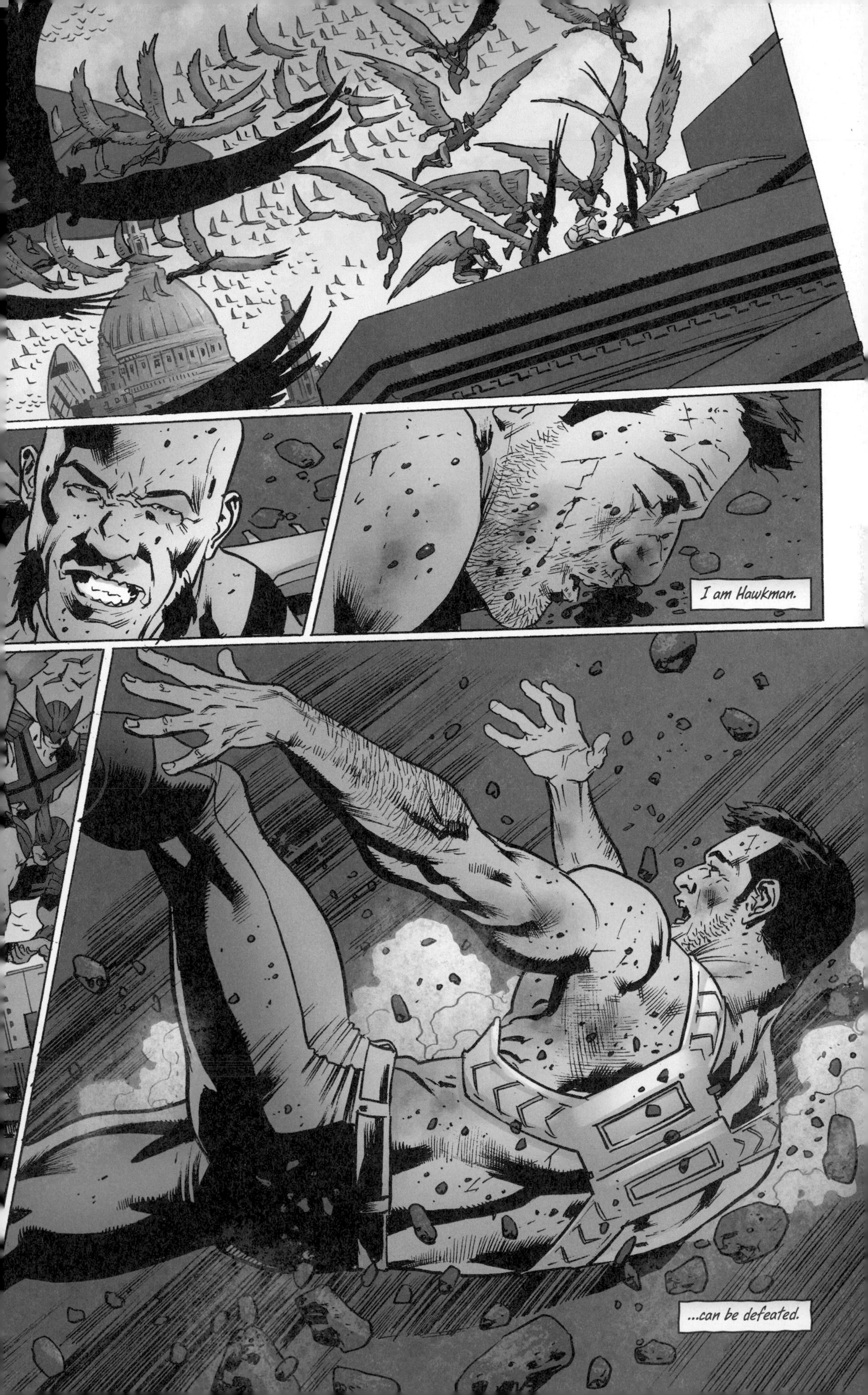
I am Hawkman.
...can be defeated.

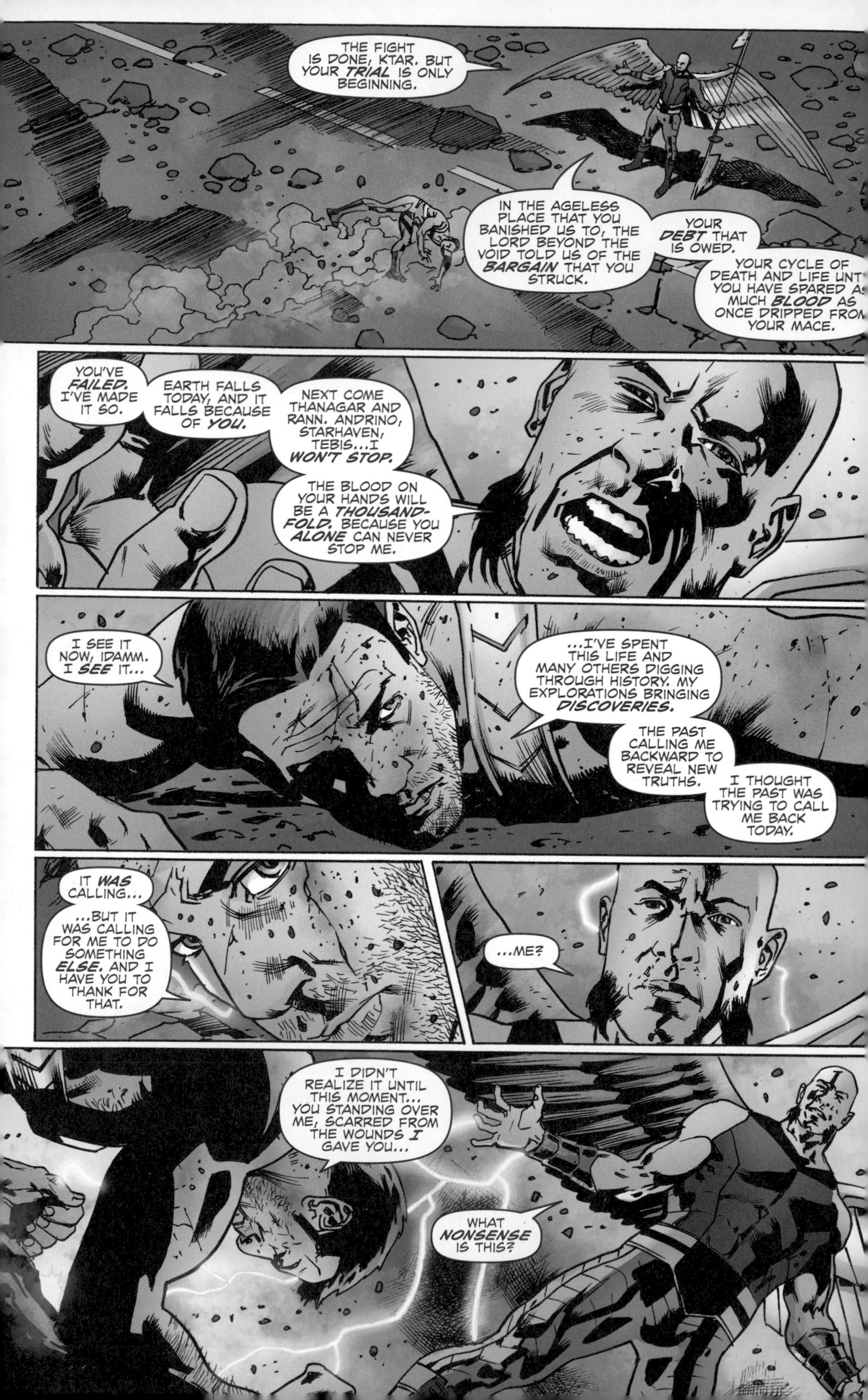
THE FIGHT IS DONE, KTAR. BUT YOUR TRIAL IS ONLY BEGINNING.
IN THE AGELESS PLACE THAT YOU BANISHED US TO, THE LORD BEYOND THE VOID TOLD US OF THE BARGAIN THAT YOU STRUCK.
YOUR DEBT THAT IS OWED.
YOUR CYCLE OF DEATH AND LIFE UNTI YOU HAVE SPARED AS MUCH BLOOD AS ONCE DRIPPED FROM YOUR MACE.
YOU'VE FAILED. I'VE MADE IT SO.
EARTH FALLS TODAY, AND IT FALLS BECAUSE OF YOU.
NEXT COME THANAGAR AND RANN. ANDRINO, STARHAVEN, TEBIS...I WON'T STOP.
THE BLOOD ON YOUR HANDS WILL BE A THOUSAND-FOLD. BECAUSE YOU ALONE CAN NEVER STOP ME.
I SEE IT NOW, IDAMM. I SEE IT...
...I'VE SPENT THIS LIFE AND MANY OTHERS DIGGING THROUGH HISTORY. MY EXPLORATIONS BRINGING DISCOVERIES.
THE PAST CALLING ME BACKWARD TO REVEAL NEW TRUTHS.
I THOUGHT THE PAST WAS TRYING TO CALL ME BACK TODAY.
IT WAS CALLING...
...BUT IT WAS CALLING FOR ME TO DO SOMETHING ELSE. AND I HAVE YOU TO THANK FOR THAT.
...ME?
I DIDN'T REALIZE IT UNTIL THIS MOMENT... YOU STANDING OVER ME, SCARRED FROM THE WOUNDS I GAVE YOU...
WHAT NONSENSE IS THIS?

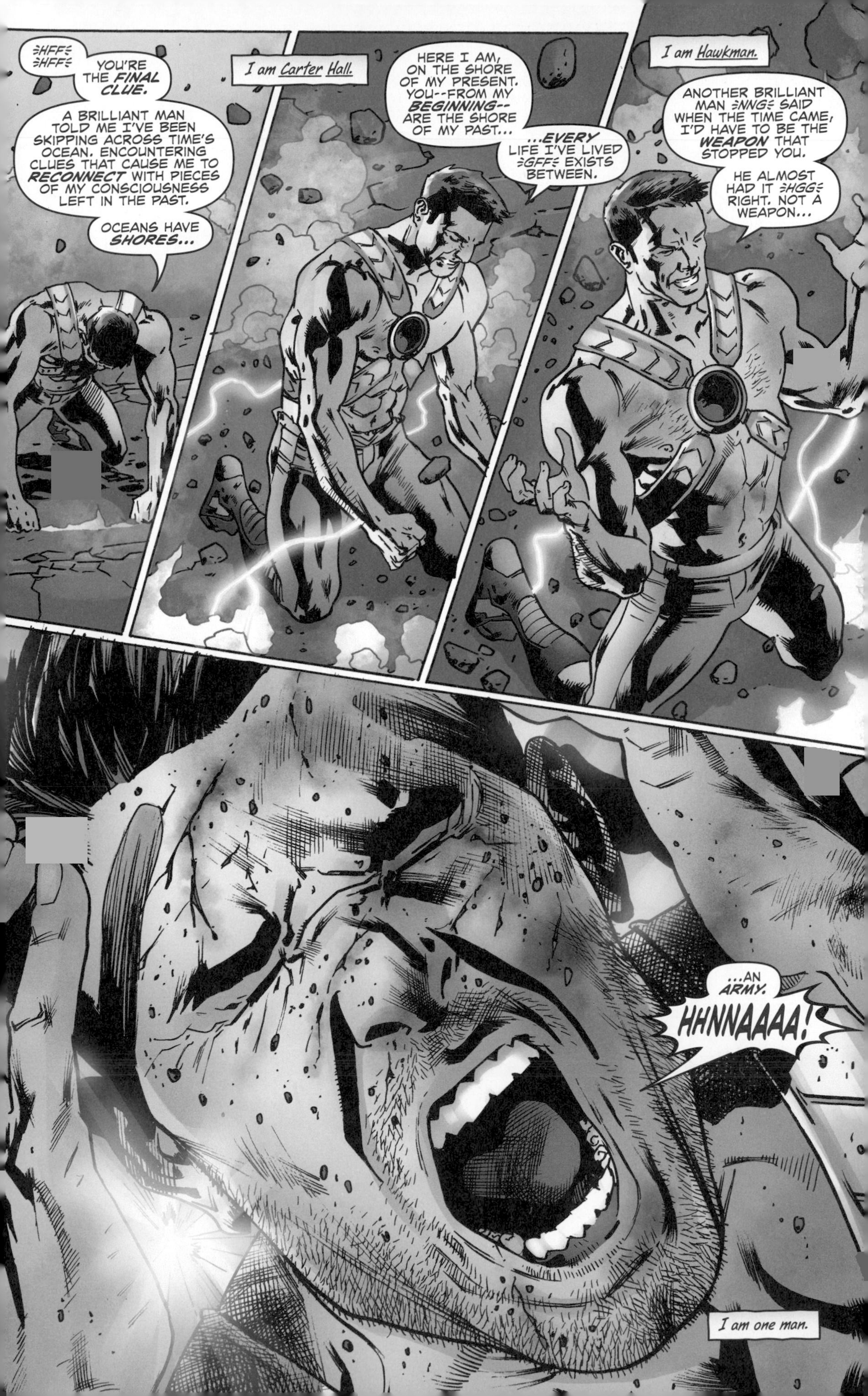
HFF HFF
YOU'RE THE FINAL CLUE.
A BRILLIANT MAN TOLD ME I'VE BEEN SKIPPING ACROSS TIME'S OCEAN. ENCOUNTERING CLUES THAT CAUSE ME TO RECONNECT WITH PIECES OF MY CONSCIOUSNESS LEFT IN THE PAST.
OCEANS HAVE SHORES...
I am Carter Hall.
HERE I AM, ON THE SHORE OF MY PRESENT. YOU--FROM MY BEGINNING--ARE THE SHORE OF MY PAST...
...EVERY LIFE I'VE LIVED GFF EXISTS BETWEEN.
I am Hawkman.
ANOTHER BRILLIANT MAN NNG SAID WHEN THE TIME CAME, I'D HAVE TO BE THE WEAPON THAT STOPPED YOU.
HE ALMOST HAD IT HGG RIGHT. NOT A WEAPON...
...AN ARMY.
HHNNAAAA!
I am one man.

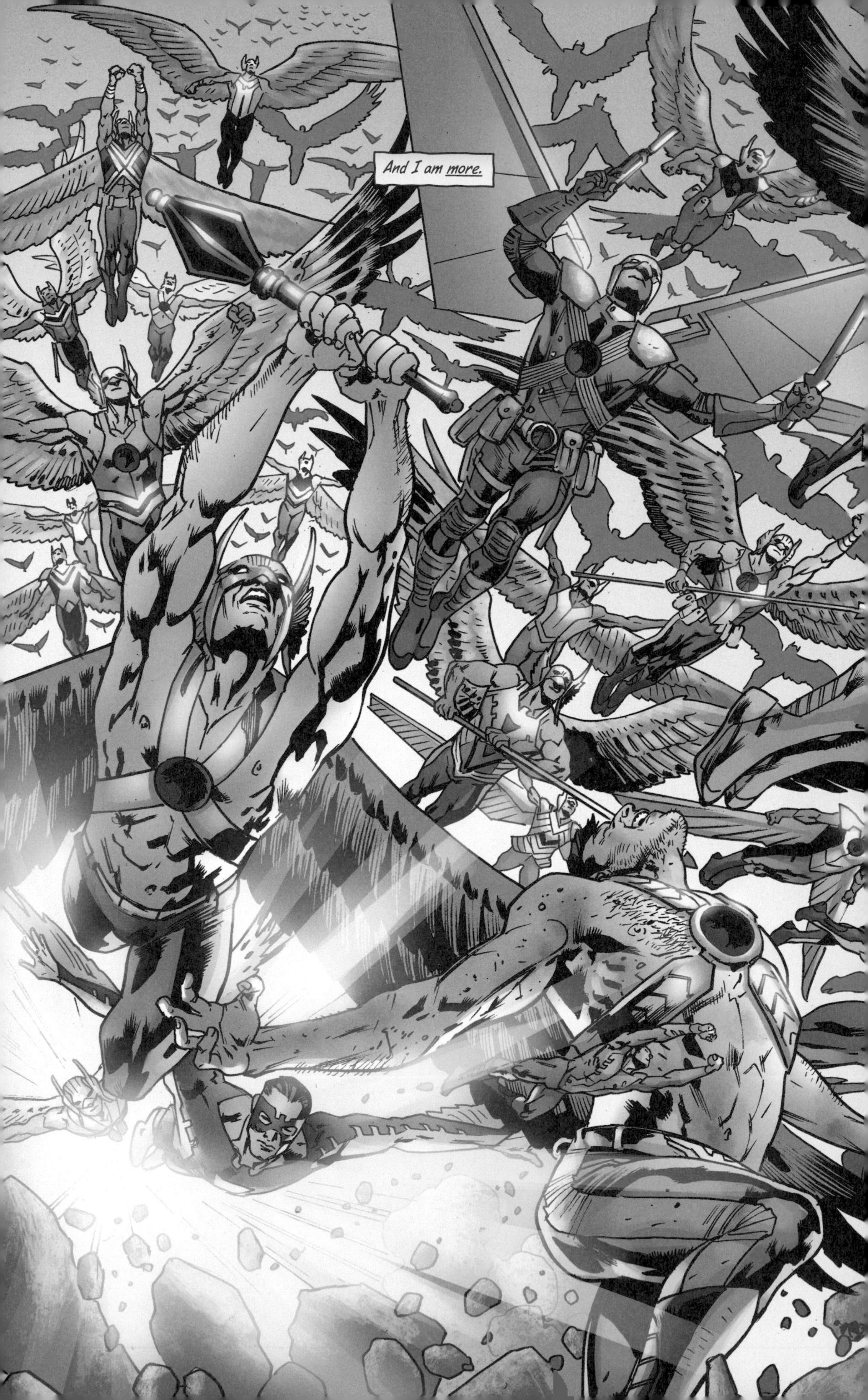
And I am more.

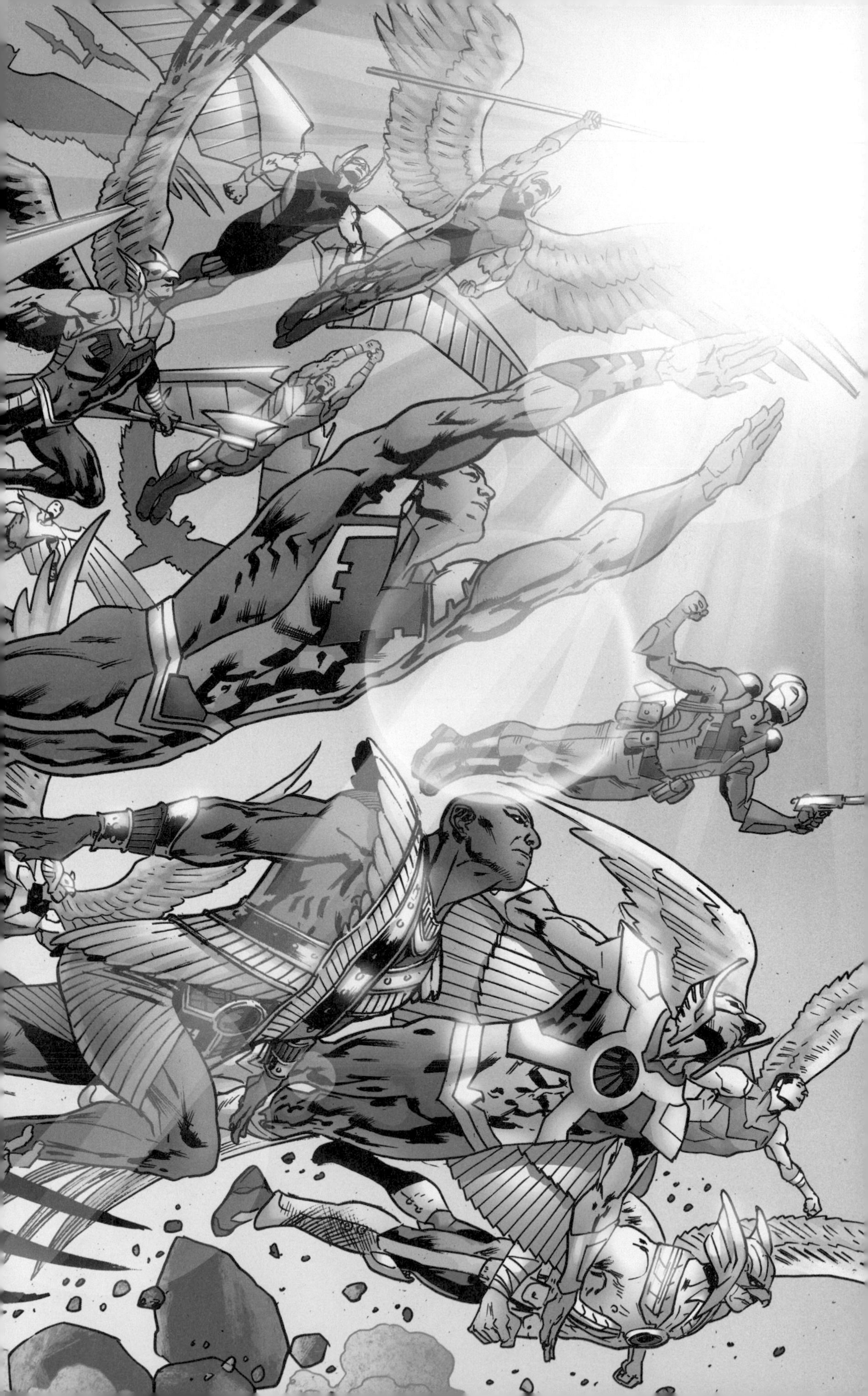

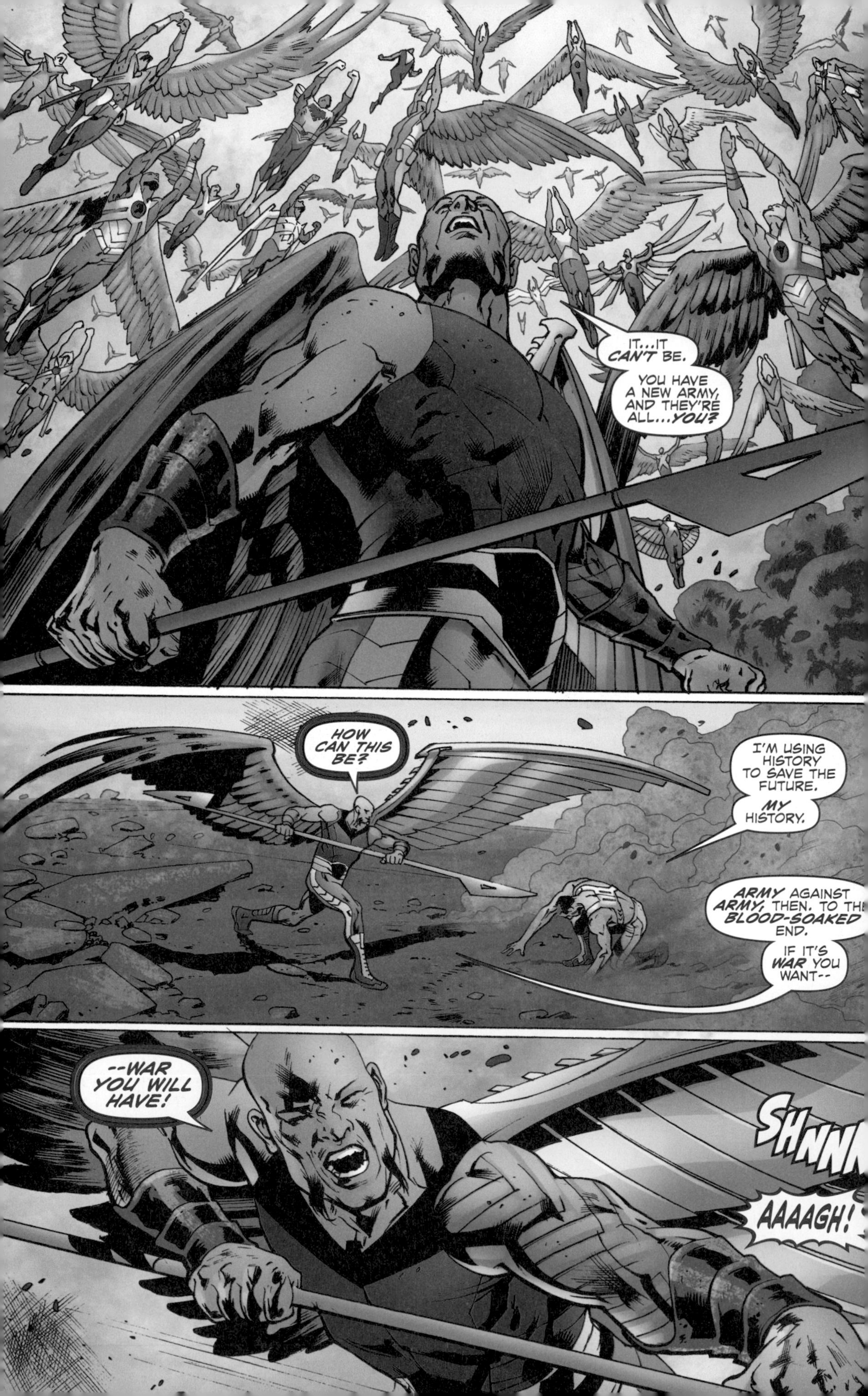
IT...IT CAN'T BE.
YOU HAVE A NEW ARMY, AND THEY'RE ALL...YOU?
HOW CAN THIS BE?
I'M USING HISTORY TO SAVE THE FUTURE.
MY HISTORY.
ARMY AGAINST ARMY, THEN. TO THE BLOOD-SOAKED END.
IF IT'S WAR YOU WANT--
--WAR YOU WILL HAVE!
SHNNN
AAAAGH!

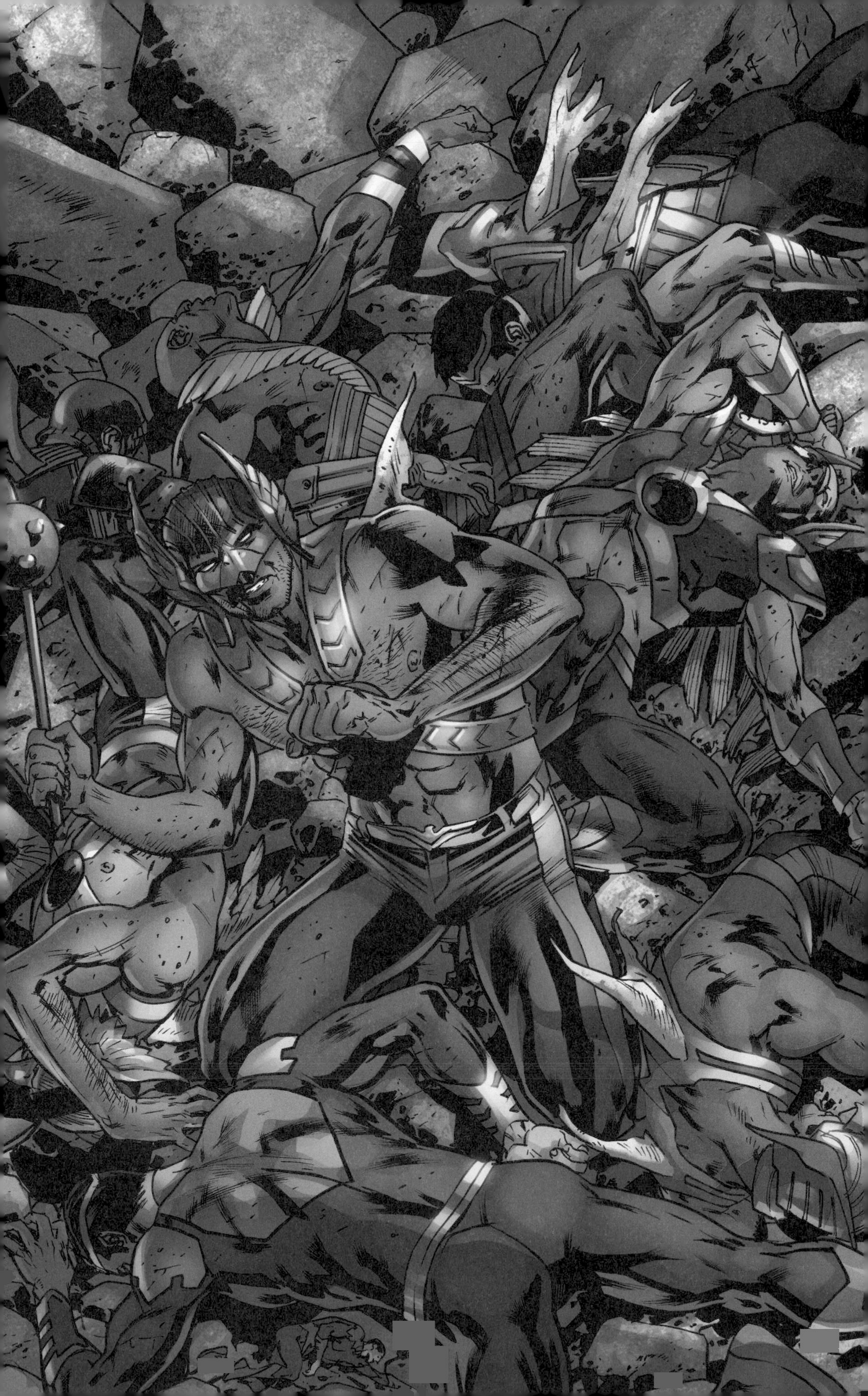

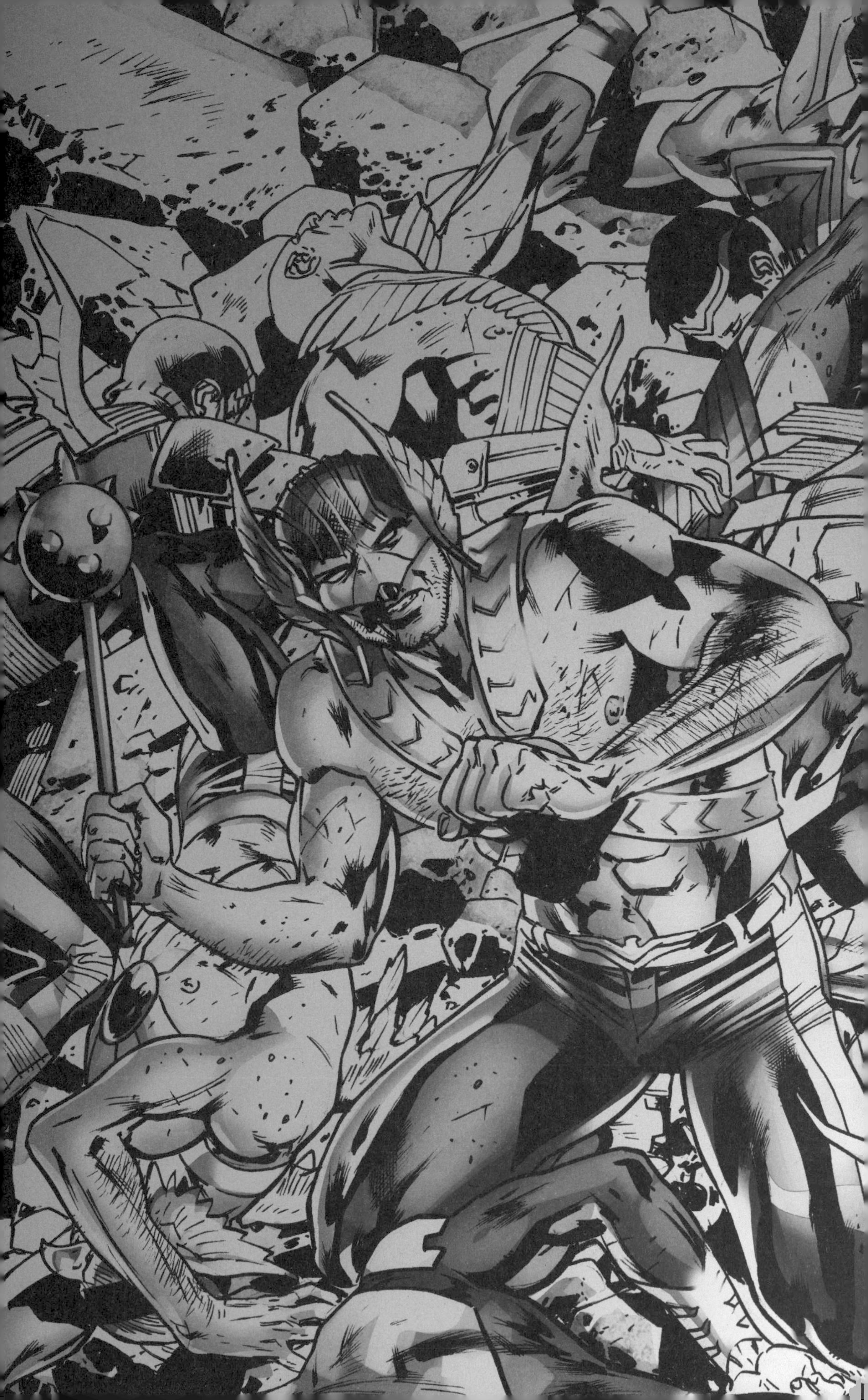

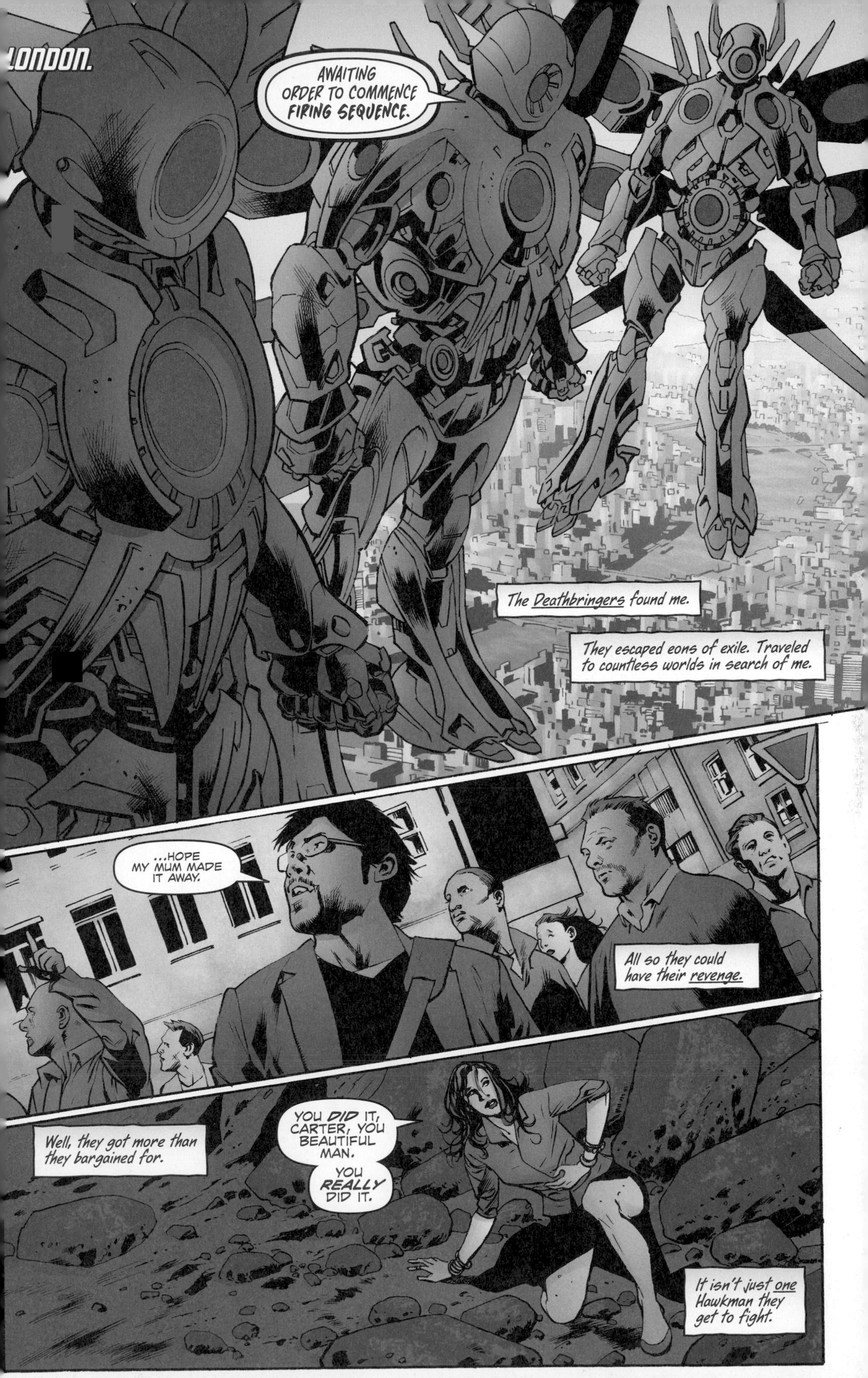
LONDON.
AWAITING ORDER TO COMMENCE FIRING SEQUENCE.
The Deathbringers found me.
They escaped eons of exile. Traveled to countless worlds in search of me.
...HOPE MY MUM MADE IT AWAY.
All so they could have their revenge.
Well, they got more than they bargained for.
YOU DID IT, CARTER, YOU BEAUTIFUL MAN.
YOU REALLY DID IT.
It isn't just one Hawkman they get to fight.

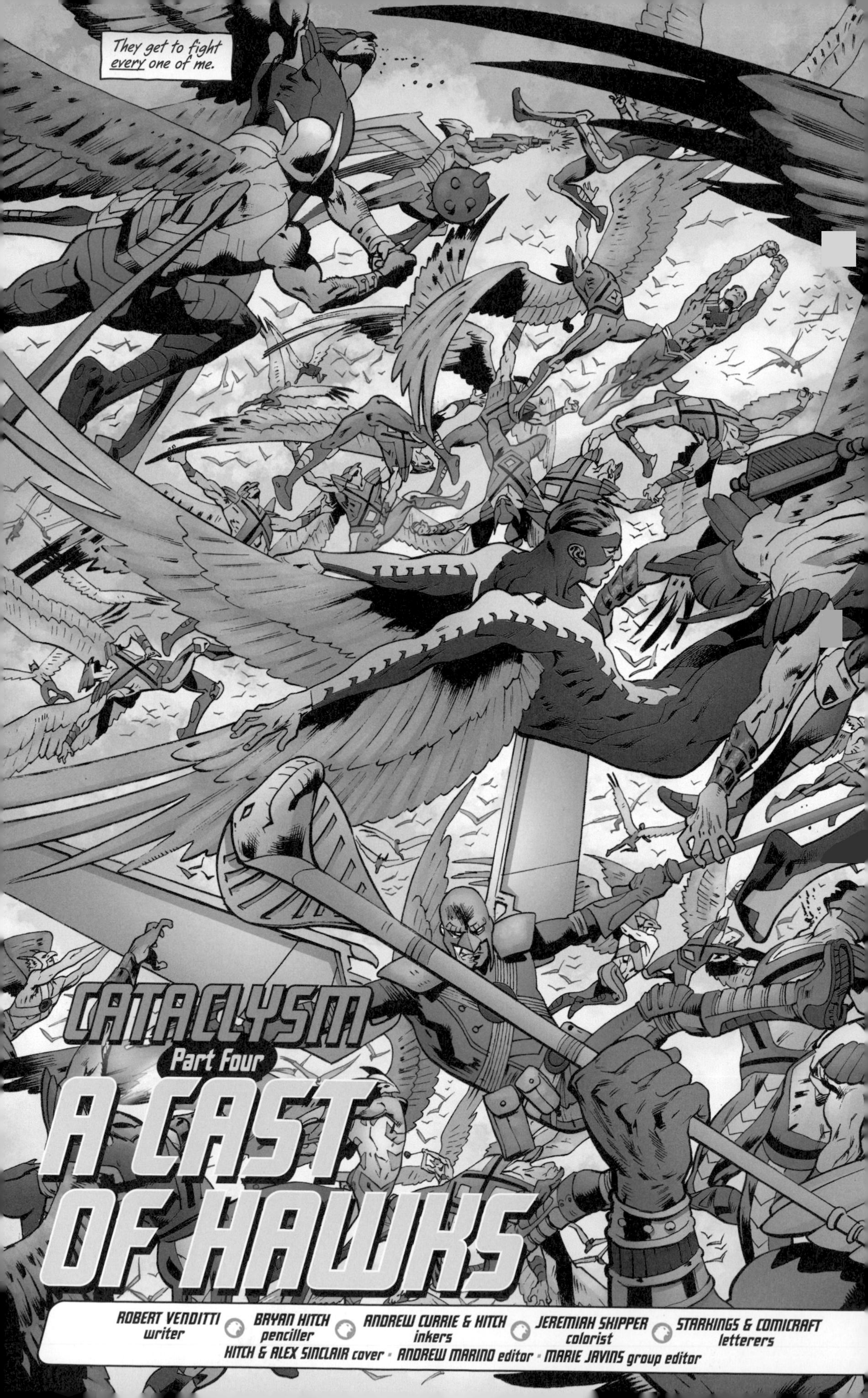
They get to fight every one of me.
CATACLYSM
Part Four
A CAST OF HAWKS
ROBERT VENDITTI writer
BRYAN HITCH penciller
ANDREW CURRIE & HITCH inkers
JEREMIAH SHIPPER colorist
STARKINGS & COMICRAFT letterers
HITCH & ALEX SINCLAIR cover • ANDREW MARINO editor • MARIE JAVINS group editor

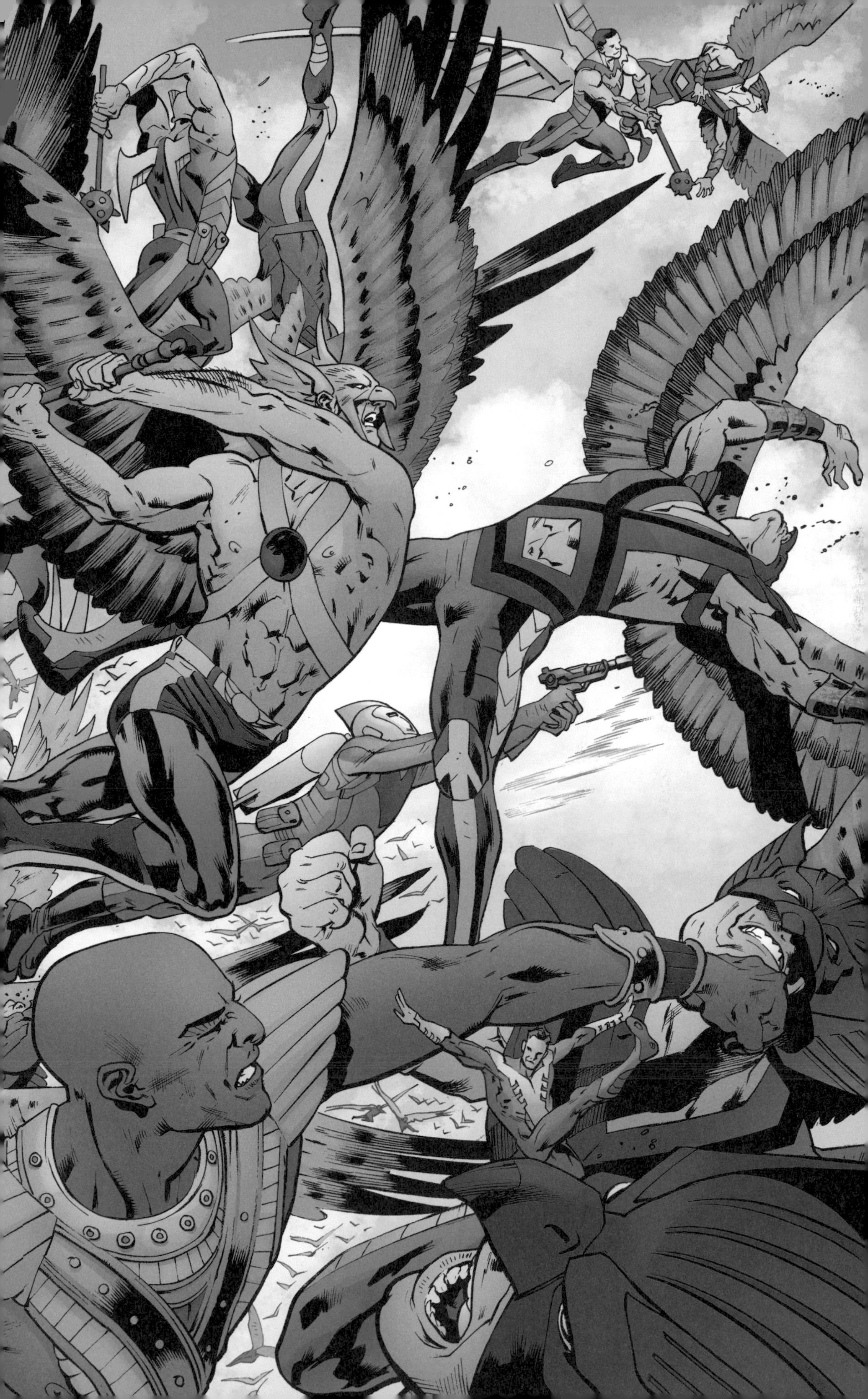

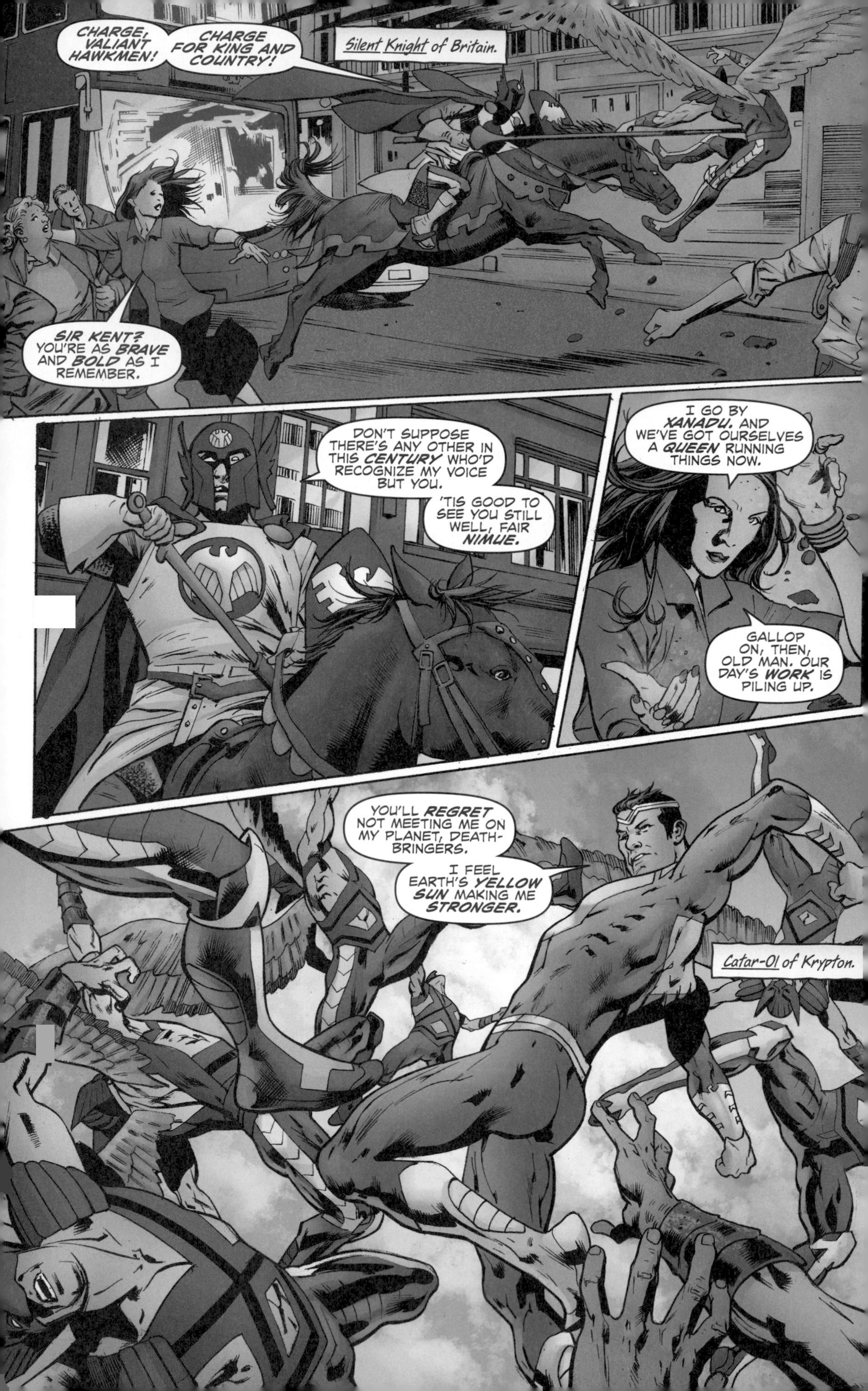
CHARGE, VALIANT HAWKMEN!
CHARGE FOR KING AND COUNTRY!
Silent Knight of Britain.
SIR KENT? YOU'RE AS BRAVE AND BOLD AS I REMEMBER.
DON'T SUPPOSE THERE'S ANY OTHER IN THIS CENTURY WHO'D RECOGNIZE MY VOICE BUT YOU.
'TIS GOOD TO SEE YOU STILL WELL, FAIR NIMUE.
I GO BY XANADU. AND WE'VE GOT OURSELVES A QUEEN RUNNING THINGS NOW.
GALLOP ON, THEN, OLD MAN. OUR DAY'S WORK IS PILING UP.
YOU'LL REGRET NOT MEETING ME ON MY PLANET, DEATH-BRINGERS.
I FEEL EARTH'S YELLOW SUN MAKING ME STRONGER.
Catar-Ol of Krypton.

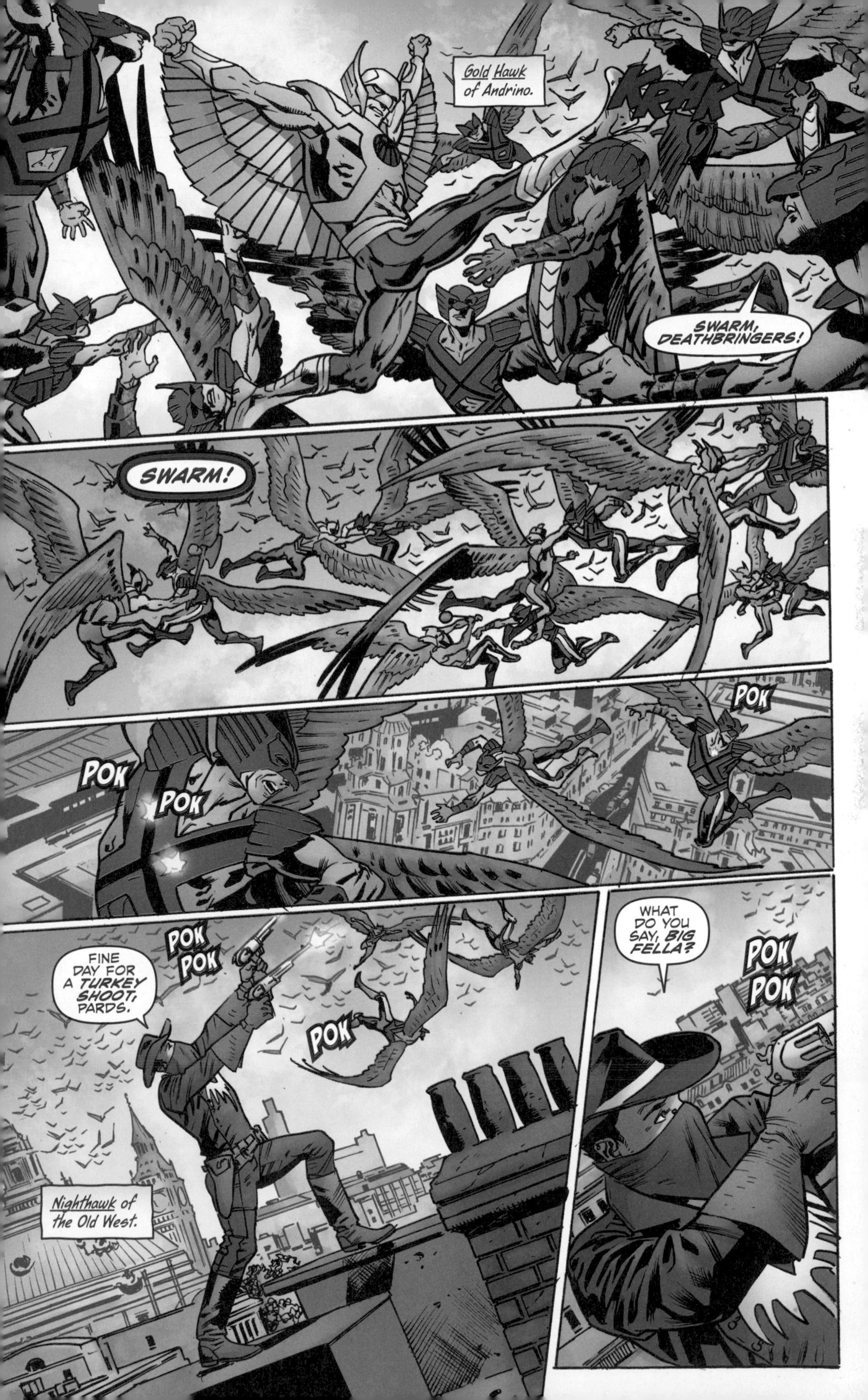
Gold Hawk of Andrino.
KRAK
SWARM, DEATHBRINGERS!
SWARM!
POK
POK
POK
POK
POK
FINE DAY FOR A TURKEY SHOOT, PARDS.
POK
Nighthawk of the Old West.
WHAT DO YOU SAY, BIG FELLA?
POK
POK

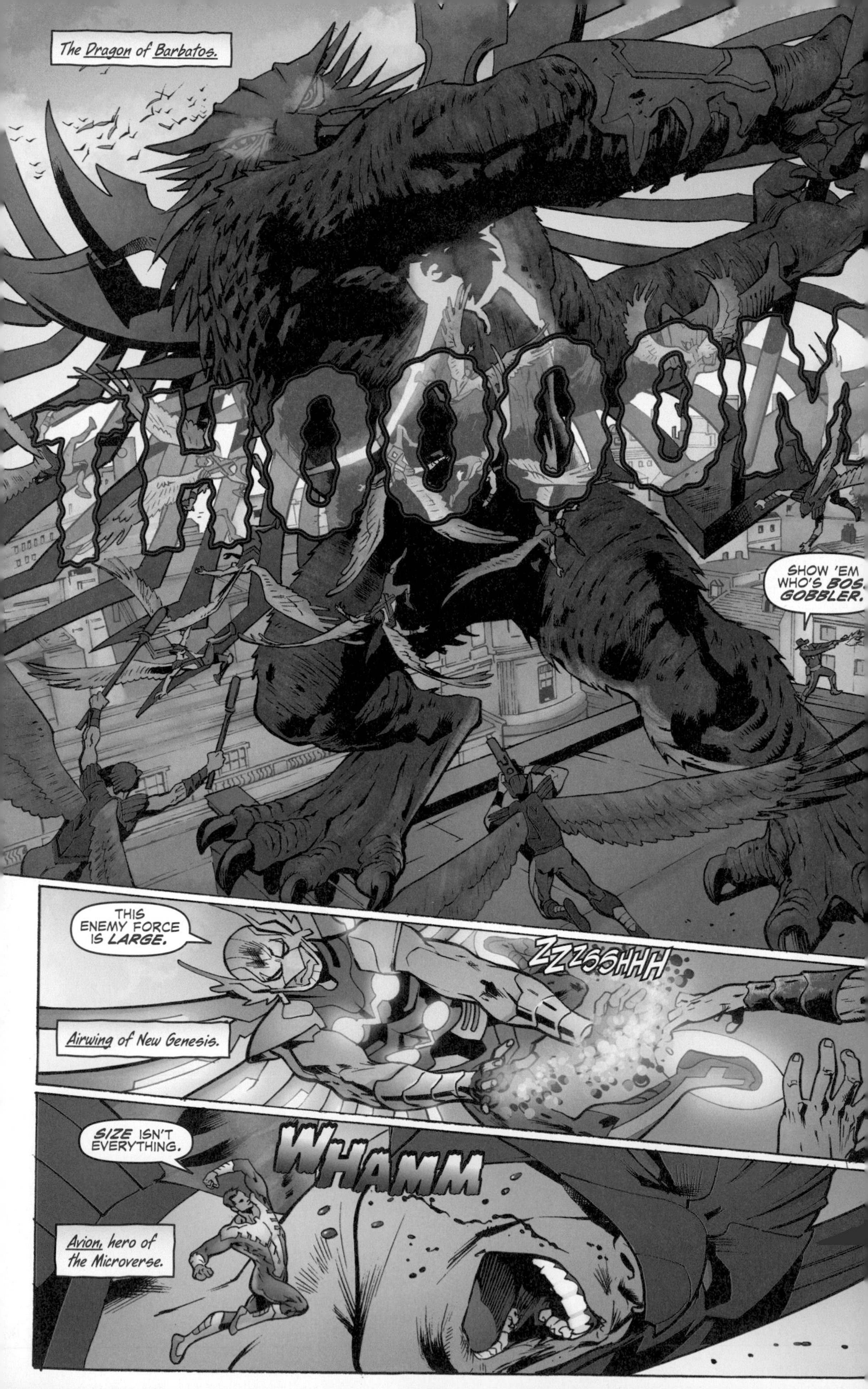
The Dragon of Barbatos.
THOOOOM
SHOW 'EM WHO'S BOS. GOBBLER.
THIS ENEMY FORCE IS LARGE.
ZZZSSHHH
Airwing of New Genesis.
SIZE ISN'T EVERYTHING.
WHAMM
Avion, hero of the Microverse.

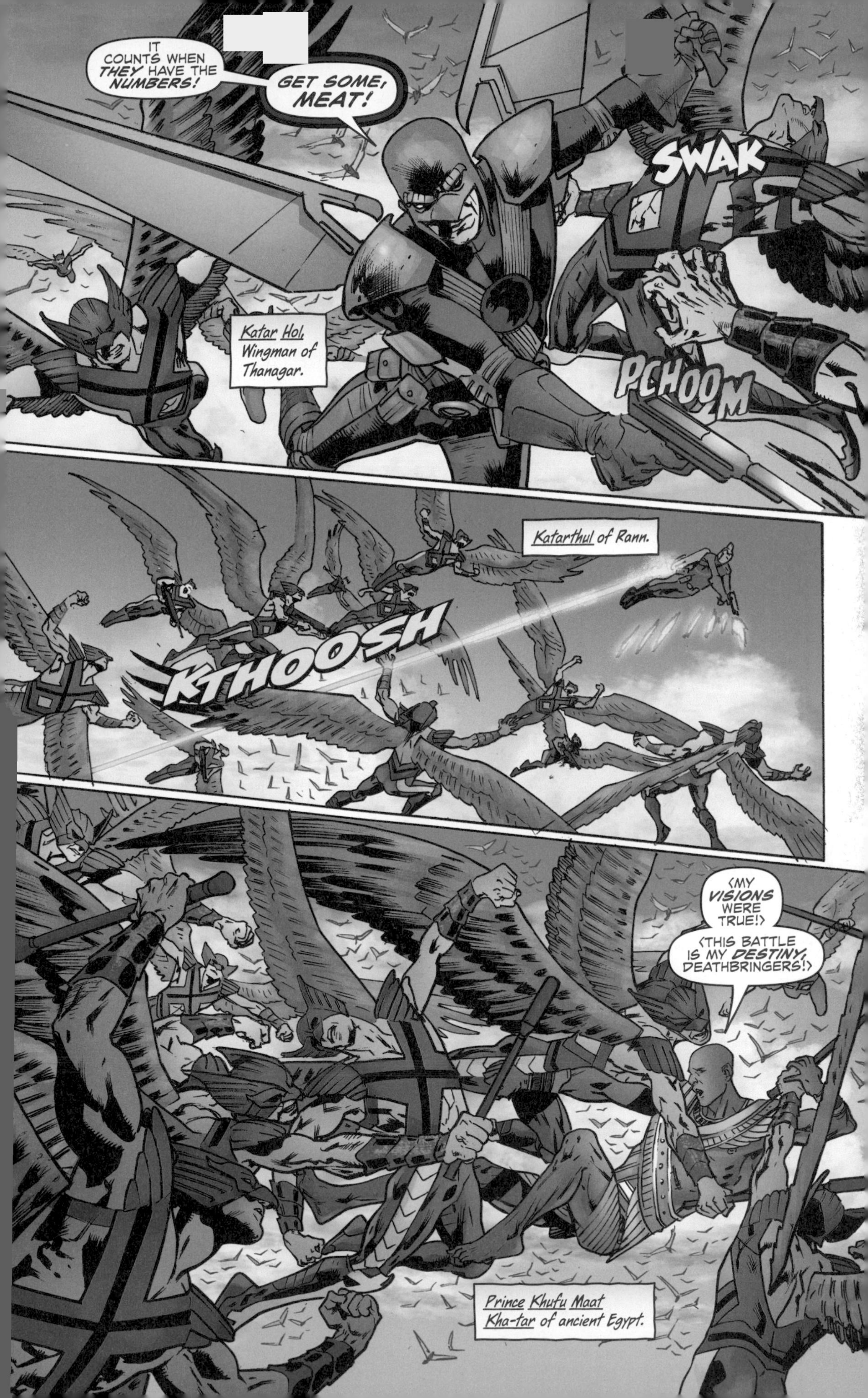
IT COUNTS WHEN THEY HAVE THE NUMBERS!
GET SOME, MEAT!
SWAK
Katar Hol, Wingman of Thanagar.
PCHOOM
Katarthul of Rann.
KTHOOSH
<MY VISIONS WERE TRUE!>
<THIS BATTLE IS MY DESTINY, DEATHBRINGERS!>
Prince Khufu Maat Kha-tar of ancient Egypt.

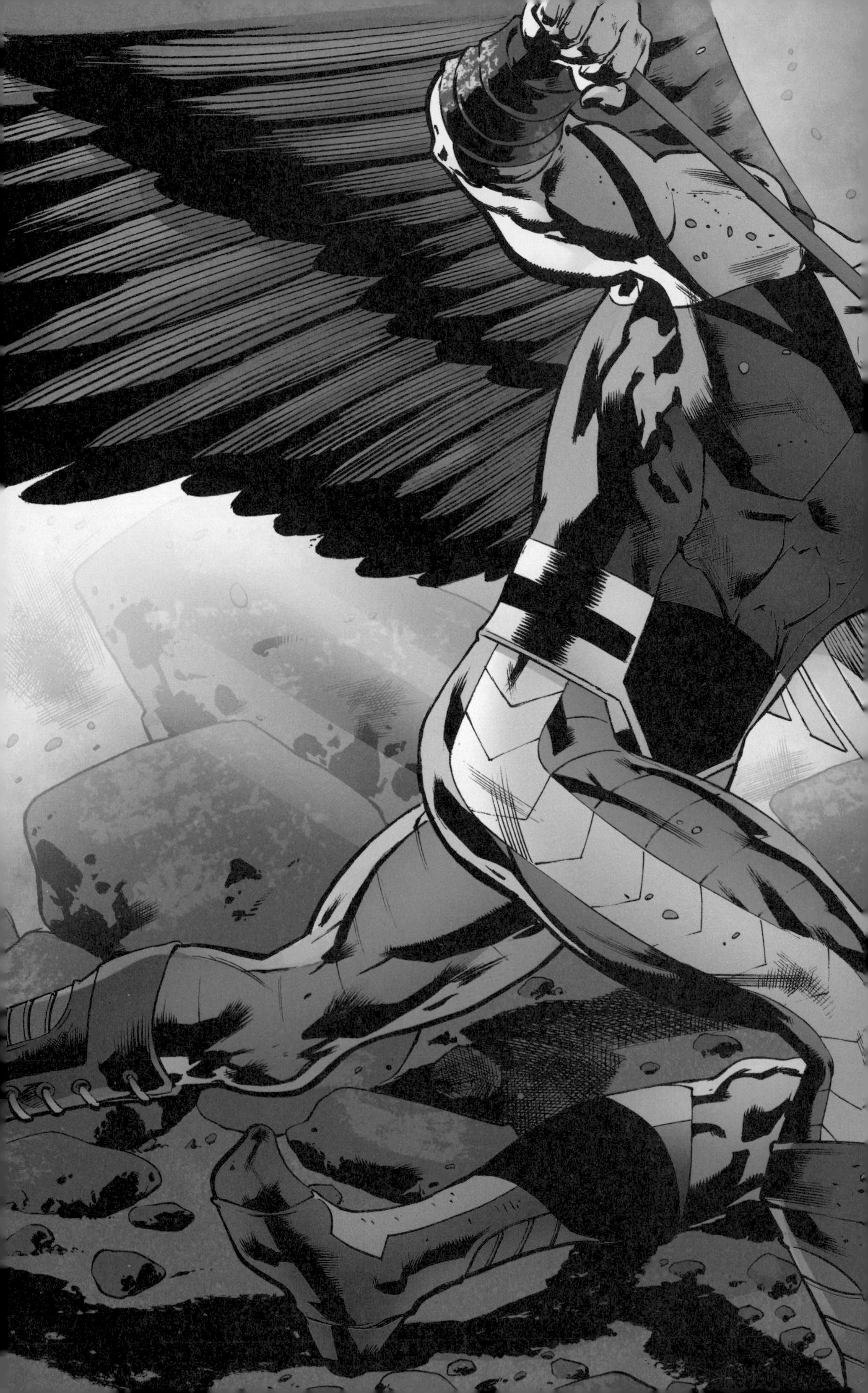

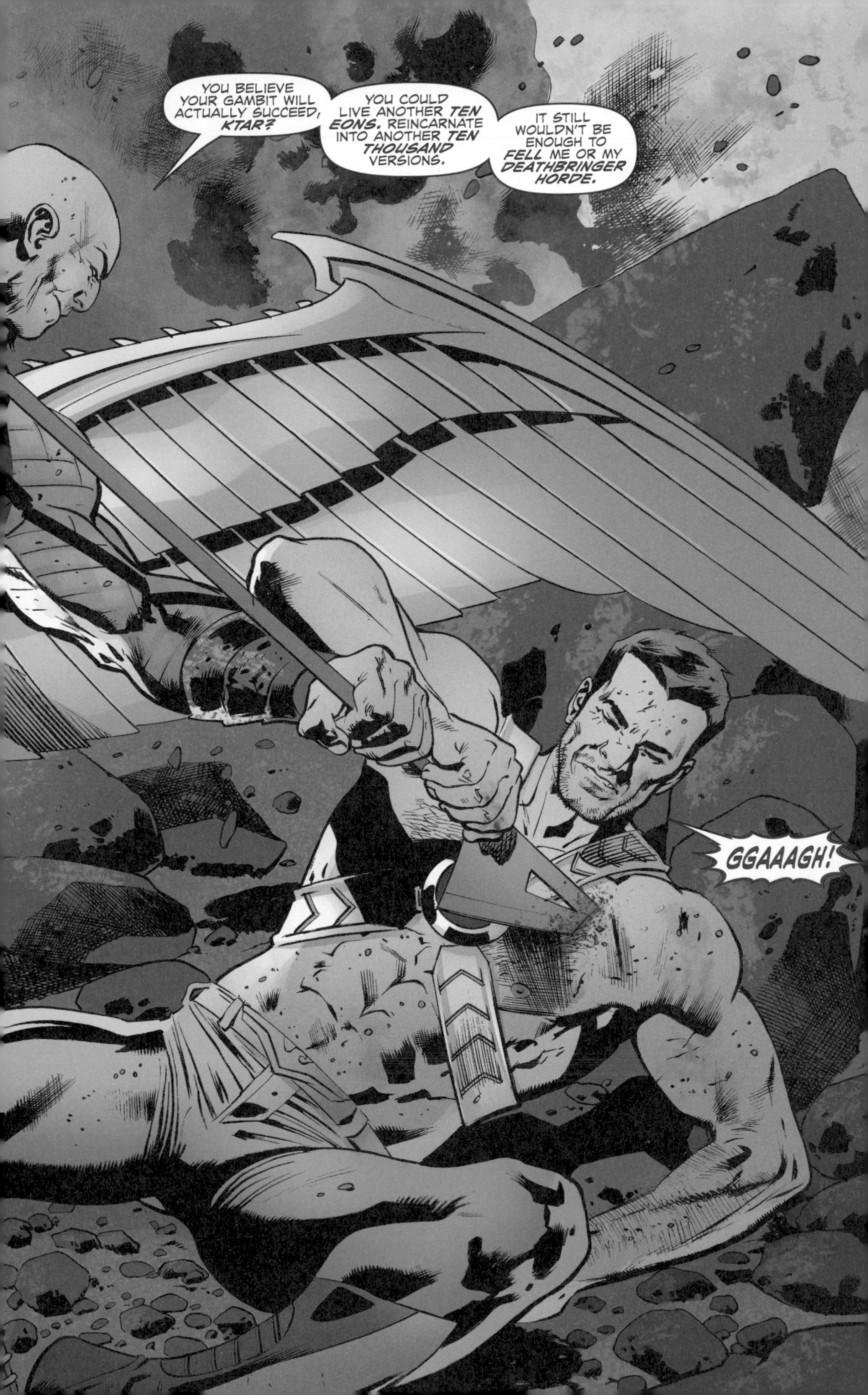
YOU BELIEVE YOUR GAMBIT WILL ACTUALLY SUCCEED, KTAR?
YOU COULD LIVE ANOTHER TEN EONS. REINCARNATE INTO ANOTHER TEN THOUSAND VERSIONS.
IT STILL WOULDN'T BE ENOUGH TO FELL ME OR MY DEATHBRINGER HORDE.
GGAAAGH!

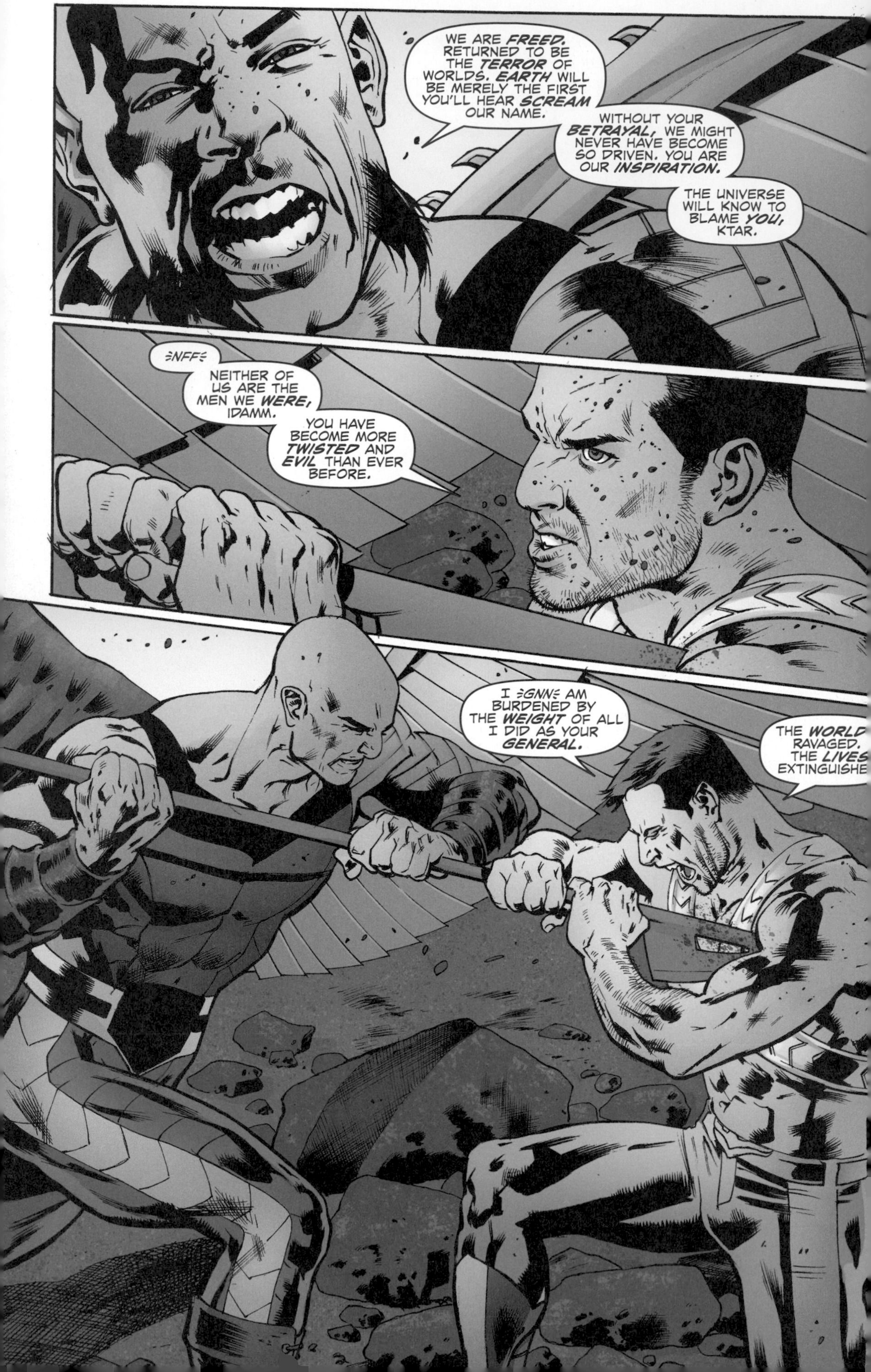
WE ARE *FREED.* RETURNED TO BE THE *TERROR* OF WORLDS. *EARTH* WILL BE MERELY THE FIRST YOU'LL HEAR *SCREAM* OUR NAME.
WITHOUT YOUR *BETRAYAL,* WE MIGHT NEVER HAVE BECOME SO DRIVEN. YOU ARE OUR *INSPIRATION.*
THE UNIVERSE WILL KNOW TO BLAME *YOU,* KTAR.
=NFF=
NEITHER OF US ARE THE MEN WE *WERE,* IDAMM.
YOU HAVE BECOME MORE *TWISTED* AND *EVIL* THAN EVER BEFORE.
I =GNN= AM BURDENED BY THE *WEIGHT* OF ALL I DID AS YOUR *GENERAL.*
THE *WORLD* RAVAGED. THE *LIVES* EXTINGUISHE

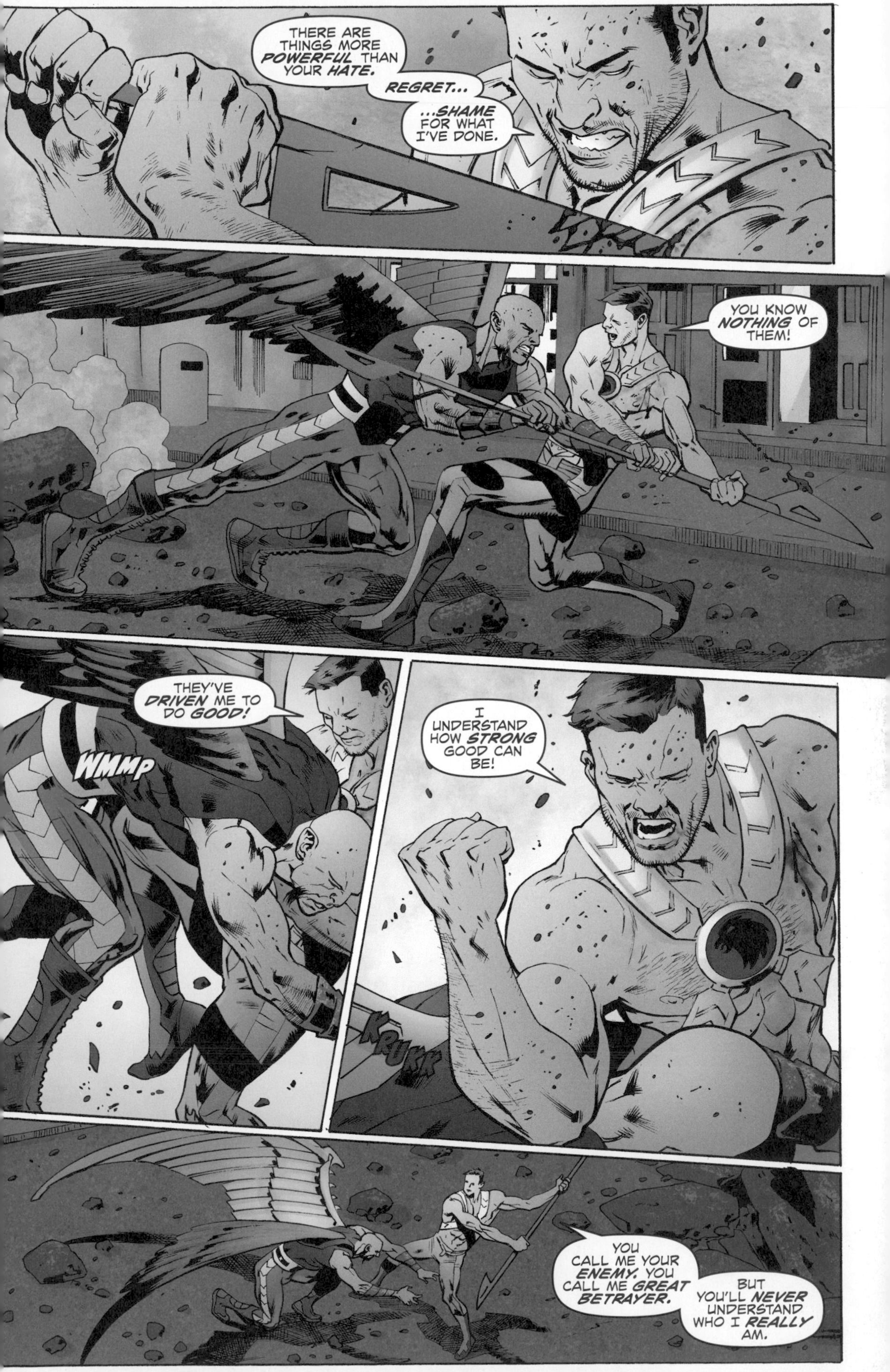
THERE ARE THINGS MORE POWERFUL THAN YOUR HATE.
REGRET...
...SHAME FOR WHAT I'VE DONE.
YOU KNOW NOTHING OF THEM!
THEY'VE DRIVEN ME TO DO GOOD!
WMMP
I UNDERSTAND HOW STRONG GOOD CAN BE!
KRUKK
YOU CALL ME YOUR ENEMY. YOU CALL ME GREAT BETRAYER.
BUT YOU'LL NEVER UNDERSTAND WHO I REALLY AM.

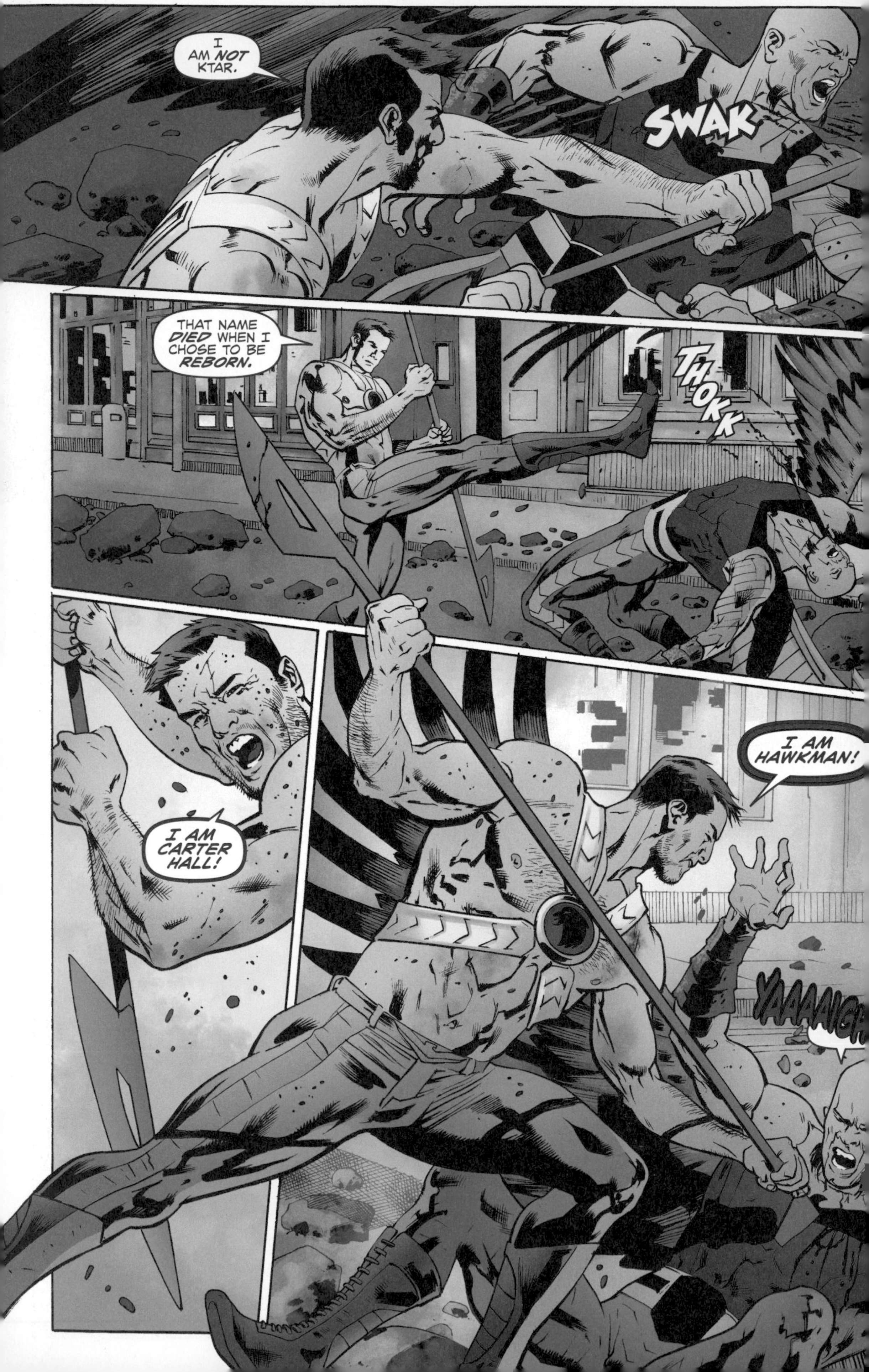
I AM NOT KTAR.
SWAK
THAT NAME DIED WHEN I CHOSE TO BE REBORN.
THOKK
I AM CARTER HALL!
I AM HAWKMAN!
YAAAAIGH

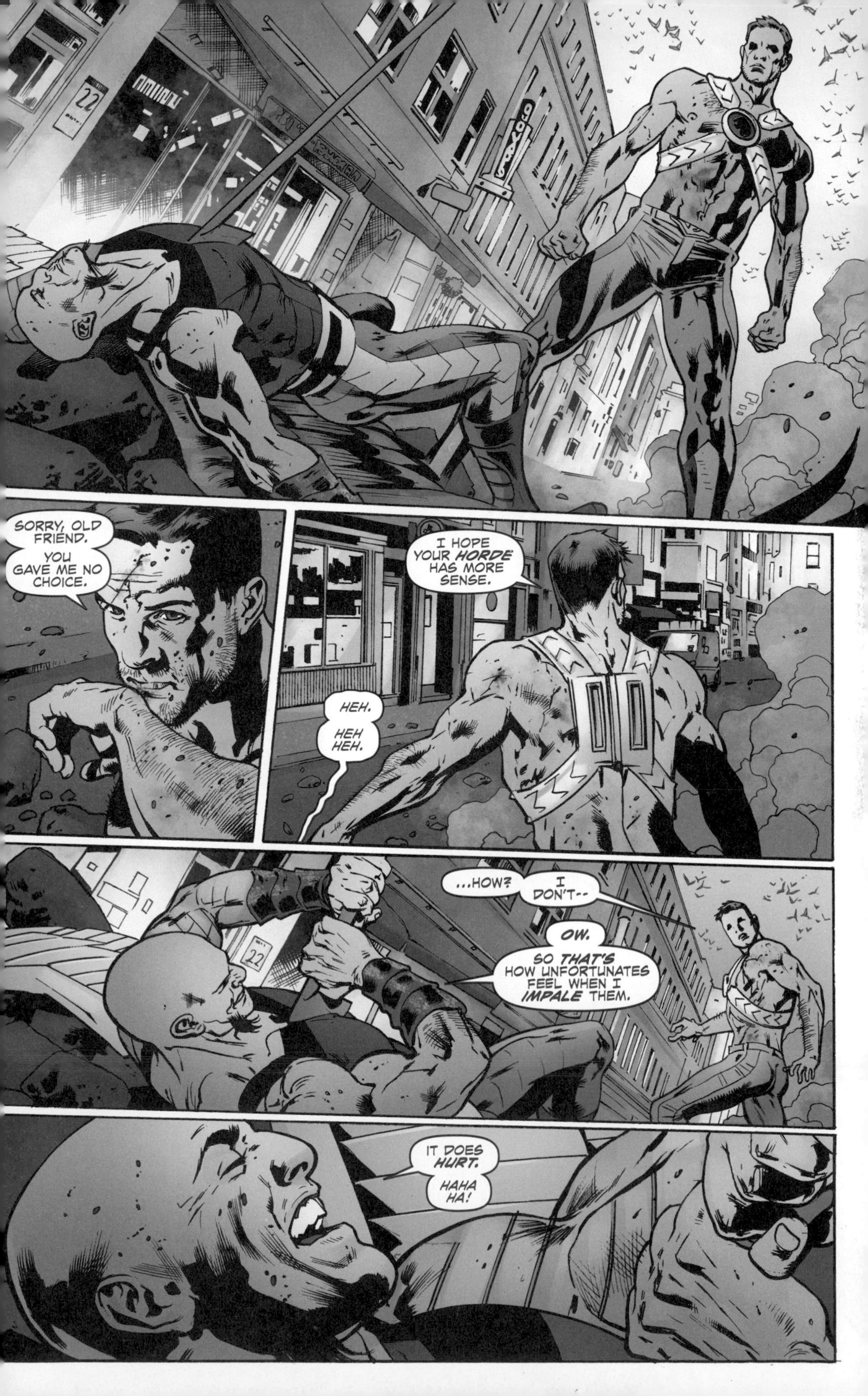

SORRY, OLD FRIEND.
YOU GAVE ME NO CHOICE.
I HOPE YOUR HORDE HAS MORE SENSE.
HEH.
HEH HEH.
...HOW?
I DON'T--
OW.
SO THAT'S HOW UNFORTUNATES FEEL WHEN I IMPALE THEM.
IT DOES HURT.
HAHA HA!

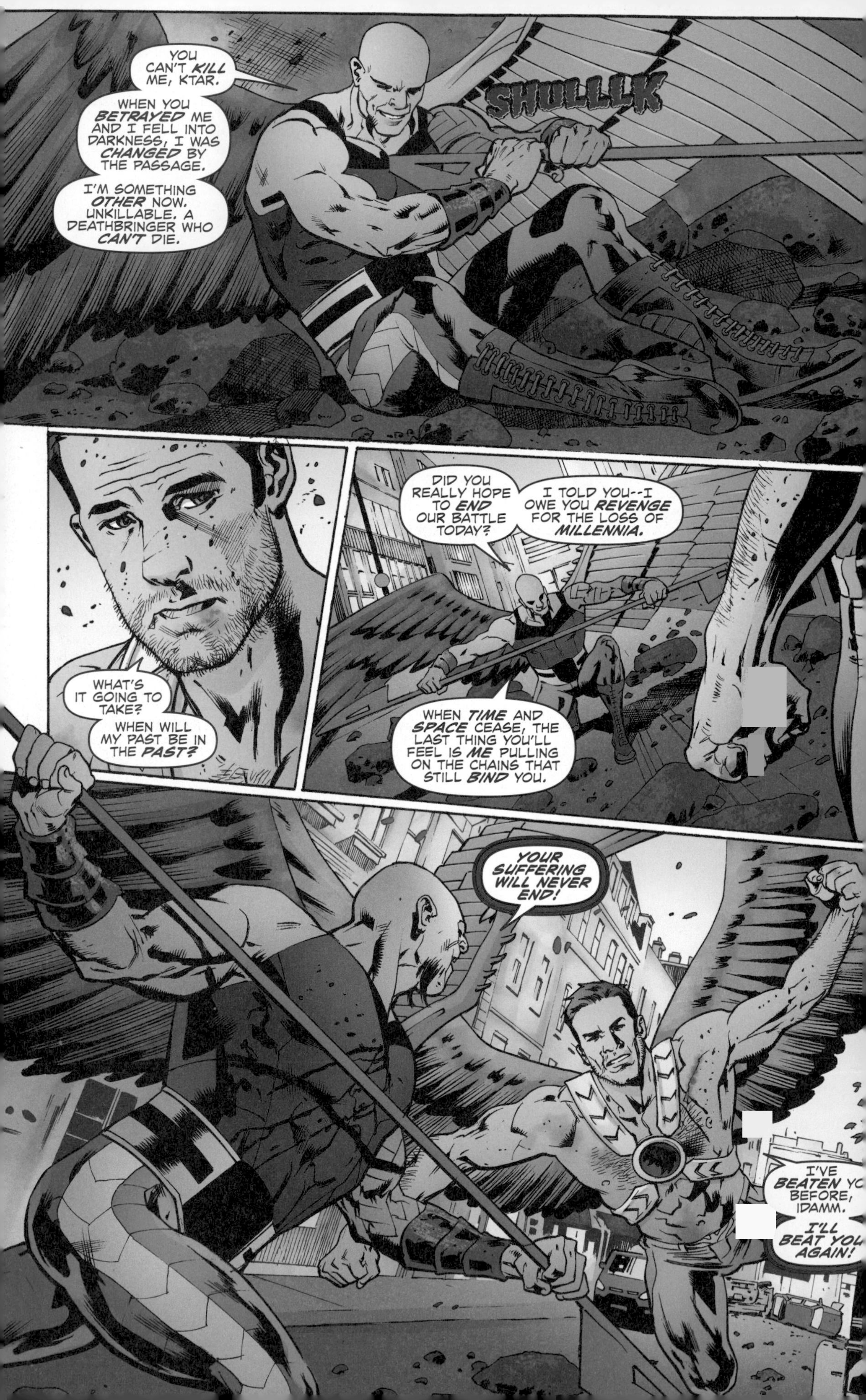
YOU CAN'T KILL ME, KTAR.
WHEN YOU BETRAYED ME AND I FELL INTO DARKNESS, I WAS CHANGED BY THE PASSAGE.
I'M SOMETHING OTHER NOW. UNKILLABLE. A DEATHBRINGER WHO CAN'T DIE.
SHULLLK
WHAT'S IT GOING TO TAKE?
WHEN WILL MY PAST BE IN THE PAST?
DID YOU REALLY HOPE TO END OUR BATTLE TODAY?
I TOLD YOU--I OWE YOU REVENGE FOR THE LOSS OF MILLENNIA.
WHEN TIME AND SPACE CEASE, THE LAST THING YOU'LL FEEL IS ME PULLING ON THE CHAINS THAT STILL BIND YOU.
YOUR SUFFERING WILL NEVER END!
I'VE BEATEN YO BEFORE, IDAMM.
I'LL BEAT YOU AGAIN!

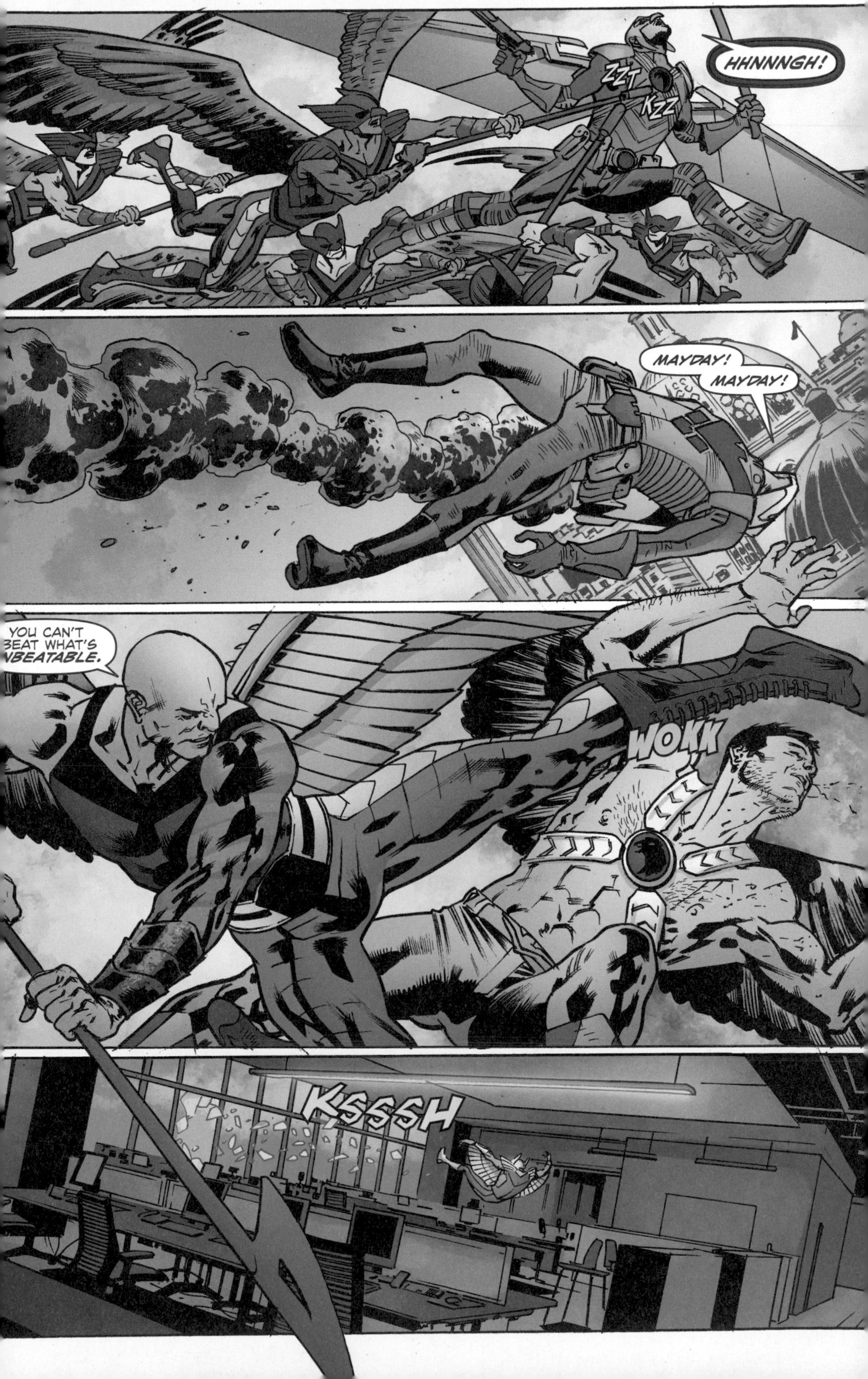
HHNNNGH!
ZZZT
KZZ
MAYDAY!
MAYDAY!
YOU CAN'T
BEAT WHAT'S
UNBEATABLE.
WOKK
KSSSH

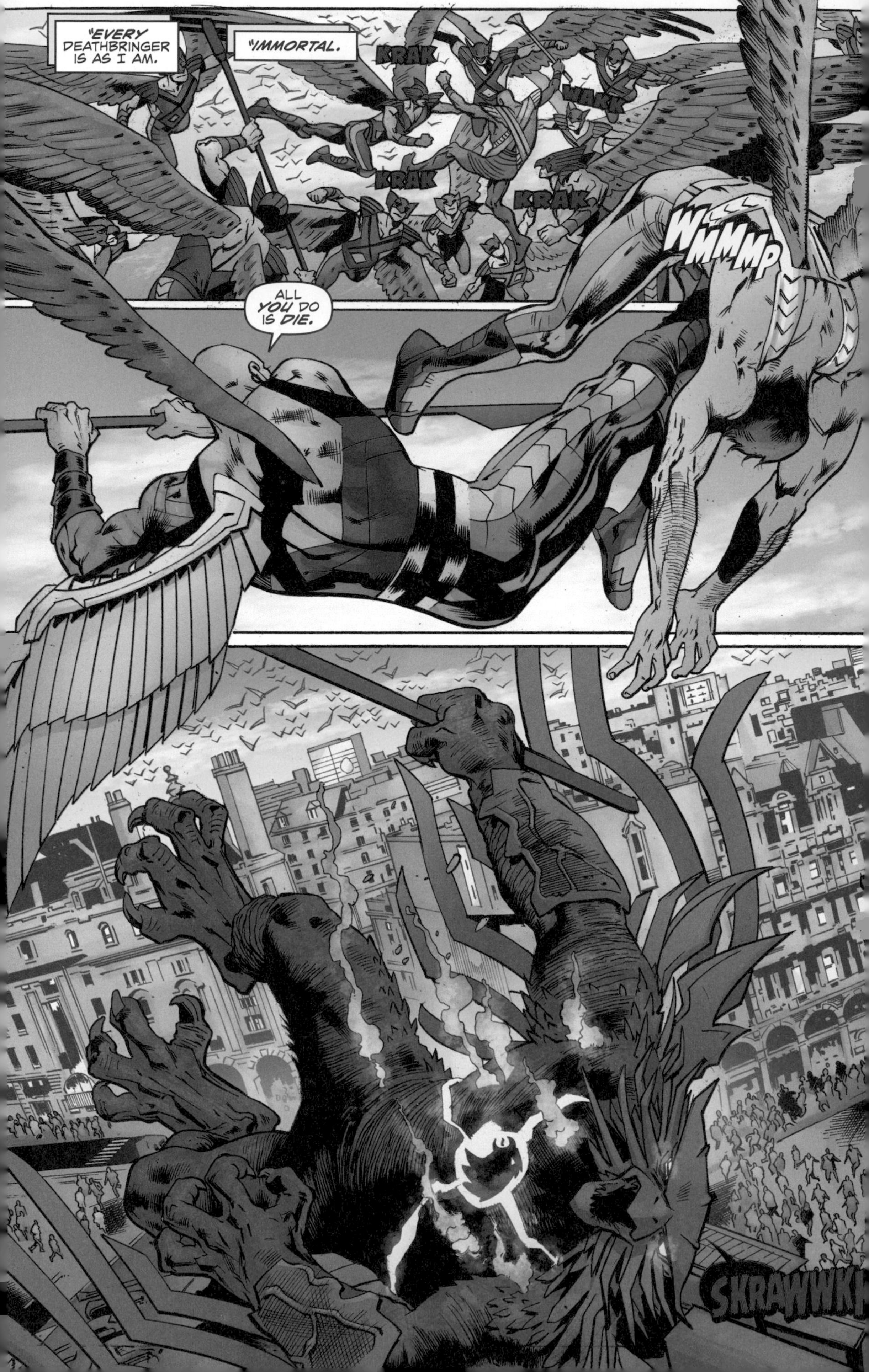
"EVERY DEATHBRINGER IS AS I AM.
"IMMORTAL.
KRAK
WAKK
KRAK
KRAK
WMMMP
ALL YOU DO IS DIE.
SKRAWWK

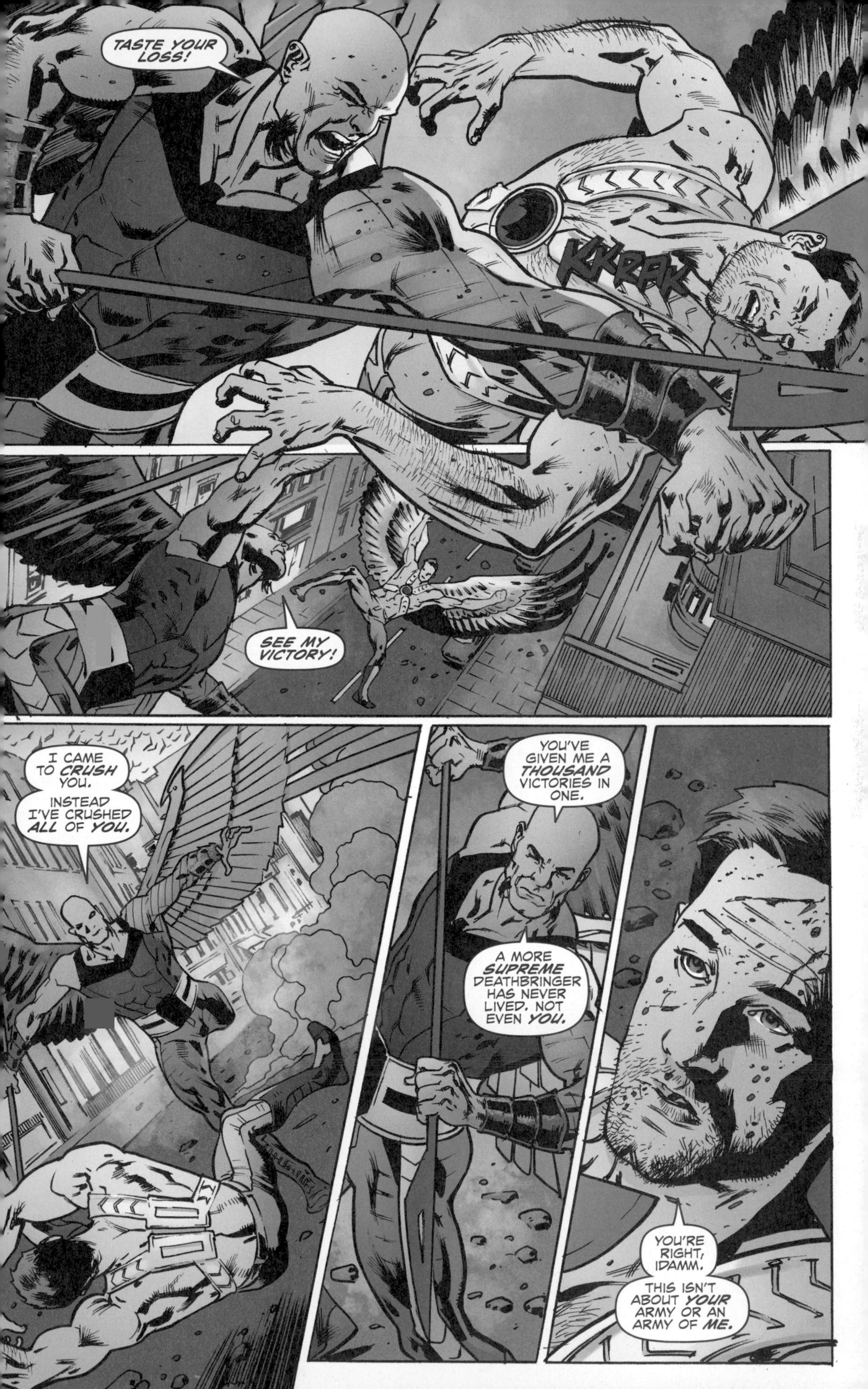
TASTE YOUR LOSS!
KKRAK
SEE MY VICTORY!
I CAME TO CRUSH YOU.
INSTEAD I'VE CRUSHED ALL OF YOU.
YOU'VE GIVEN ME A THOUSAND VICTORIES IN ONE.
A MORE SUPREME DEATHBRINGER HAS NEVER LIVED. NOT EVEN YOU.
YOU'RE RIGHT, IDAMM.
THIS ISN'T ABOUT YOUR ARMY OR AN ARMY OF ME.

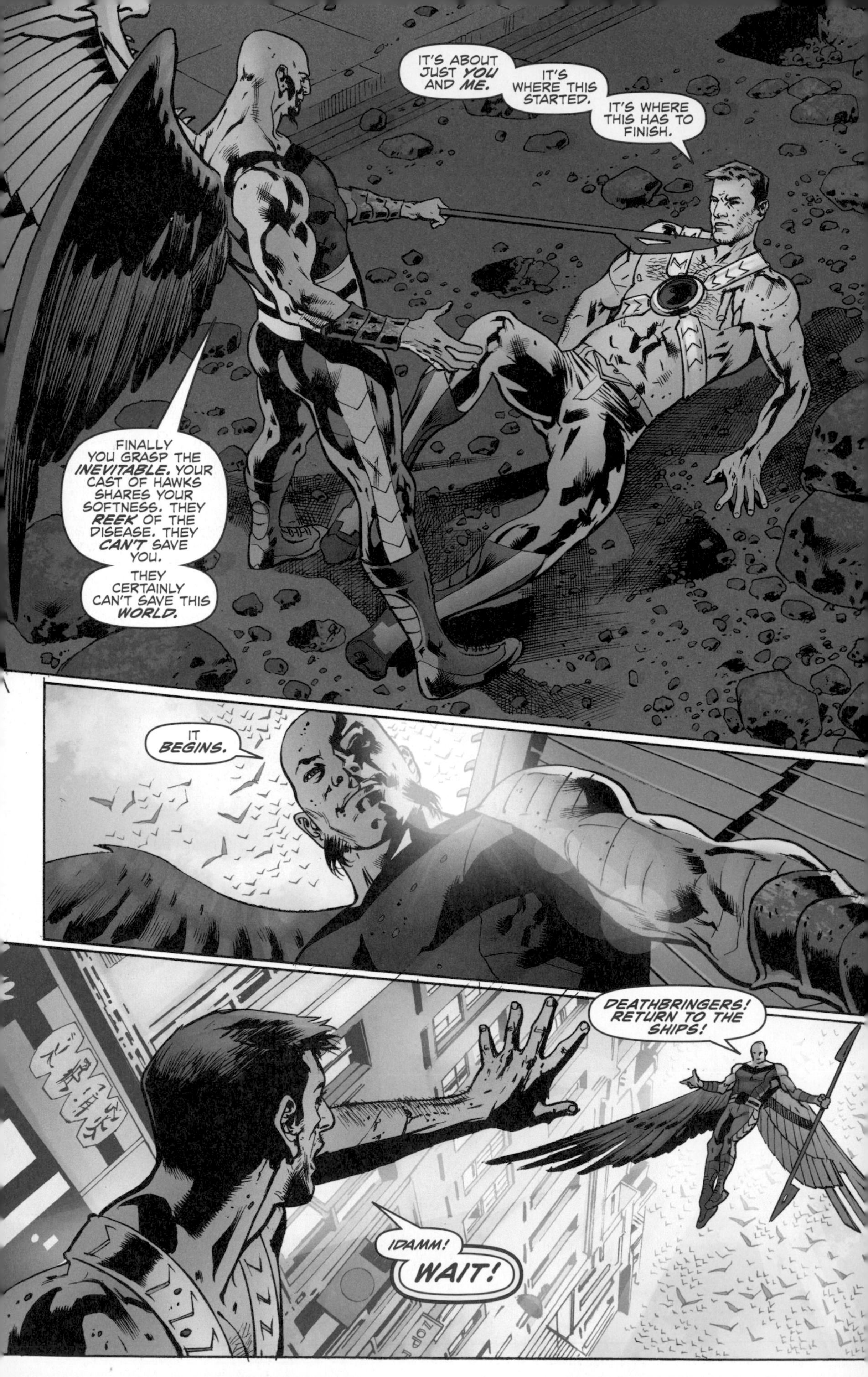
IT'S ABOUT JUST YOU AND ME.
IT'S WHERE THIS STARTED.
IT'S WHERE THIS HAS TO FINISH.
FINALLY YOU GRASP THE INEVITABLE. YOUR CAST OF HAWKS SHARES YOUR SOFTNESS. THEY REEK OF THE DISEASE. THEY CAN'T SAVE YOU.
THEY CERTAINLY CAN'T SAVE THIS WORLD.
IT BEGINS.
DEATHBRINGERS! RETURN TO THE SHIPS!
¡DAMM!
WAIT!

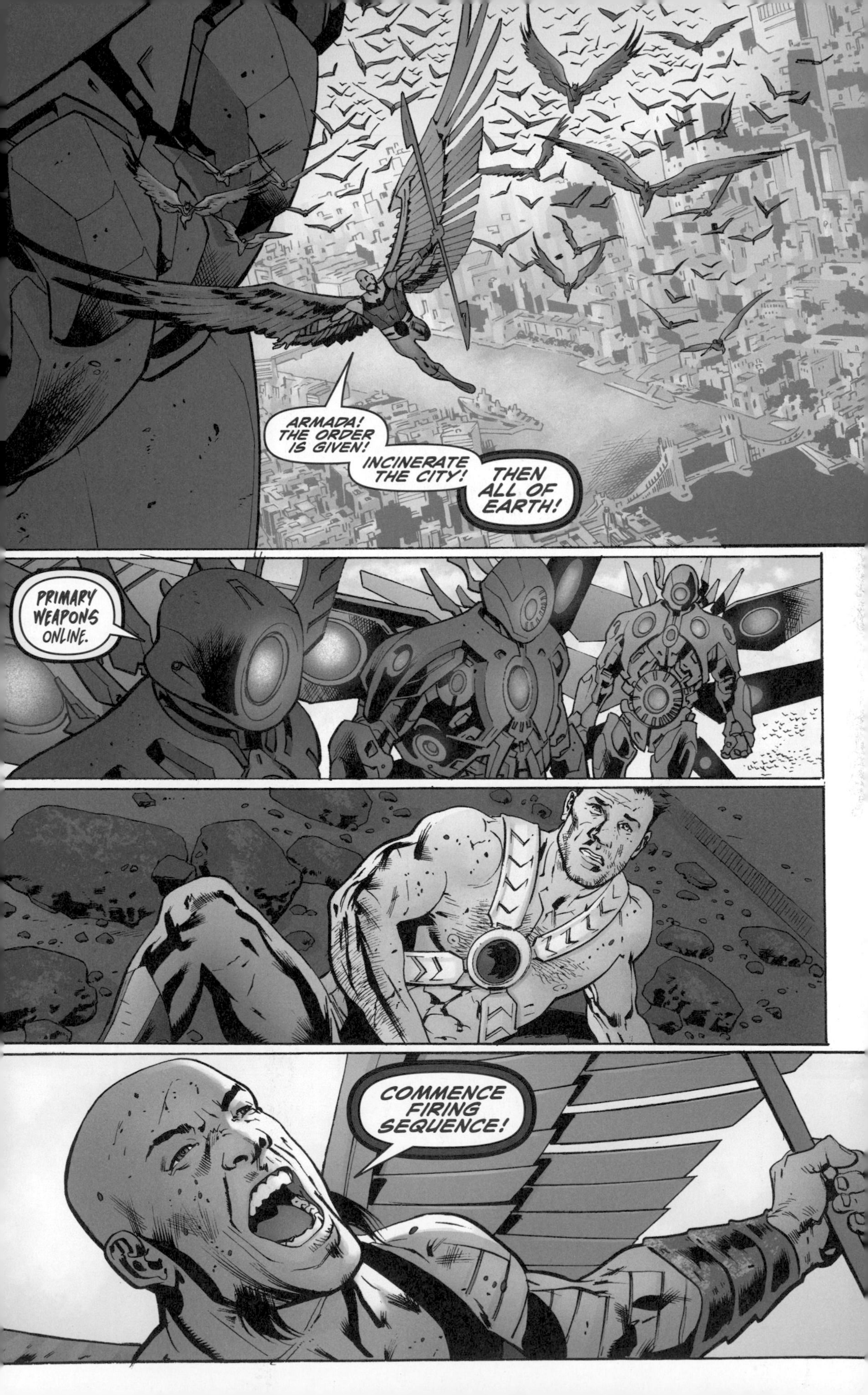
ARMADA! THE ORDER IS GIVEN!
INCINERATE THE CITY!
THEN ALL OF EARTH!
PRIMARY WEAPONS ONLINE.
COMMENCE FIRING SEQUENCE!

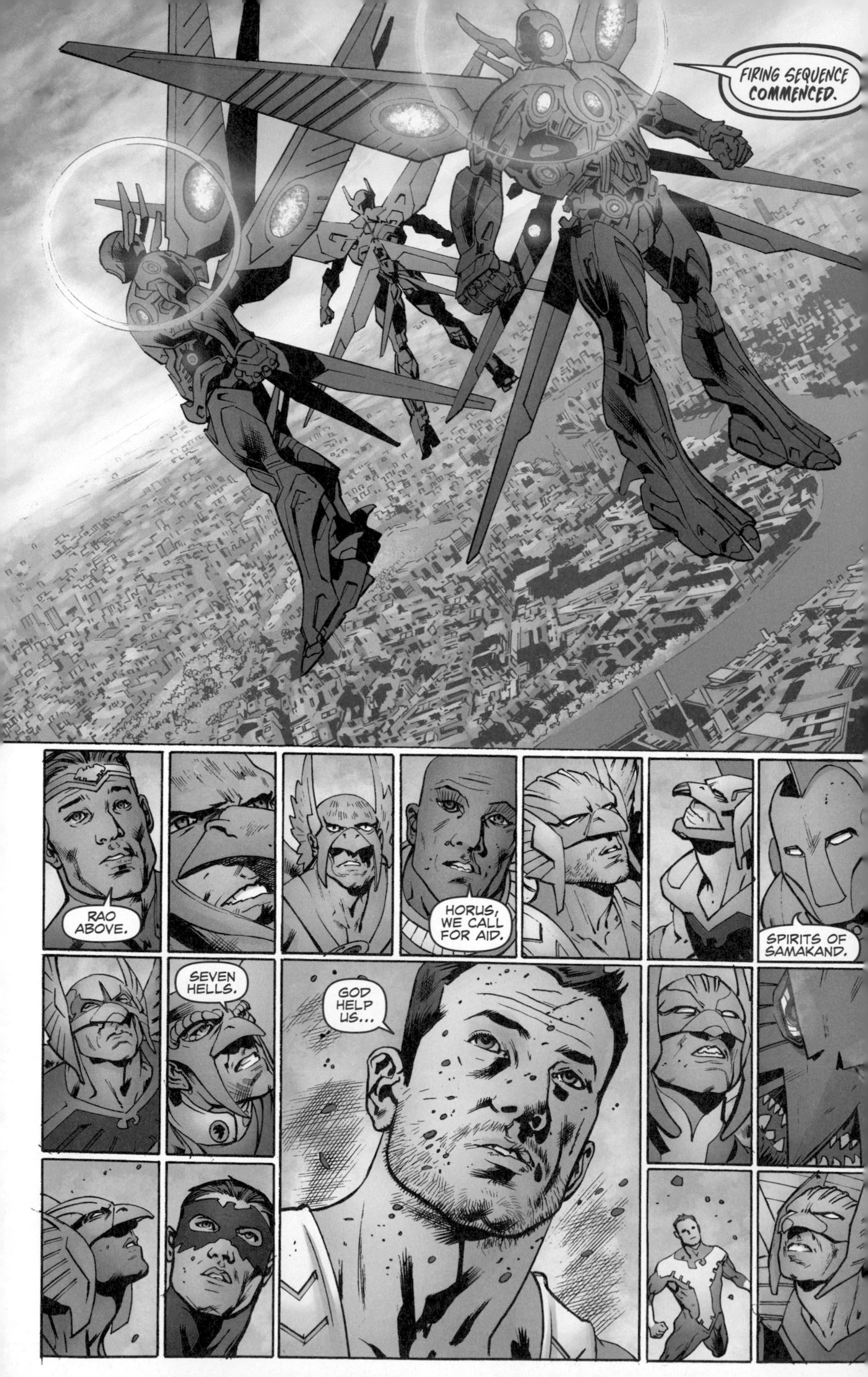
FIRING SEQUENCE COMMENCED.
RAO ABOVE.
HORUS, WE CALL FOR AID.
SPIRITS OF SAMAKAND.
SEVEN HELLS.
GOD HELP US...

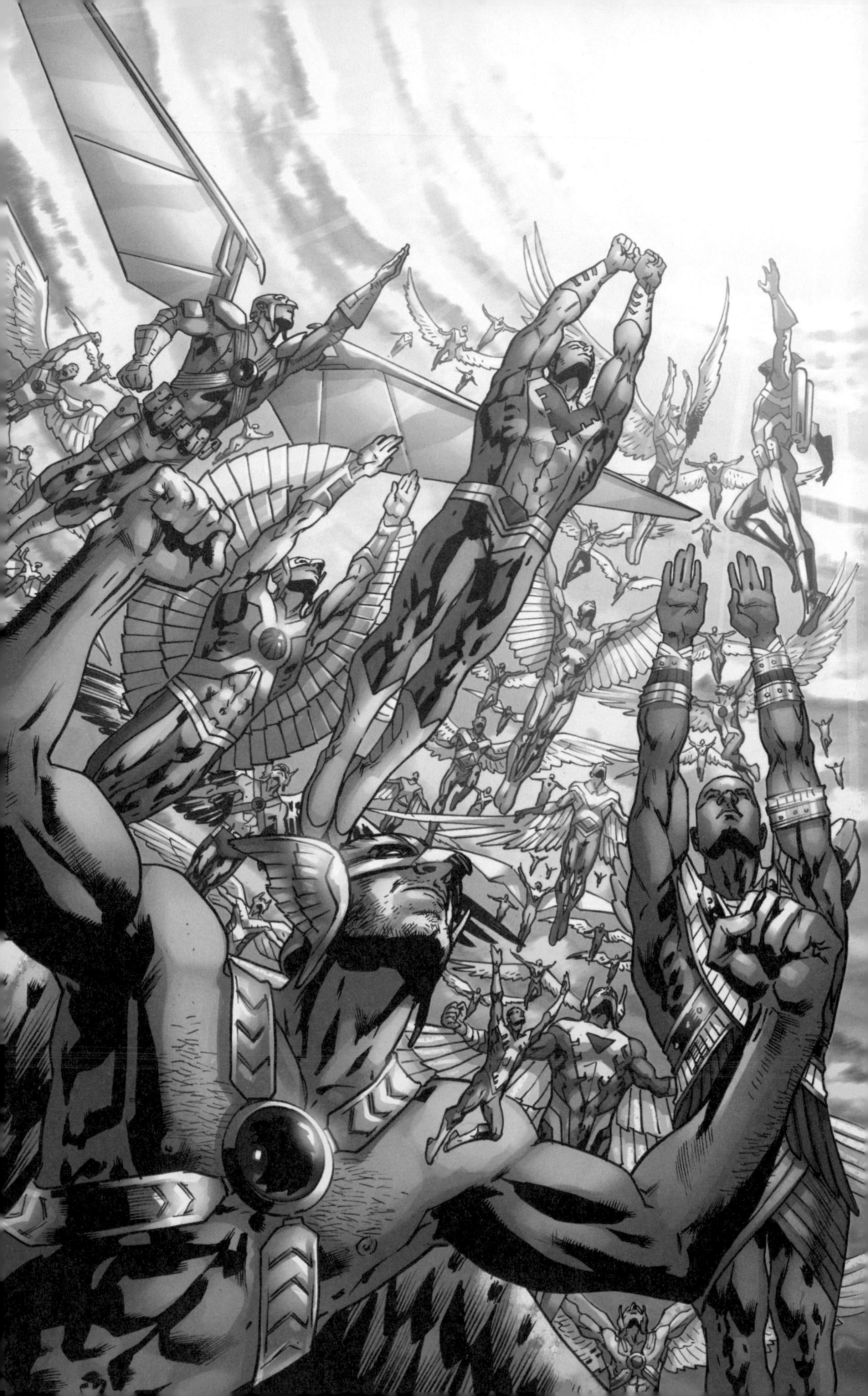

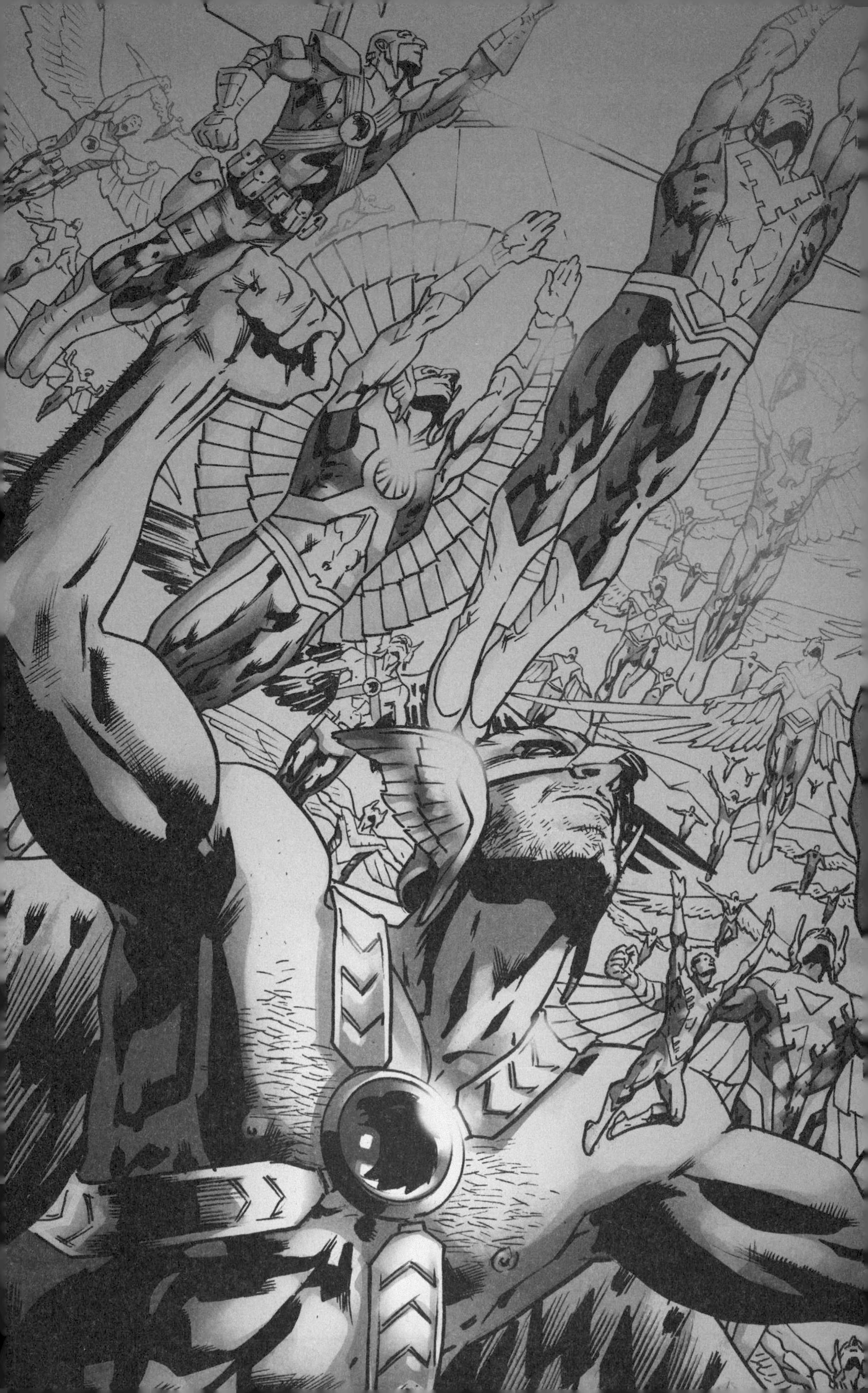

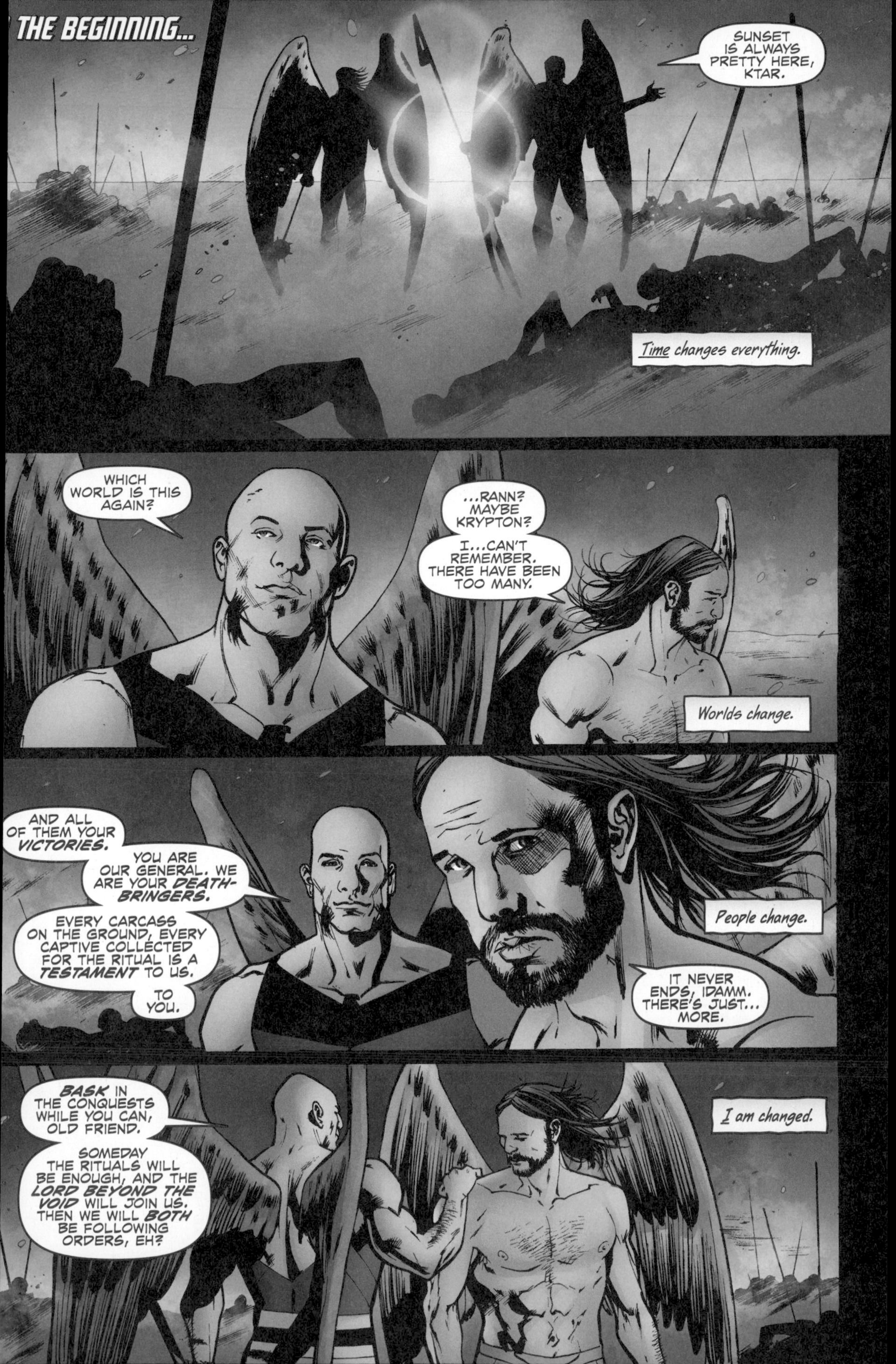
THE BEGINNING...
SUNSET IS ALWAYS PRETTY HERE, KTAR.
Time changes everything.
WHICH WORLD IS THIS AGAIN?
...RANN? MAYBE KRYPTON?
I...CAN'T REMEMBER. THERE HAVE BEEN TOO MANY.
Worlds change.
AND ALL OF THEM YOUR VICTORIES.
YOU ARE OUR GENERAL. WE ARE YOUR DEATH-BRINGERS.
EVERY CARCASS ON THE GROUND, EVERY CAPTIVE COLLECTED FOR THE RITUAL IS A TESTAMENT TO US.
TO YOU.
People change.
IT NEVER ENDS, IDAMM. THERE'S JUST... MORE.
BASK IN THE CONQUESTS WHILE YOU CAN, OLD FRIEND.
I am changed.
SOMEDAY THE RITUALS WILL BE ENOUGH, AND THE LORD BEYOND THE VOID WILL JOIN US. THEN WE WILL BOTH BE FOLLOWING ORDERS, EH?

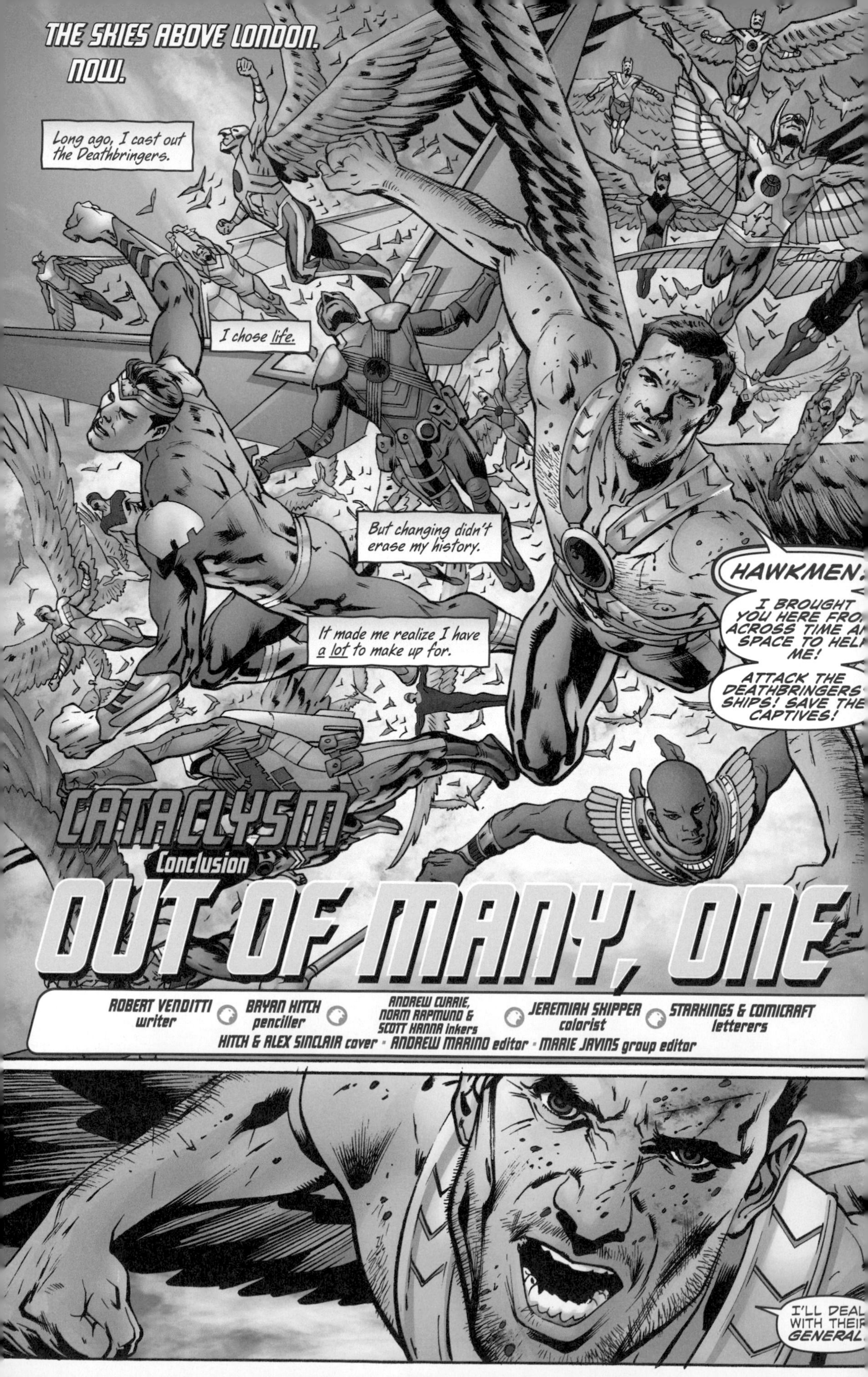
THE SKIES ABOVE LONDON. NOW.
Long ago, I cast out the Deathbringers.
I chose life.
But changing didn't erase my history.
It made me realize I have a lot to make up for.
HAWKMEN!
I BROUGHT YOU HERE FROM ACROSS TIME AND SPACE TO HELP ME!
ATTACK THE DEATHBRINGERS' SHIPS! SAVE THE CAPTIVES!
CATACLYSM Conclusion
OUT OF MANY, ONE
ROBERT VENDITTI writer
BRYAN HITCH penciller
ANDREW CURRIE, NORM RAPMUND & SCOTT HANNA inkers
JEREMIAH SKIPPER colorist
STARKINGS & COMICRAFT letterers
HITCH & ALEX SINCLAIR cover • ANDREW MARINO editor • MARIE JAVINS group editor
I'LL DEAL WITH THEIR GENERAL.

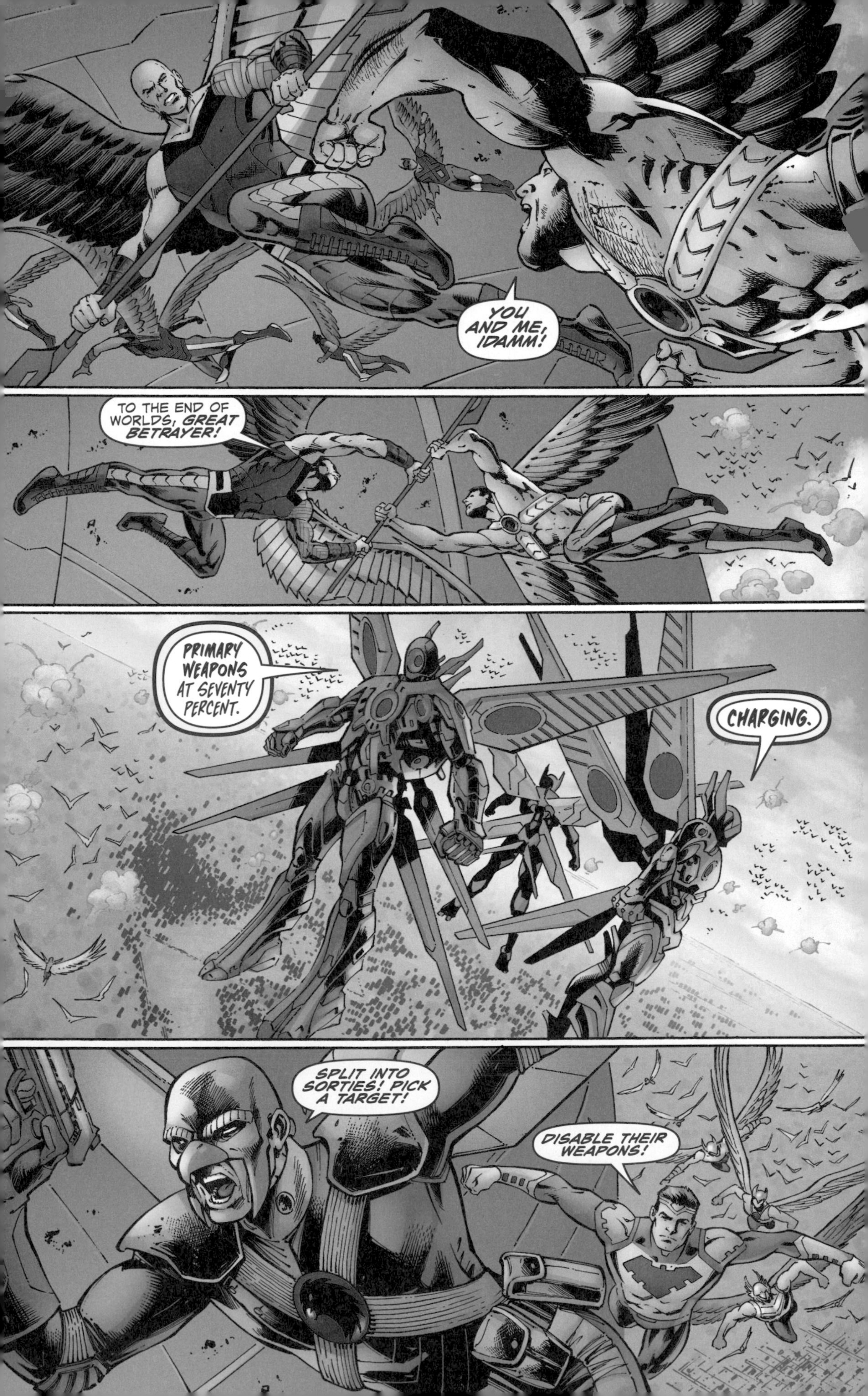
YOU AND ME, IDAMM!
TO THE END OF WORLDS, GREAT BETRAYER!
PRIMARY WEAPONS AT SEVENTY PERCENT.
CHARGING.
SPLIT INTO SORTIES! PICK A TARGET!
DISABLE THEIR WEAPONS!

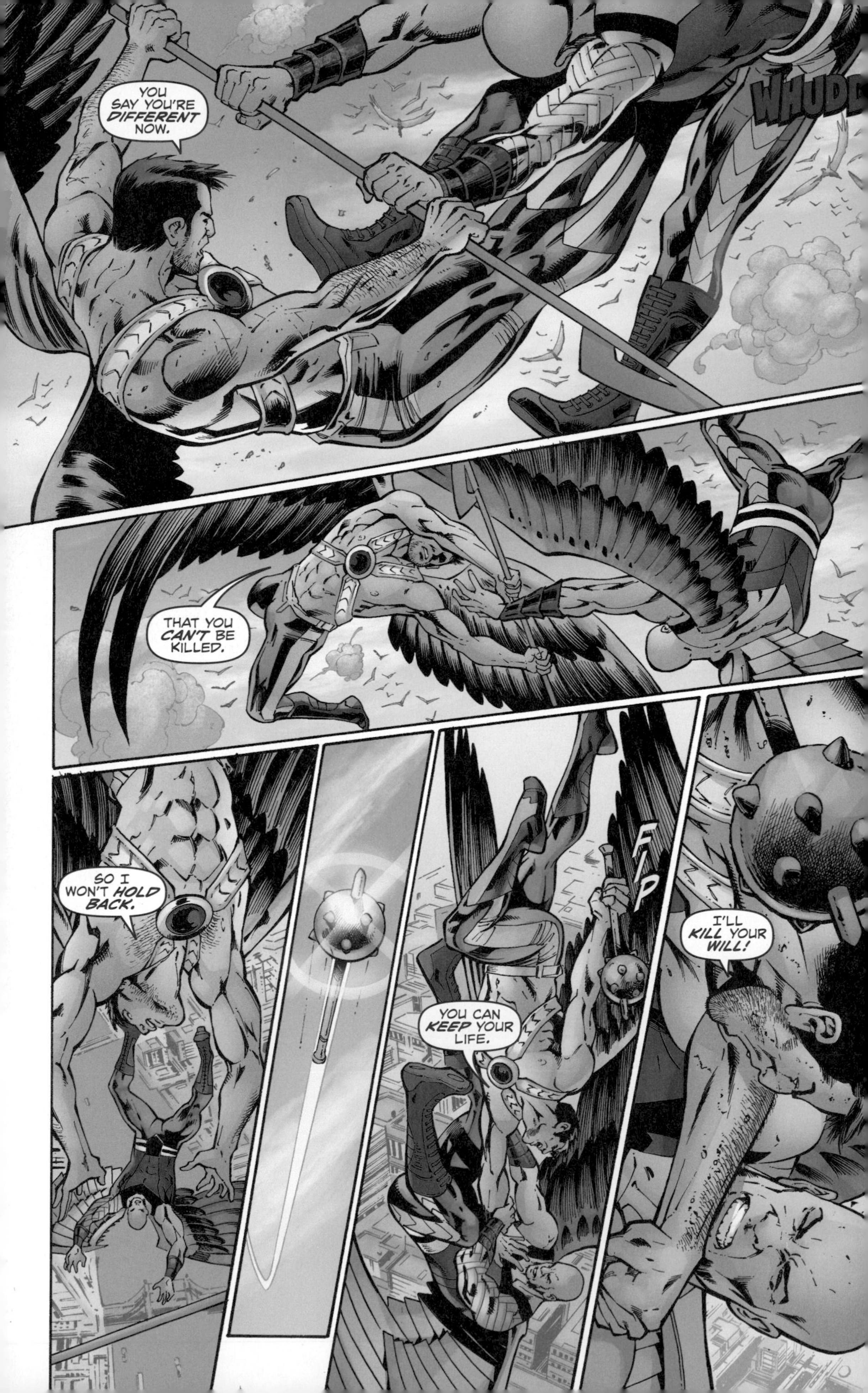

WHUDD
YOU SAY YOU'RE *DIFFERENT* NOW.
THAT YOU *CAN'T* BE KILLED.
SO I WON'T *HOLD BACK.*
FIP
YOU CAN *KEEP* YOUR LIFE.
I'LL *KILL* YOUR *WILL!*

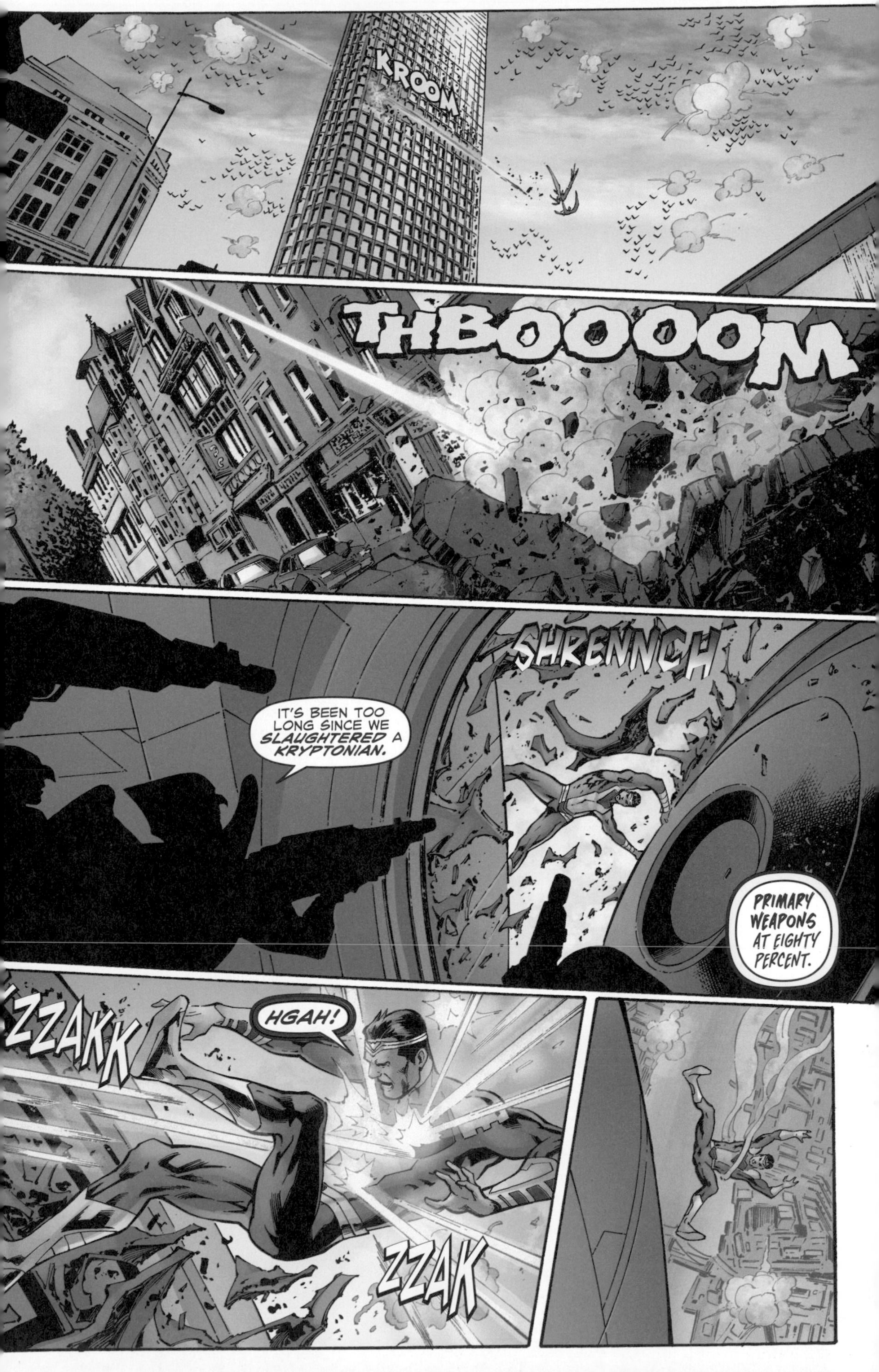

KROOM
THBOOOOM
SHRENNCH
IT'S BEEN TOO LONG SINCE WE SLAUGHTERED A KRYPTONIAN.
PRIMARY WEAPONS AT EIGHTY PERCENT.
ZZAKK
HGAH!
ZZAK

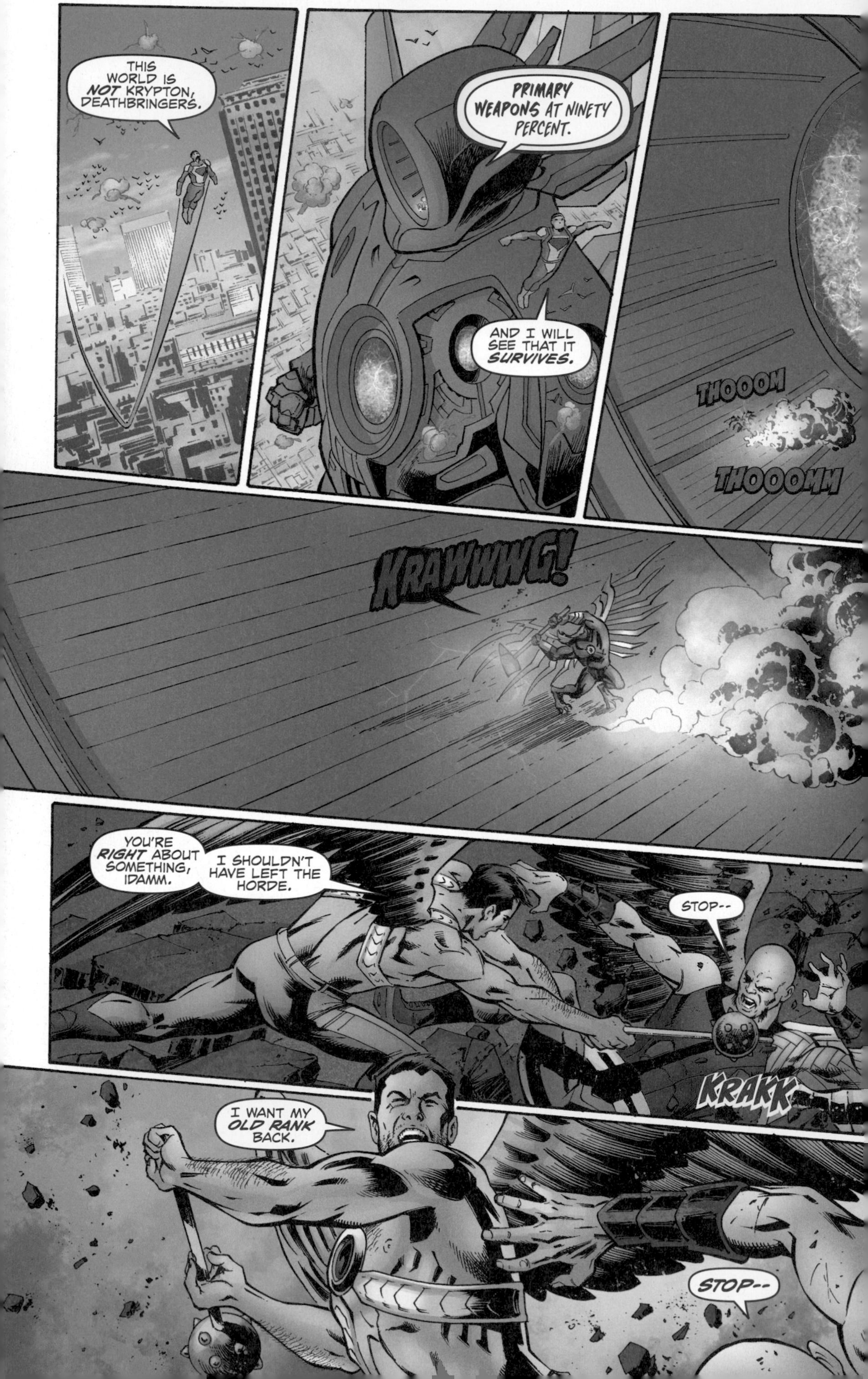
THIS WORLD IS NOT KRYPTON, DEATHBRINGERS.
PRIMARY WEAPONS AT NINETY PERCENT.
AND I WILL SEE THAT IT SURVIVES.
THOOOM
THOOOMM
KRAWWWG!
YOU'RE RIGHT ABOUT SOMETHING, IDAMM.
I SHOULDN'T HAVE LEFT THE HORDE.
STOP--
KRAKK
I WANT MY OLD RANK BACK.
STOP--

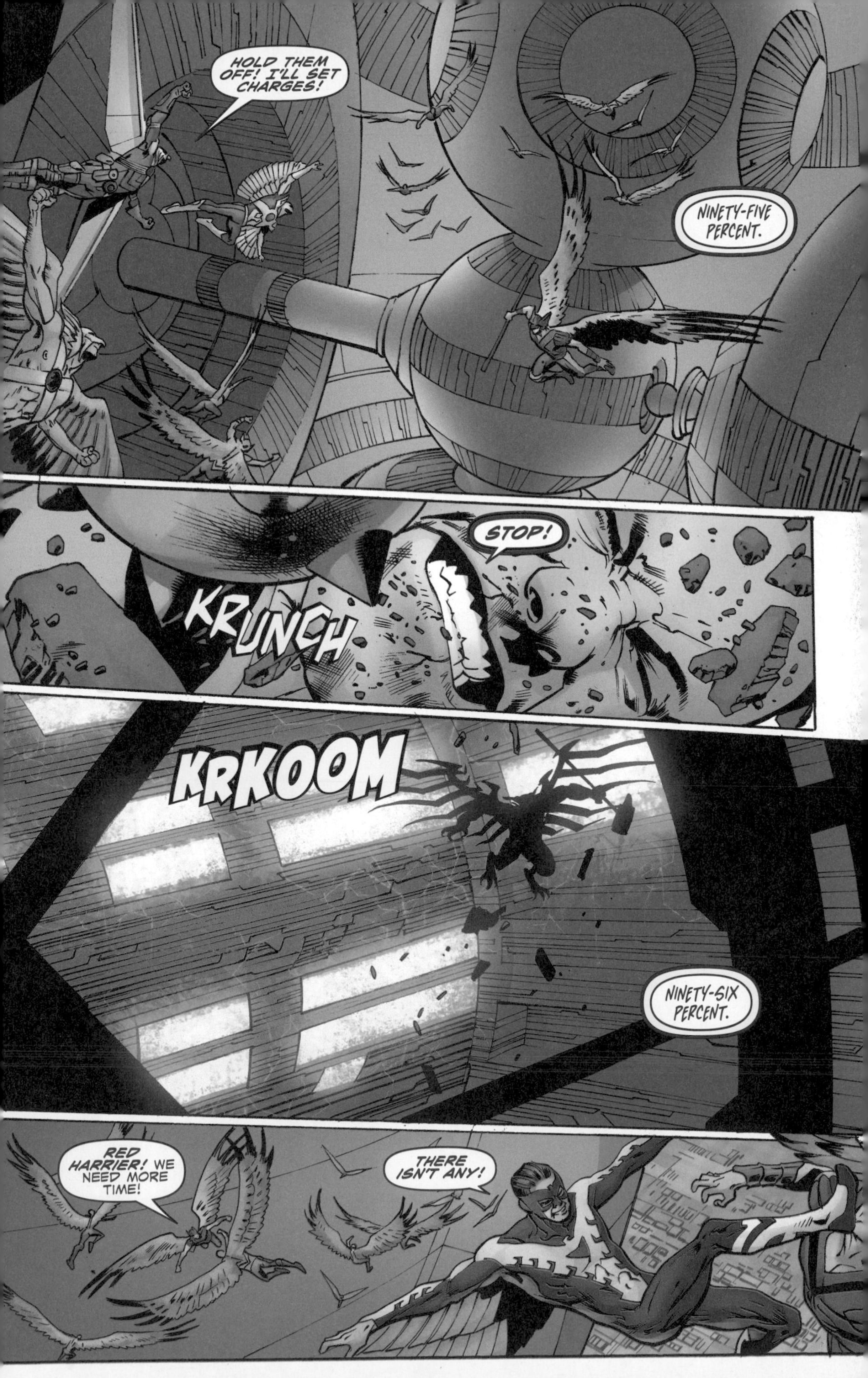
HOLD THEM OFF! I'LL SET CHARGES!
NINETY-FIVE PERCENT.
STOP!
KRUNCH
KRKOOM
NINETY-SIX PERCENT.
RED HARRIER! WE NEED MORE TIME!
THERE ISN'T ANY!

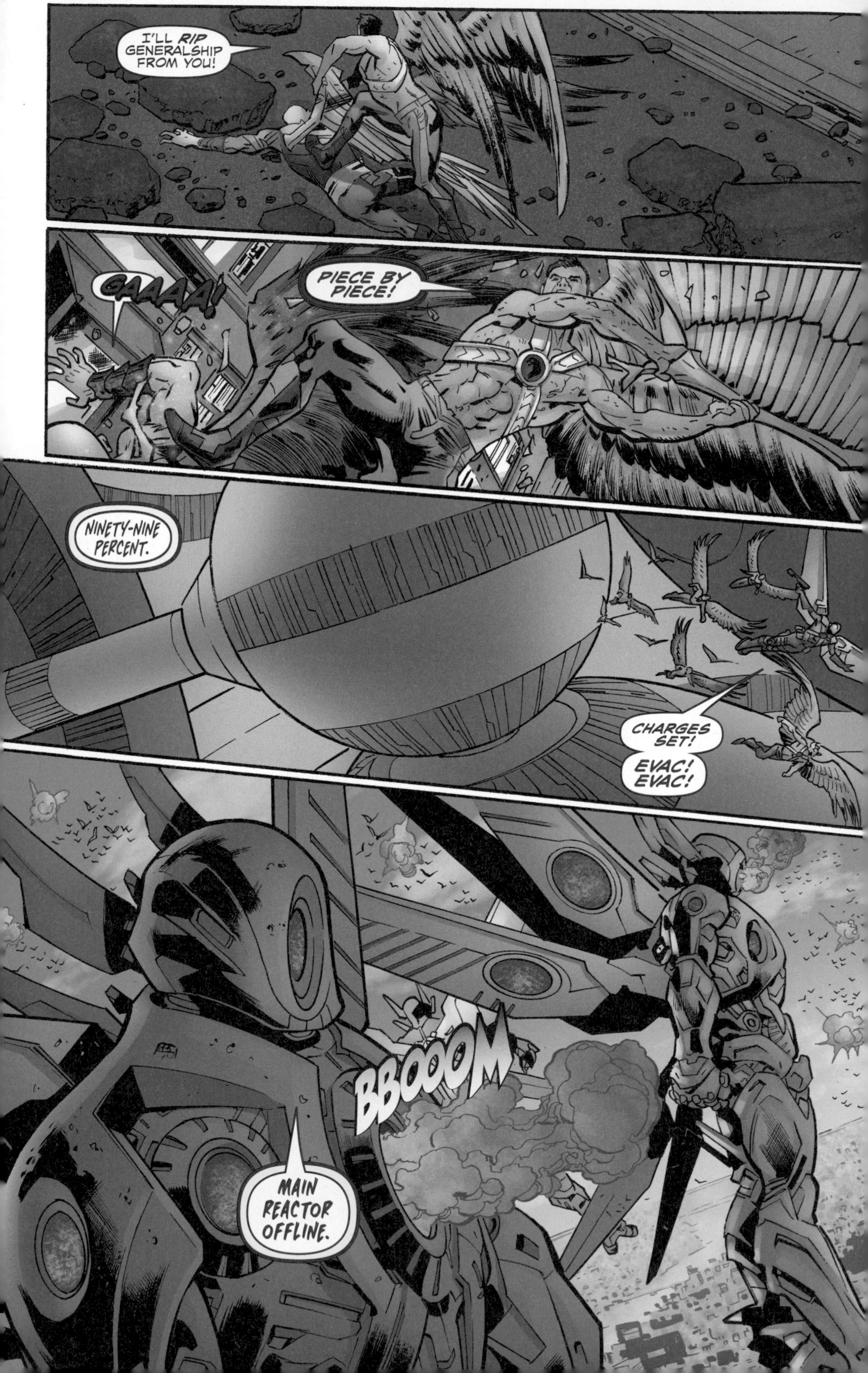
I'LL RIP GENERALSHIP FROM YOU!
GAAAAA!
PIECE BY PIECE!
NINETY-NINE PERCENT.
CHARGES SET!
EVAC! EVAC!
BBOOOM
MAIN REACTOR OFFLINE.

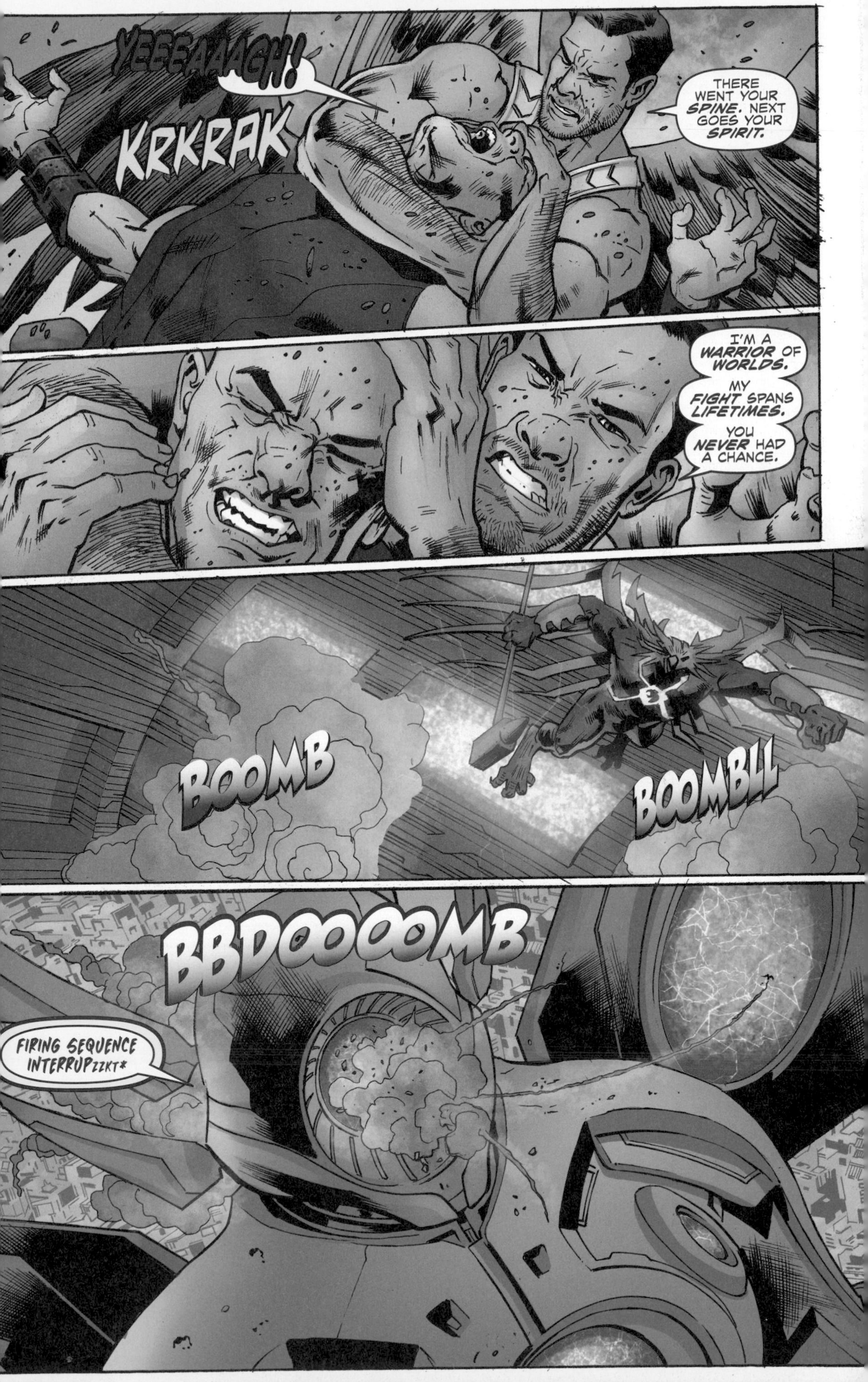
YEEEAAAGH!
KRKRAK
THERE WENT YOUR SPINE. NEXT GOES YOUR SPIRIT.
I'M A WARRIOR OF WORLDS.
MY FIGHT SPANS LIFETIMES.
YOU NEVER HAD A CHANCE.
BOOMB
BOOMBLL
BBDOOOOOMB
FIRING SEQUENCE INTERRUPzzkt*

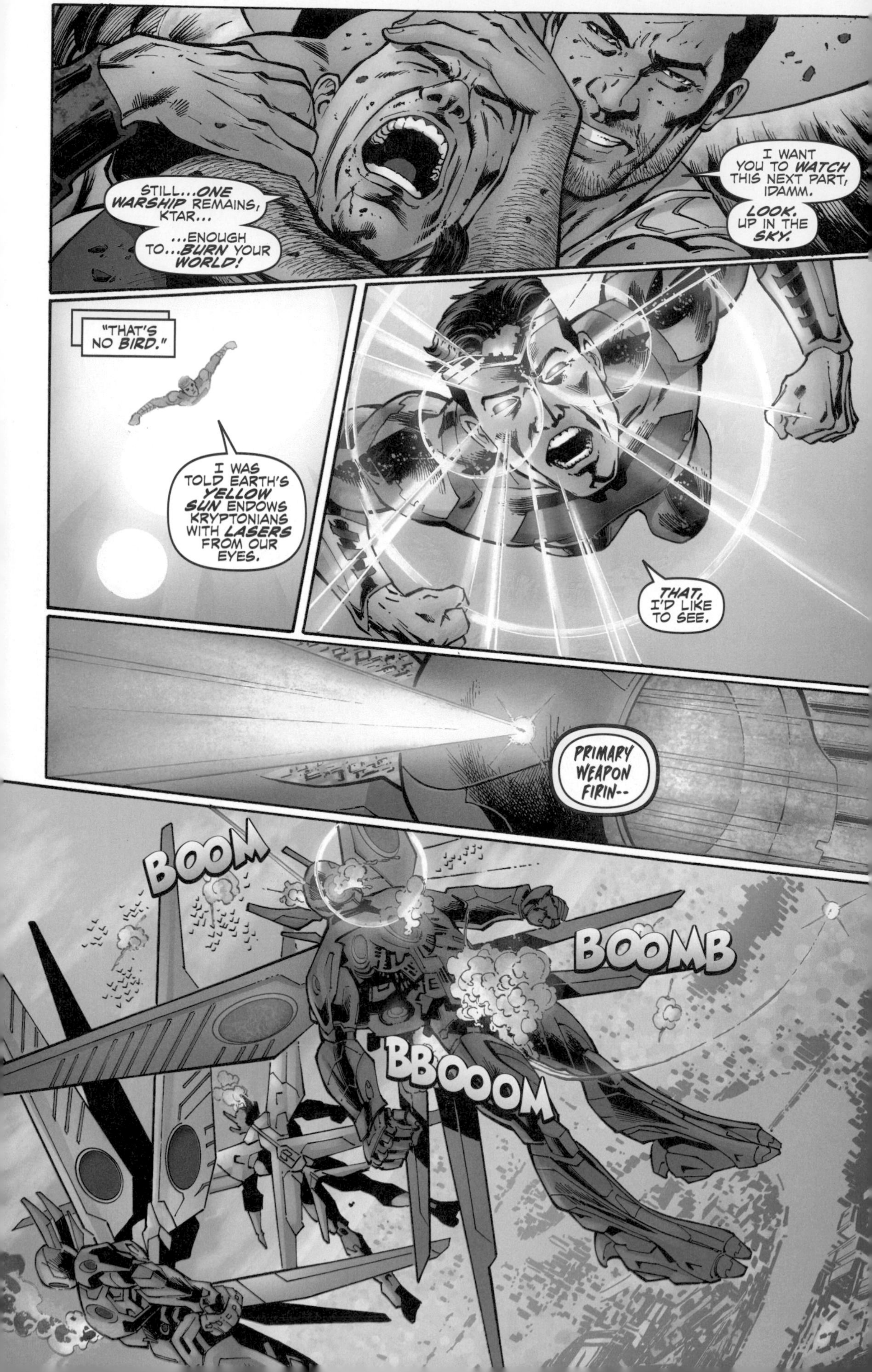
STILL...ONE WARSHIP REMAINS, KTAR...
...ENOUGH TO...BURN YOUR WORLD!
I WANT YOU TO WATCH THIS NEXT PART, IDAMM.
LOOK. UP IN THE SKY.
"THAT'S NO BIRD."
I WAS TOLD EARTH'S YELLOW SUN ENDOWS KRYPTONIANS WITH LASERS FROM OUR EYES.
THAT, I'D LIKE TO SEE.
PRIMARY WEAPON FIRIN--
BOOM
BOOMB
BBOOOM

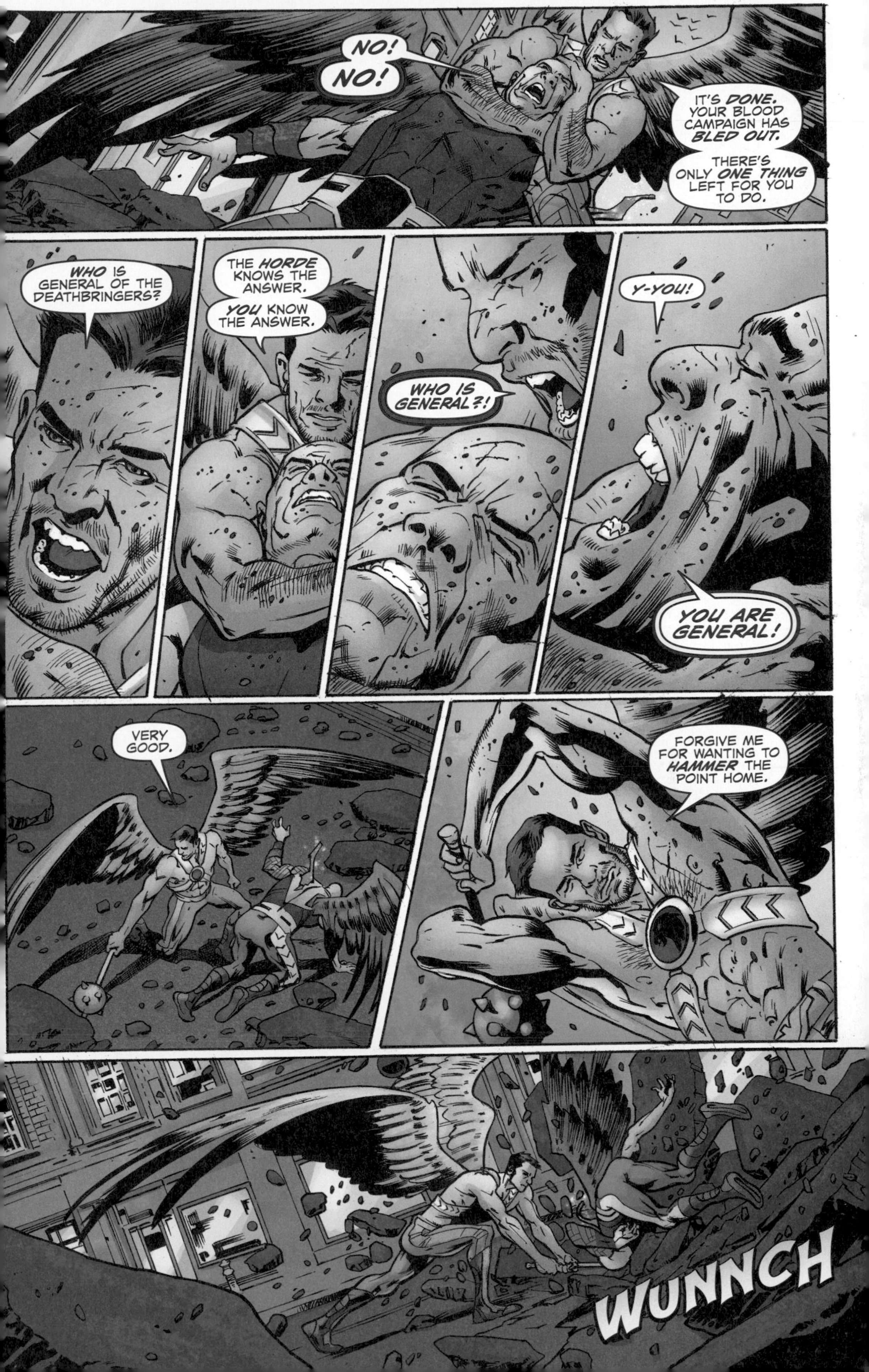
NO!
NO!
IT'S DONE. YOUR BLOOD CAMPAIGN HAS BLED OUT.
THERE'S ONLY ONE THING LEFT FOR YOU TO DO.
WHO IS GENERAL OF THE DEATHBRINGERS?
THE HORDE KNOWS THE ANSWER.
YOU KNOW THE ANSWER.
WHO IS GENERAL?!
Y-YOU!
YOU ARE GENERAL!
VERY GOOD.
FORGIVE ME FOR WANTING TO HAMMER THE POINT HOME.
WUNNCH

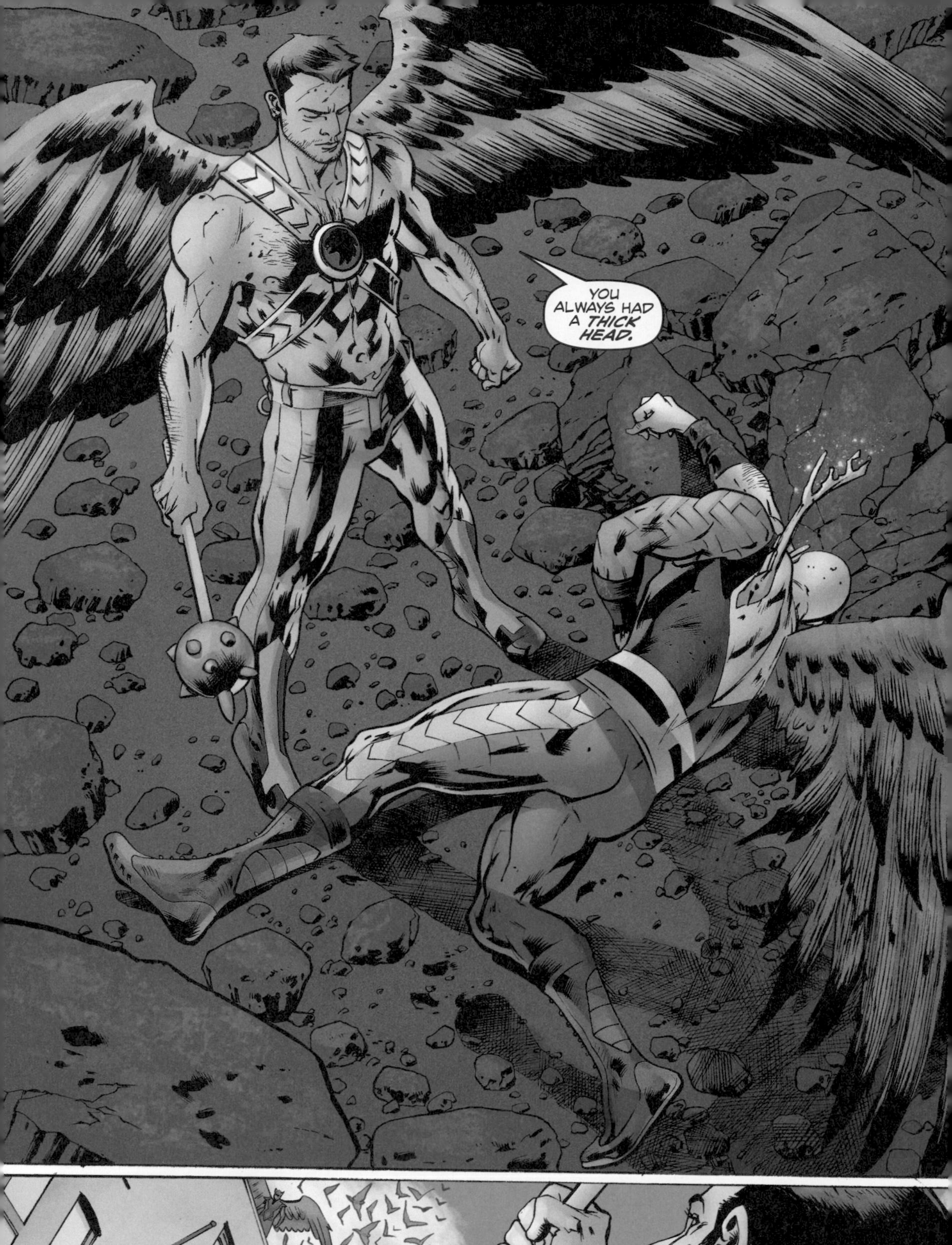
YOU ALWAYS HAD A THICK HEAD.

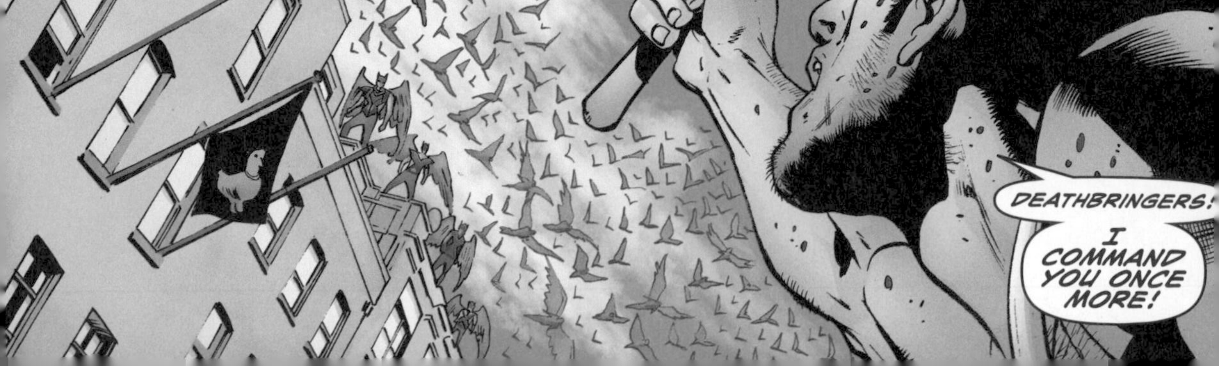
DEATHBRINGERS!
I COMMAND YOU ONCE MORE!

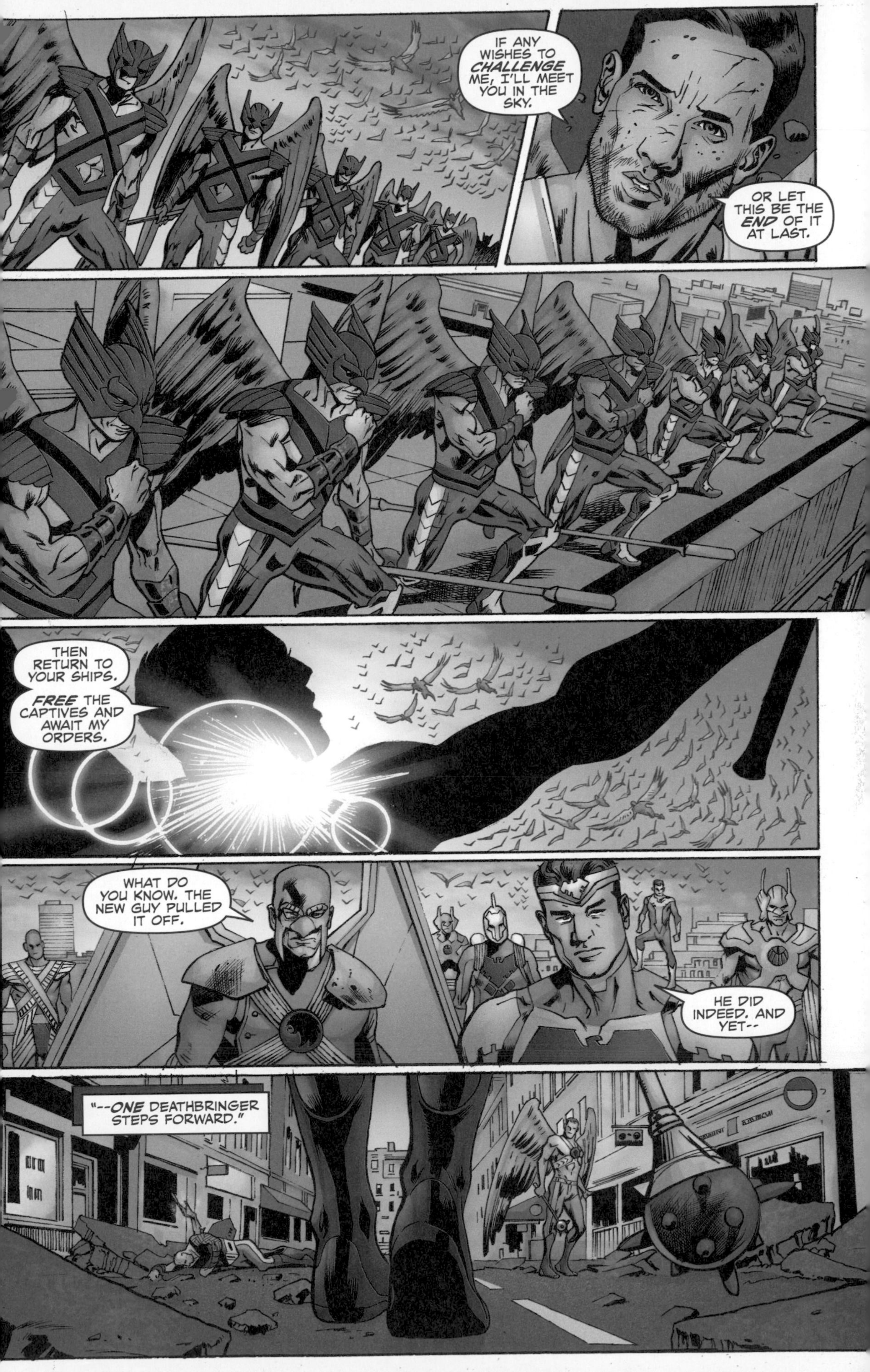
IF ANY WISHES TO CHALLENGE ME, I'LL MEET YOU IN THE SKY.
OR LET THIS BE THE END OF IT AT LAST.
THEN RETURN TO YOUR SHIPS.
FREE THE CAPTIVES AND AWAIT MY ORDERS.
WHAT DO YOU KNOW. THE NEW GUY PULLED IT OFF.
HE DID INDEED. AND YET--
"--ONE DEATHBRINGER STEPS FORWARD."

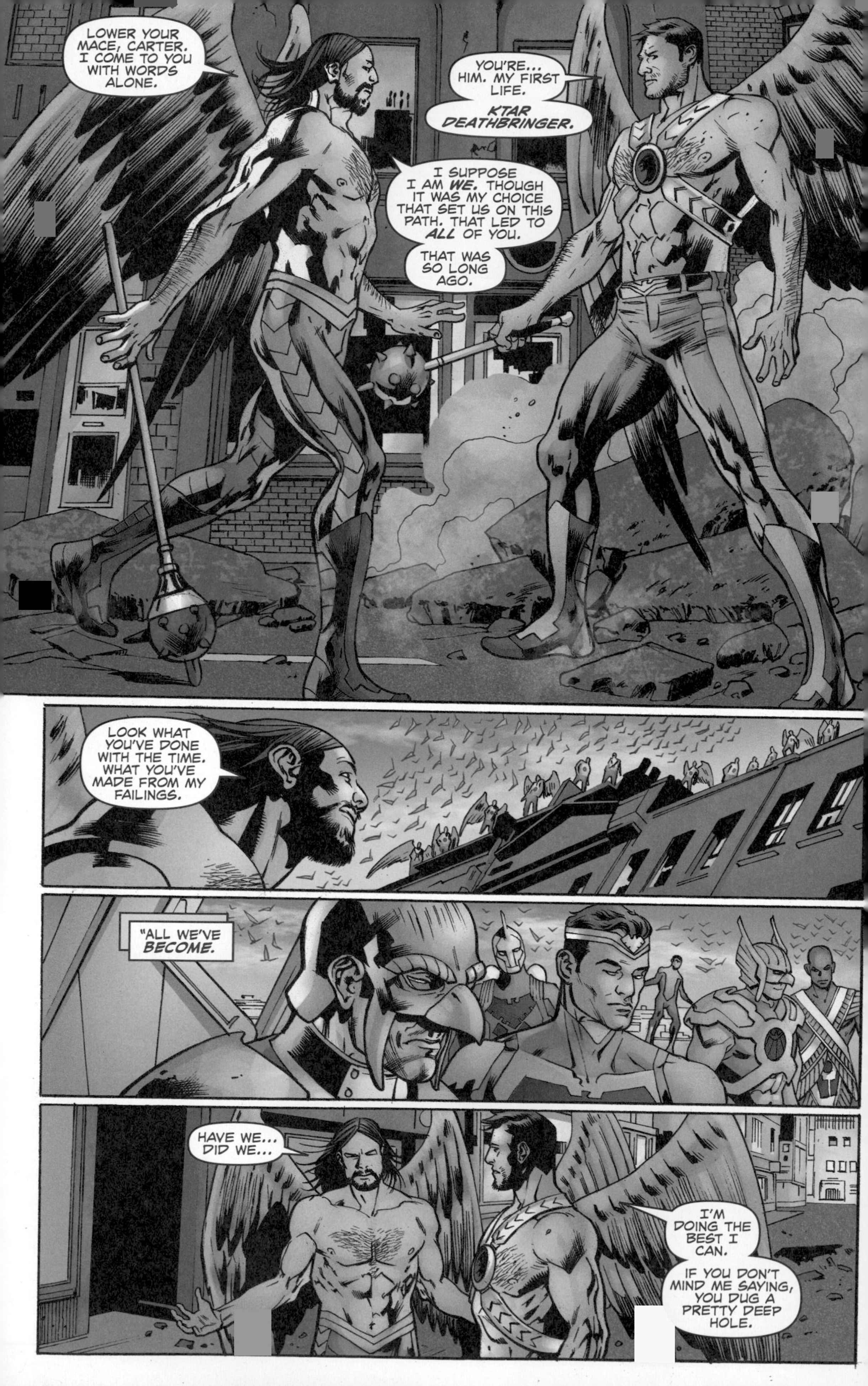
LOWER YOUR MACE, CARTER. I COME TO YOU WITH WORDS ALONE.
YOU'RE... HIM. MY FIRST LIFE.
KTAR DEATHBRINGER.
I SUPPOSE I AM WE. THOUGH IT WAS MY CHOICE THAT SET US ON THIS PATH. THAT LED TO ALL OF YOU.
THAT WAS SO LONG AGO.
LOOK WHAT YOU'VE DONE WITH THE TIME. WHAT YOU'VE MADE FROM MY FAILINGS.
"ALL WE'VE BECOME.
HAVE WE... DID WE...
I'M DOING THE BEST I CAN.
IF YOU DON'T MIND ME SAYING, YOU DUG A PRETTY DEEP HOLE.

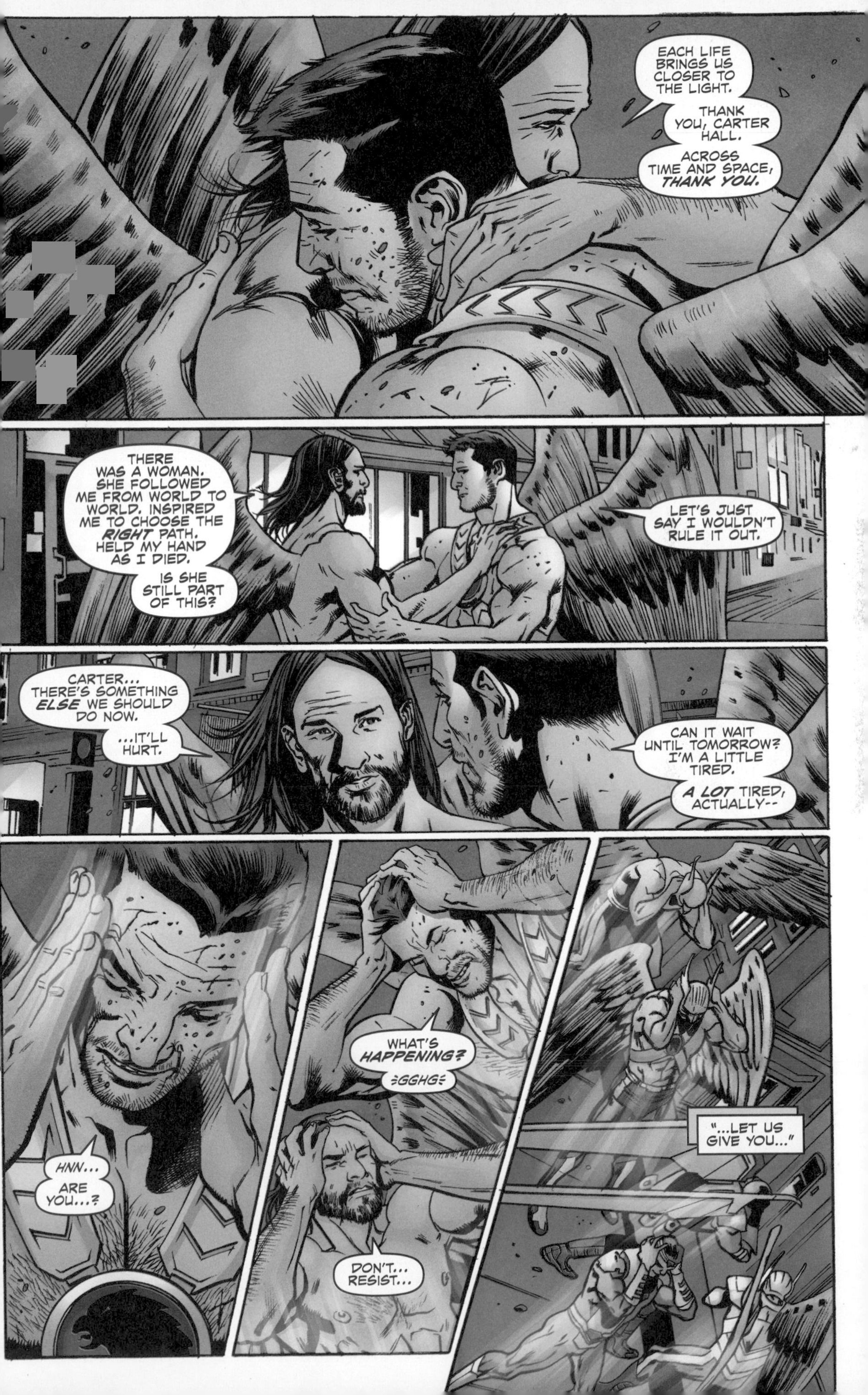

EACH LIFE BRINGS US CLOSER TO THE LIGHT.
THANK YOU, CARTER HALL.
ACROSS TIME AND SPACE, *THANK YOU.*
THERE WAS A WOMAN. SHE FOLLOWED ME FROM WORLD TO WORLD. INSPIRED ME TO CHOOSE THE *RIGHT* PATH. HELD MY HAND AS I DIED.
IS SHE STILL PART OF THIS?
LET'S JUST SAY I WOULDN'T RULE IT OUT.
CARTER... THERE'S SOMETHING *ELSE* WE SHOULD DO NOW.
...IT'LL HURT.
CAN IT WAIT UNTIL TOMORROW? I'M A LITTLE TIRED.
A LOT TIRED, ACTUALLY--
HNN...
ARE YOU...?
WHAT'S *HAPPENING?*
GGHG
DON'T... RESIST...
"...LET US GIVE YOU..."

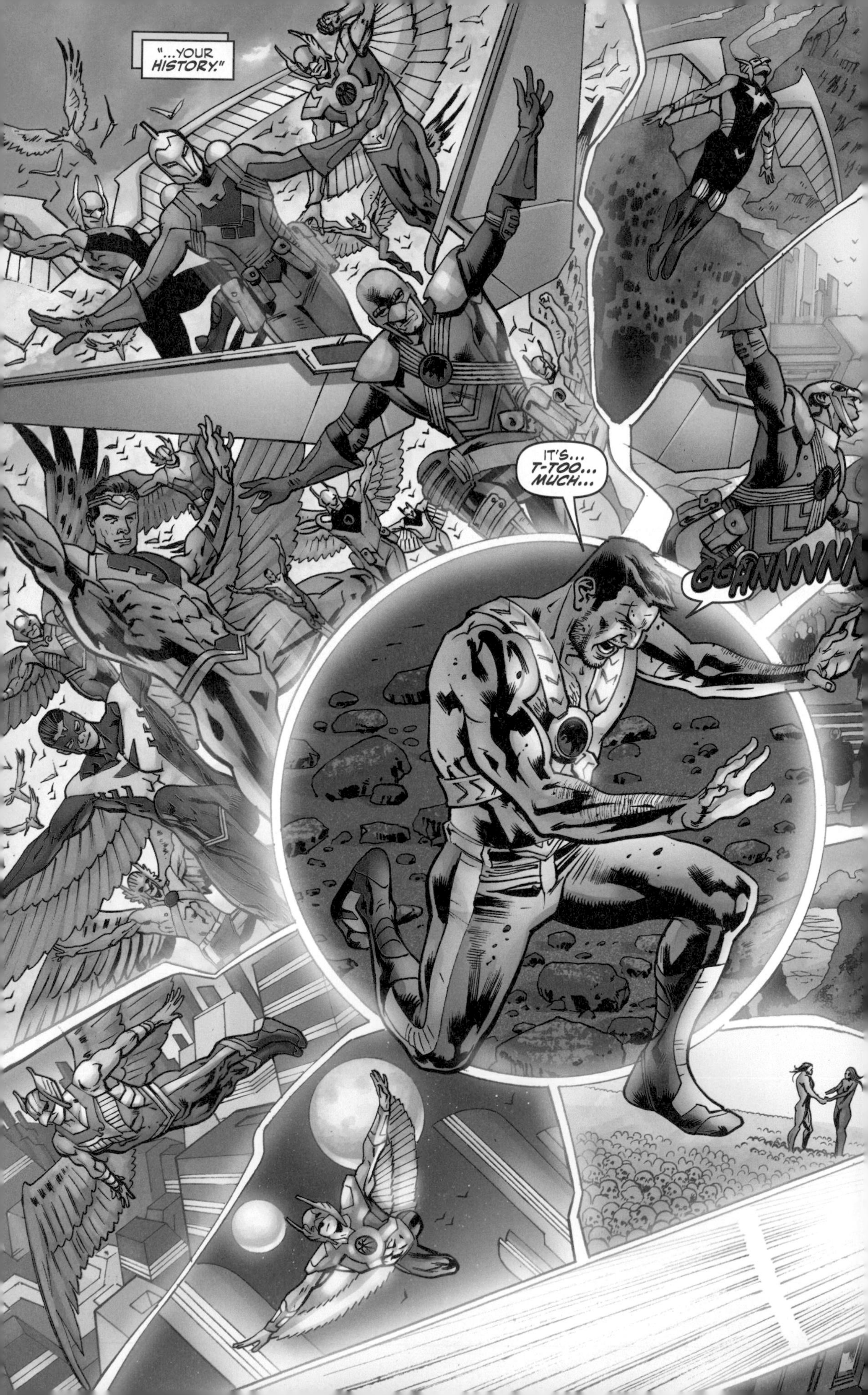
"...YOUR HISTORY."
IT'S... T-TOO... MUCH...
GGHNNNNN

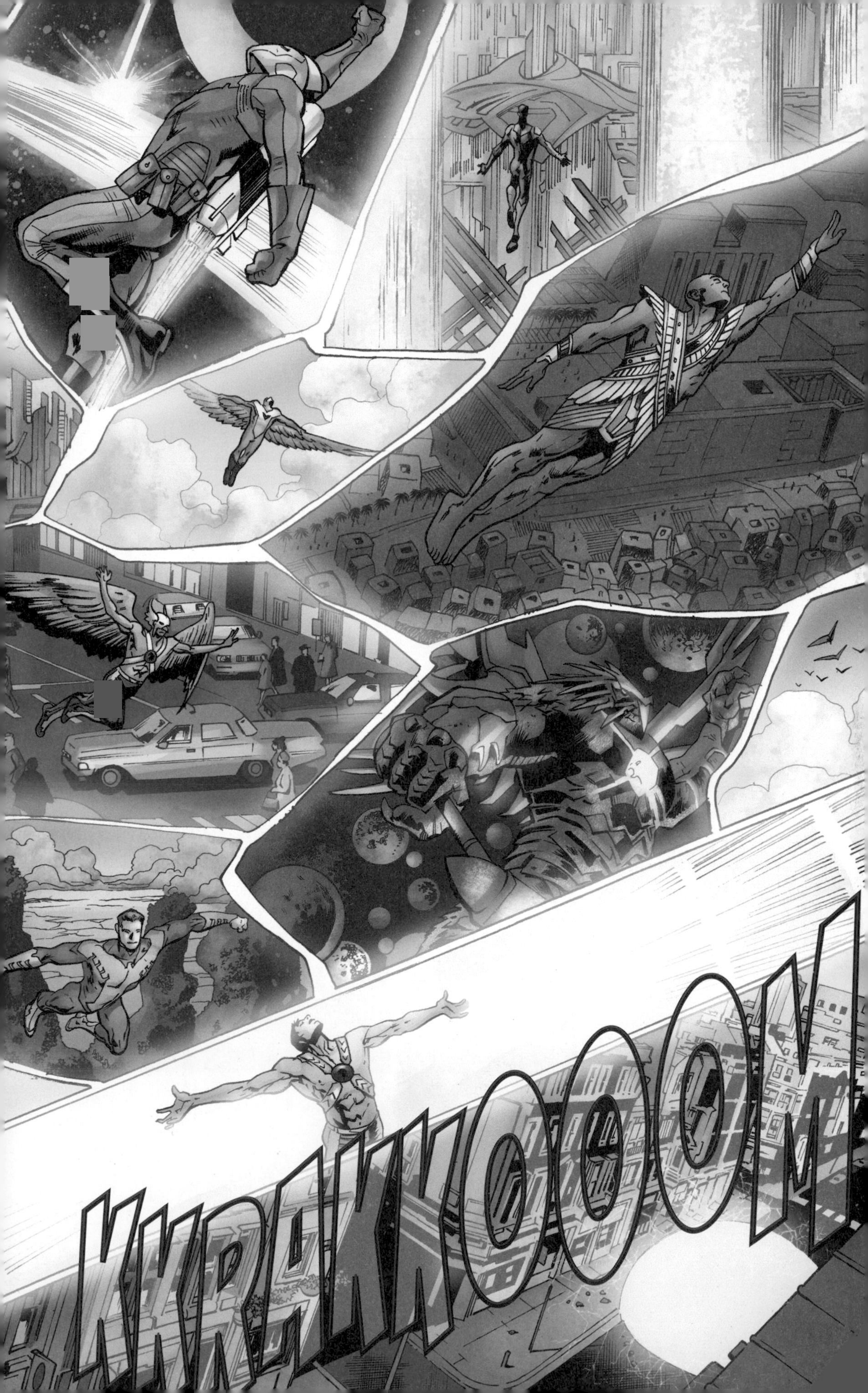
KRAKOOOM

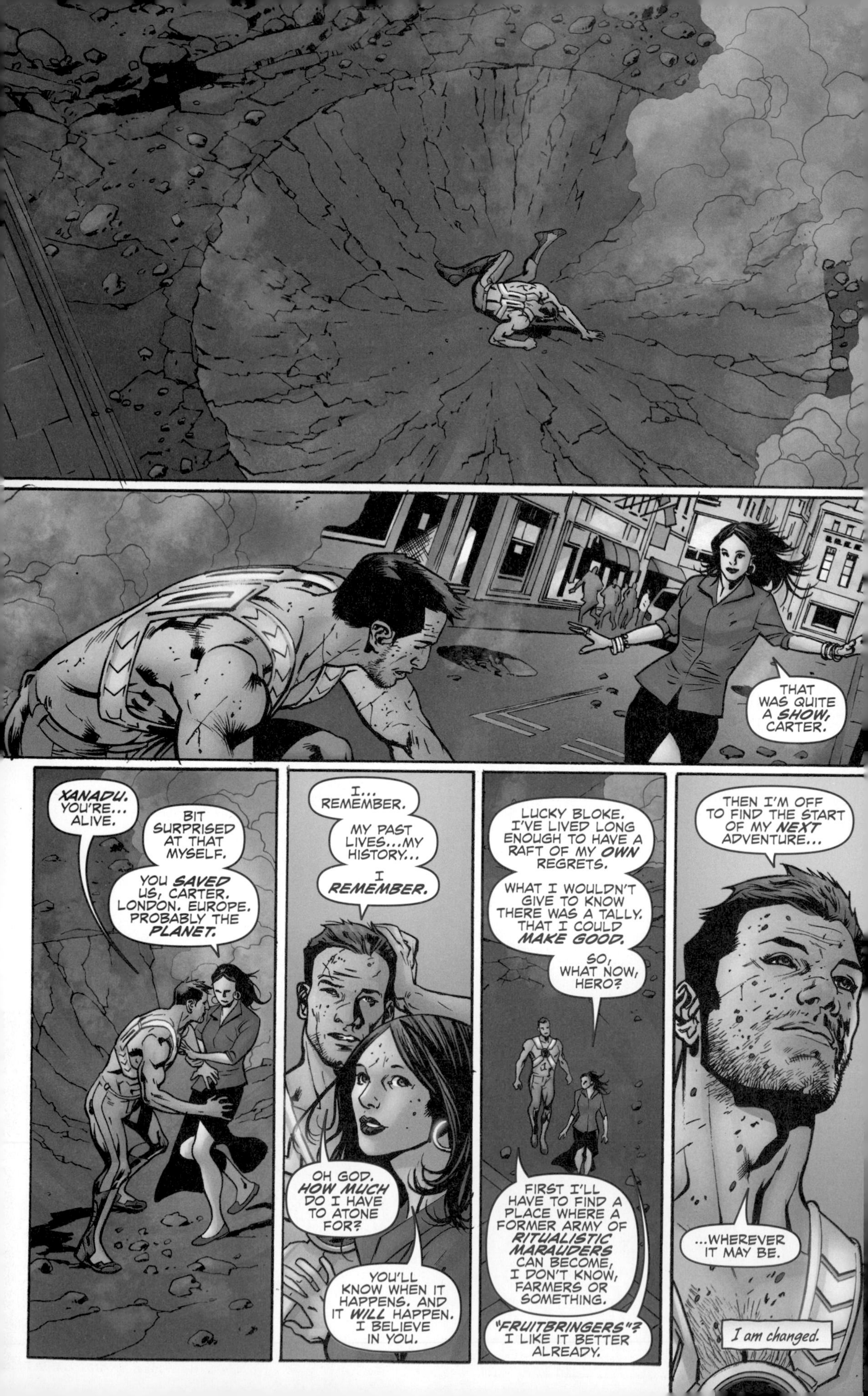
THAT WAS QUITE A SHOW, CARTER.
XANADU. YOU'RE... ALIVE.
BIT SURPRISED AT THAT MYSELF.
YOU SAVED US, CARTER. LONDON. EUROPE. PROBABLY THE PLANET.
I... REMEMBER.
MY PAST LIVES...MY HISTORY...
I REMEMBER.
OH GOD. HOW MUCH DO I HAVE TO ATONE FOR?
YOU'LL KNOW WHEN IT HAPPENS. AND IT WILL HAPPEN. I BELIEVE IN YOU.
LUCKY BLOKE. I'VE LIVED LONG ENOUGH TO HAVE A RAFT OF MY OWN REGRETS.
WHAT I WOULDN'T GIVE TO KNOW THERE WAS A TALLY. THAT I COULD MAKE GOOD.
SO, WHAT NOW, HERO?
FIRST I'LL HAVE TO FIND A PLACE WHERE A FORMER ARMY OF RITUALISTIC MARAUDERS CAN BECOME, I DON'T KNOW, FARMERS OR SOMETHING.
"FRUITBRINGERS"? I LIKE IT BETTER ALREADY.
THEN I'M OFF TO FIND THE START OF MY NEXT ADVENTURE...
...WHEREVER IT MAY BE.
I am changed.

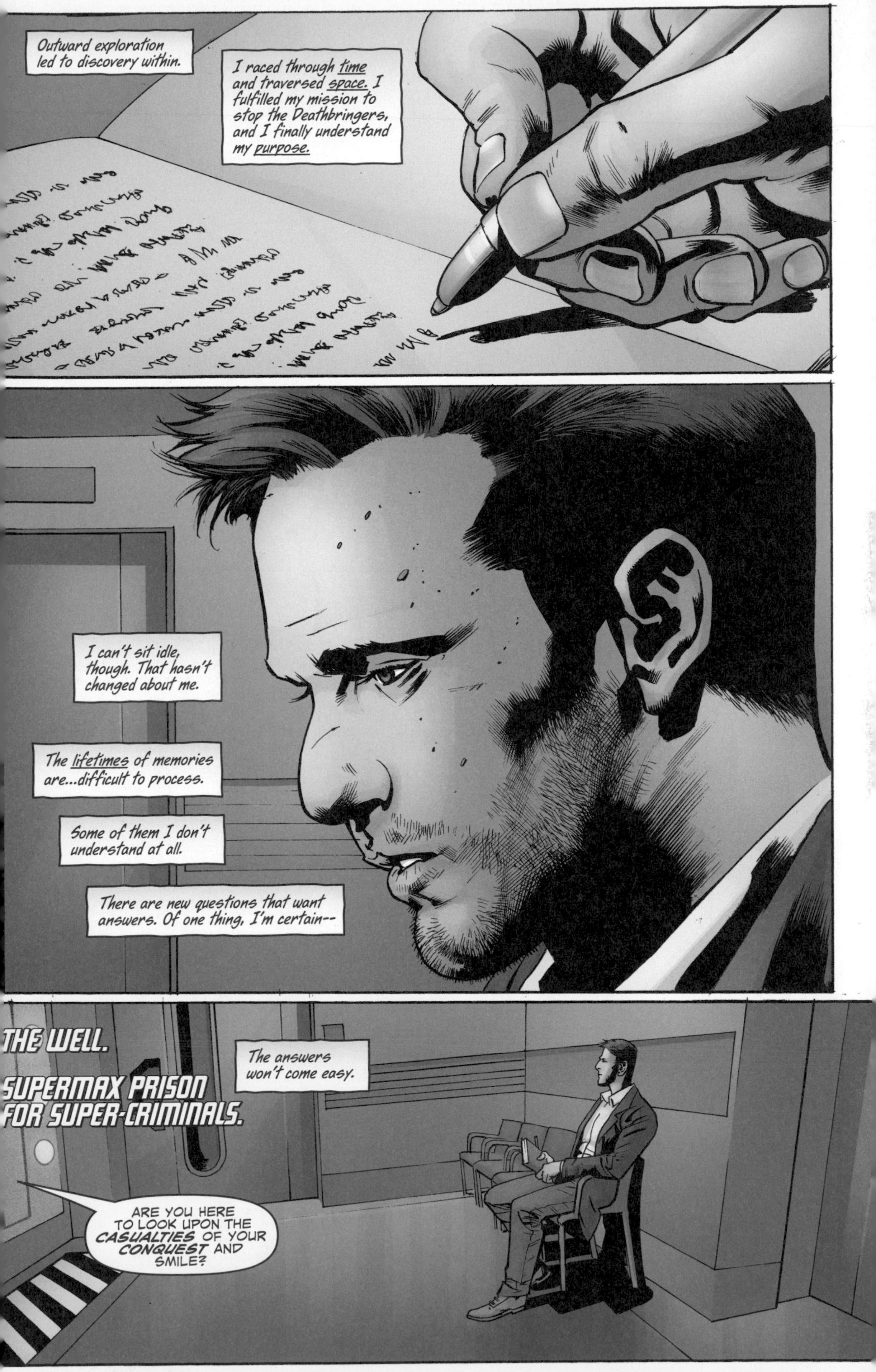
Outward exploration led to discovery within.
I raced through time and traversed space. I fulfilled my mission to stop the Deathbringers, and I finally understand my purpose.
I can't sit idle, though. That hasn't changed about me.
The lifetimes of memories are...difficult to process.
Some of them I don't understand at all.
There are new questions that want answers. Of one thing, I'm certain--
THE WELL.
SUPERMAX PRISON FOR SUPER-CRIMINALS.
The answers won't come easy.
ARE YOU HERE TO LOOK UPON THE CASUALTIES OF YOUR CONQUEST AND SMILE?

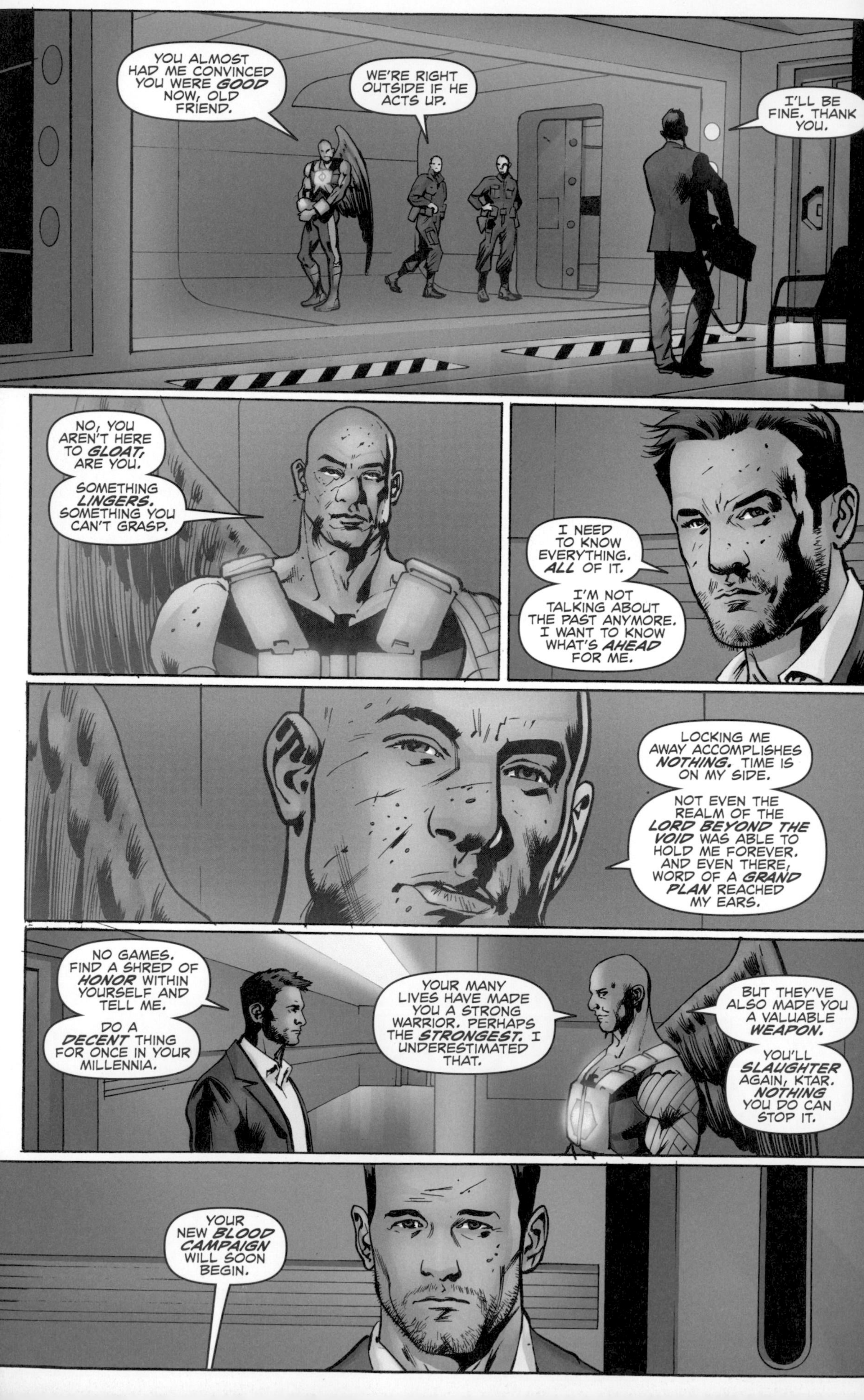
YOU ALMOST HAD ME CONVINCED YOU WERE GOOD NOW, OLD FRIEND.
WE'RE RIGHT OUTSIDE IF HE ACTS UP.
I'LL BE FINE. THANK YOU.
NO, YOU AREN'T HERE TO GLOAT, ARE YOU.
SOMETHING LINGERS. SOMETHING YOU CAN'T GRASP.
I NEED TO KNOW EVERYTHING. ALL OF IT.
I'M NOT TALKING ABOUT THE PAST ANYMORE. I WANT TO KNOW WHAT'S AHEAD FOR ME.
LOCKING ME AWAY ACCOMPLISHES NOTHING. TIME IS ON MY SIDE.
NOT EVEN THE REALM OF THE LORD BEYOND THE VOID WAS ABLE TO HOLD ME FOREVER. AND EVEN THERE, WORD OF A GRAND PLAN REACHED MY EARS.
NO GAMES. FIND A SHRED OF HONOR WITHIN YOURSELF AND TELL ME.
DO A DECENT THING FOR ONCE IN YOUR MILLENNIA.
YOUR MANY LIVES HAVE MADE YOU A STRONG WARRIOR. PERHAPS THE STRONGEST. I UNDERESTIMATED THAT.
BUT THEY'VE ALSO MADE YOU A VALUABLE WEAPON.
YOU'LL SLAUGHTER AGAIN, KTAR. NOTHING YOU DO CAN STOP IT.
YOUR NEW BLOOD CAMPAIGN WILL SOON BEGIN.

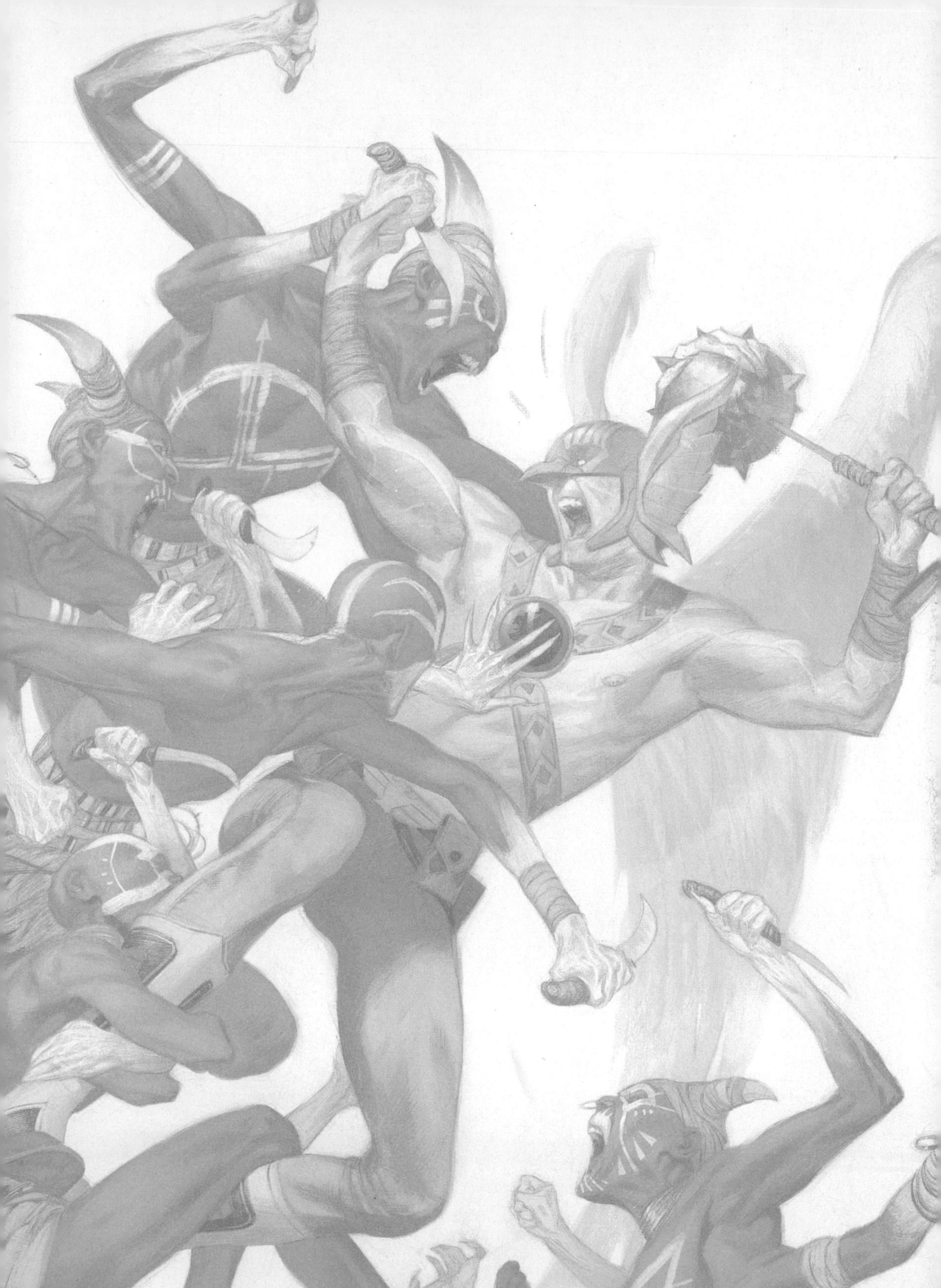

VARIANT COVER GALLERY

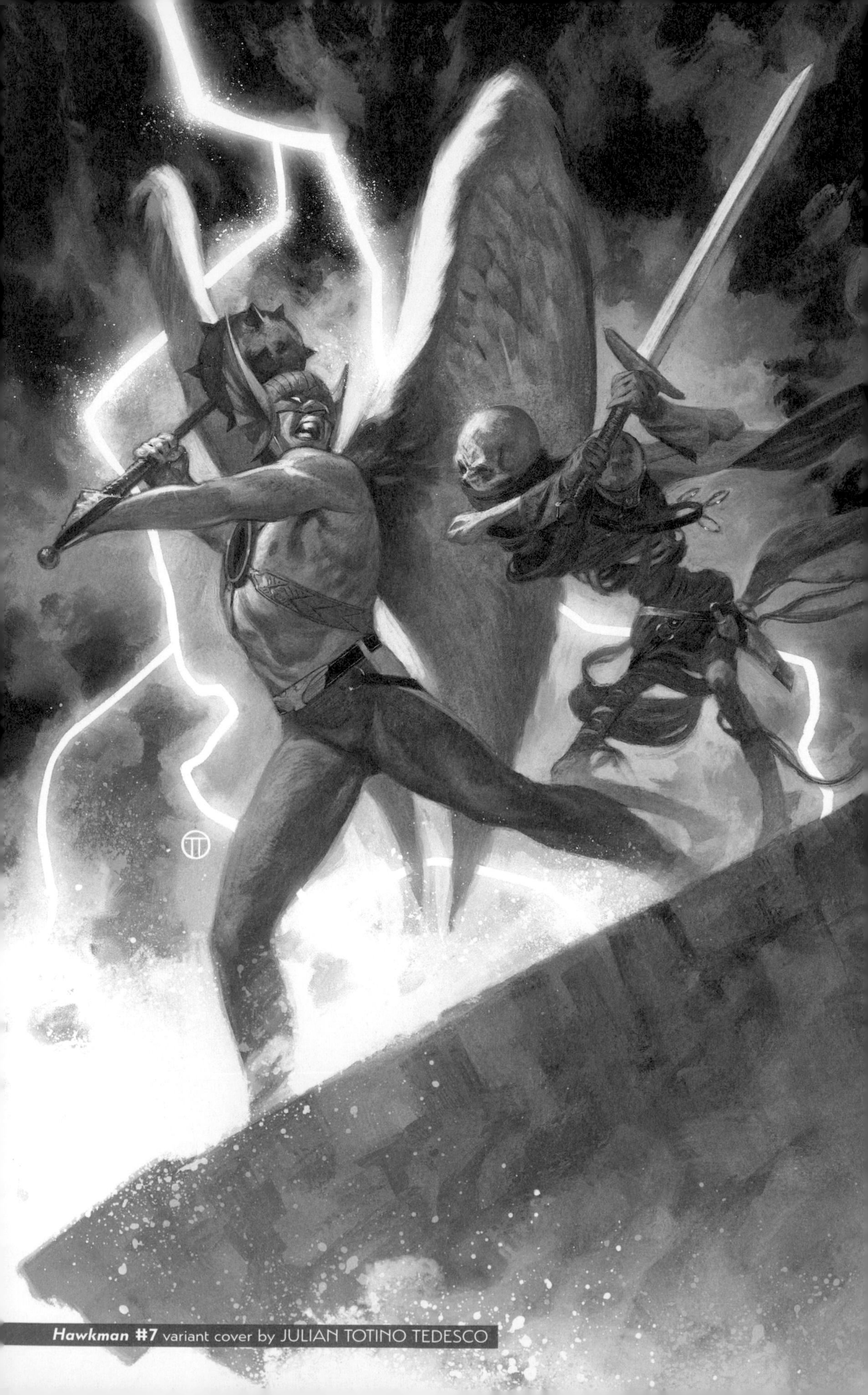

***Hawkman* #7** variant cover by JULIAN TOTINO TEDESCO

***Hawkman* #8** variant cover by BILL SIENKIEWICZ

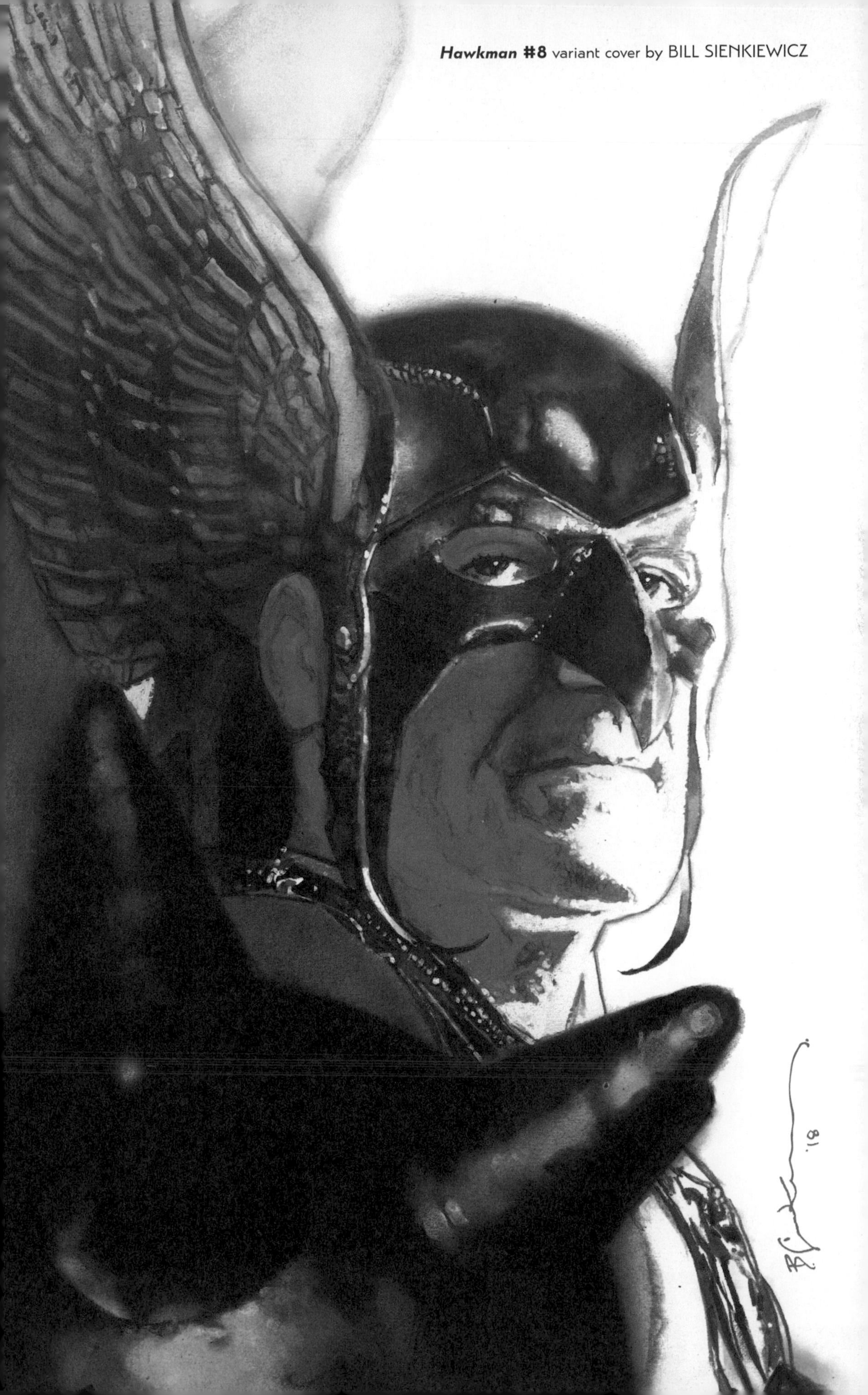

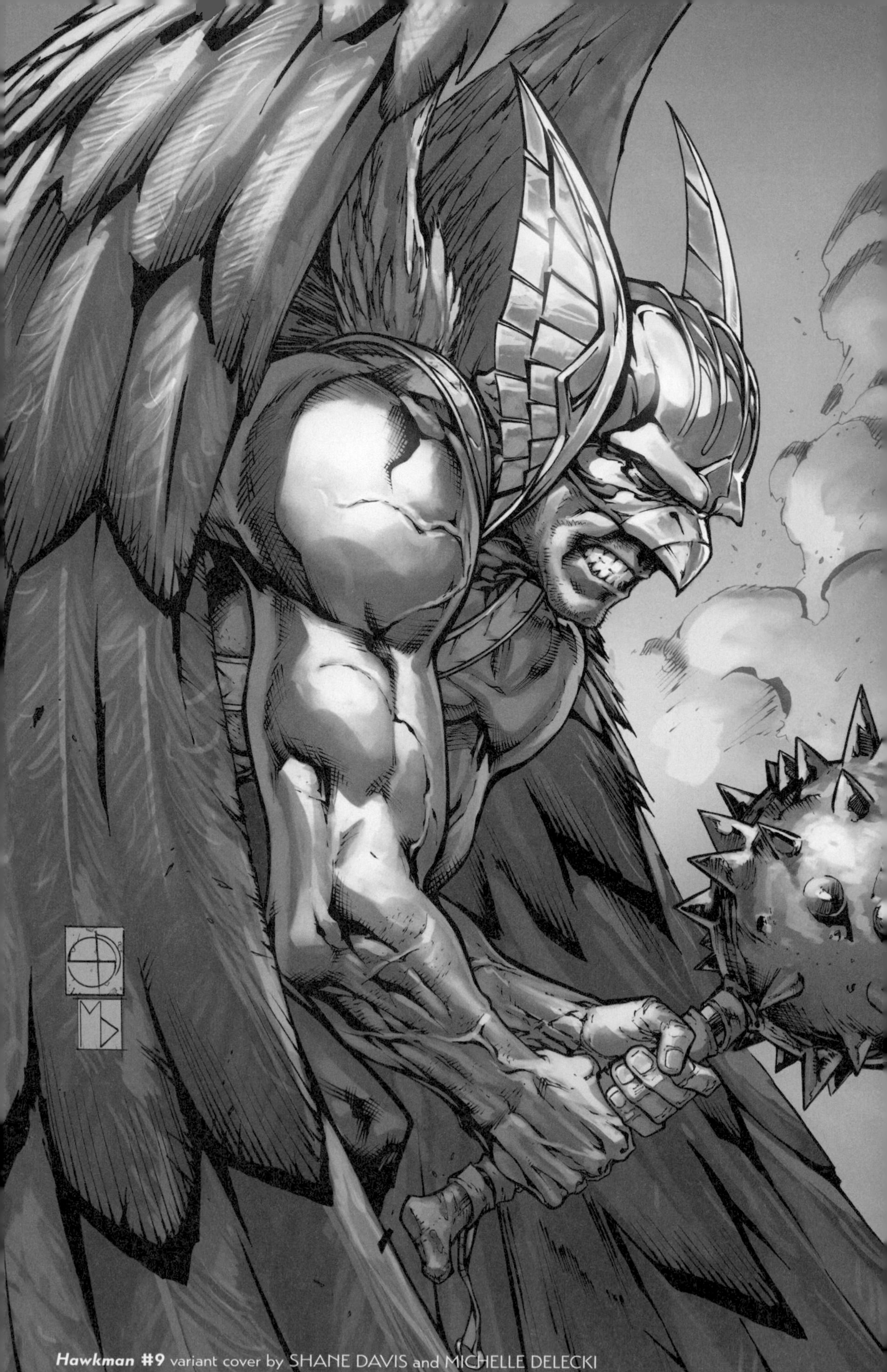

***Hawkman* #9** variant cover by SHANE DAVIS and MICHELLE DELECKI

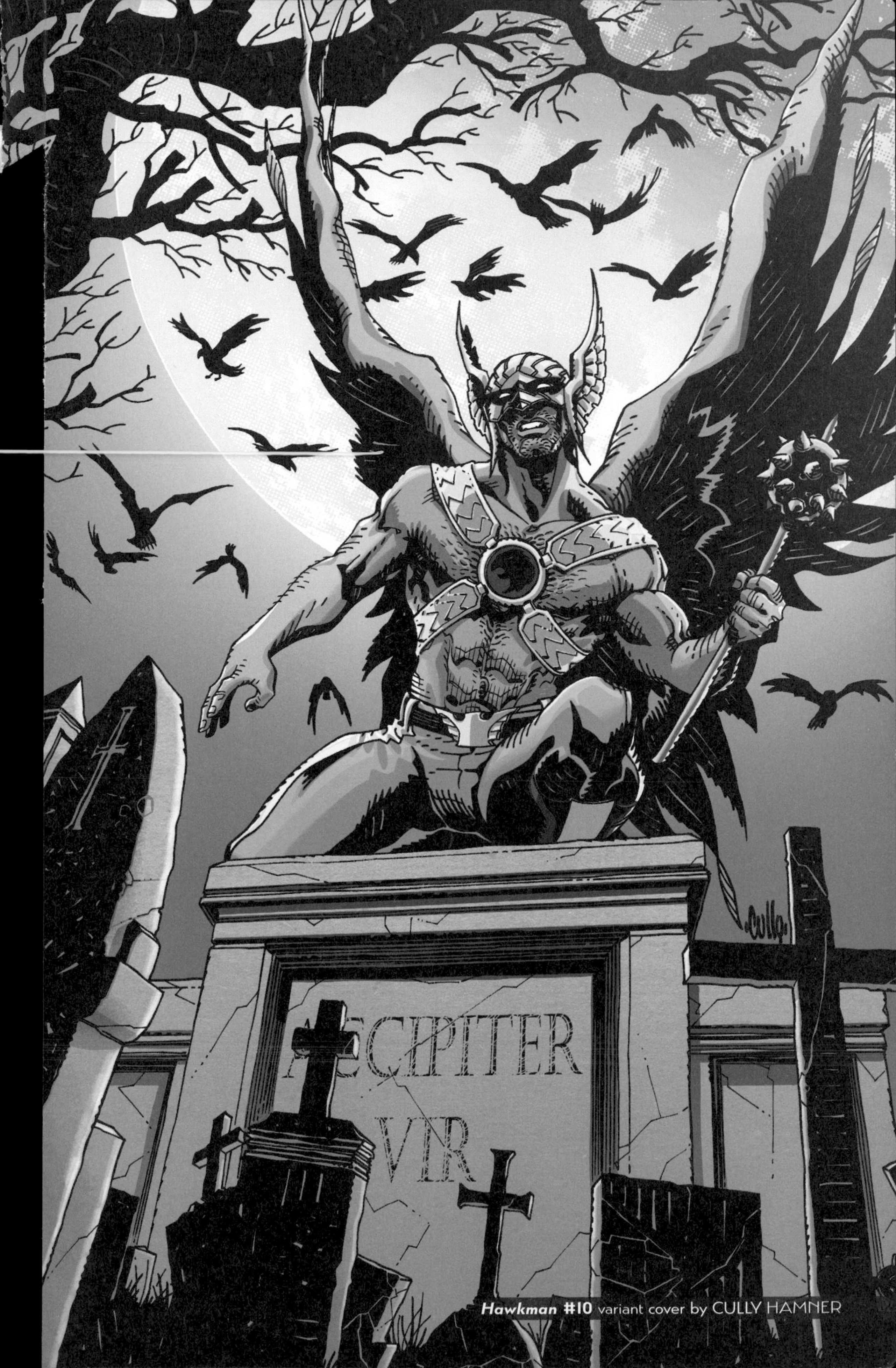
ECIPITER
VIR

***Hawkman* #10** variant cover by CULLY HAMNER

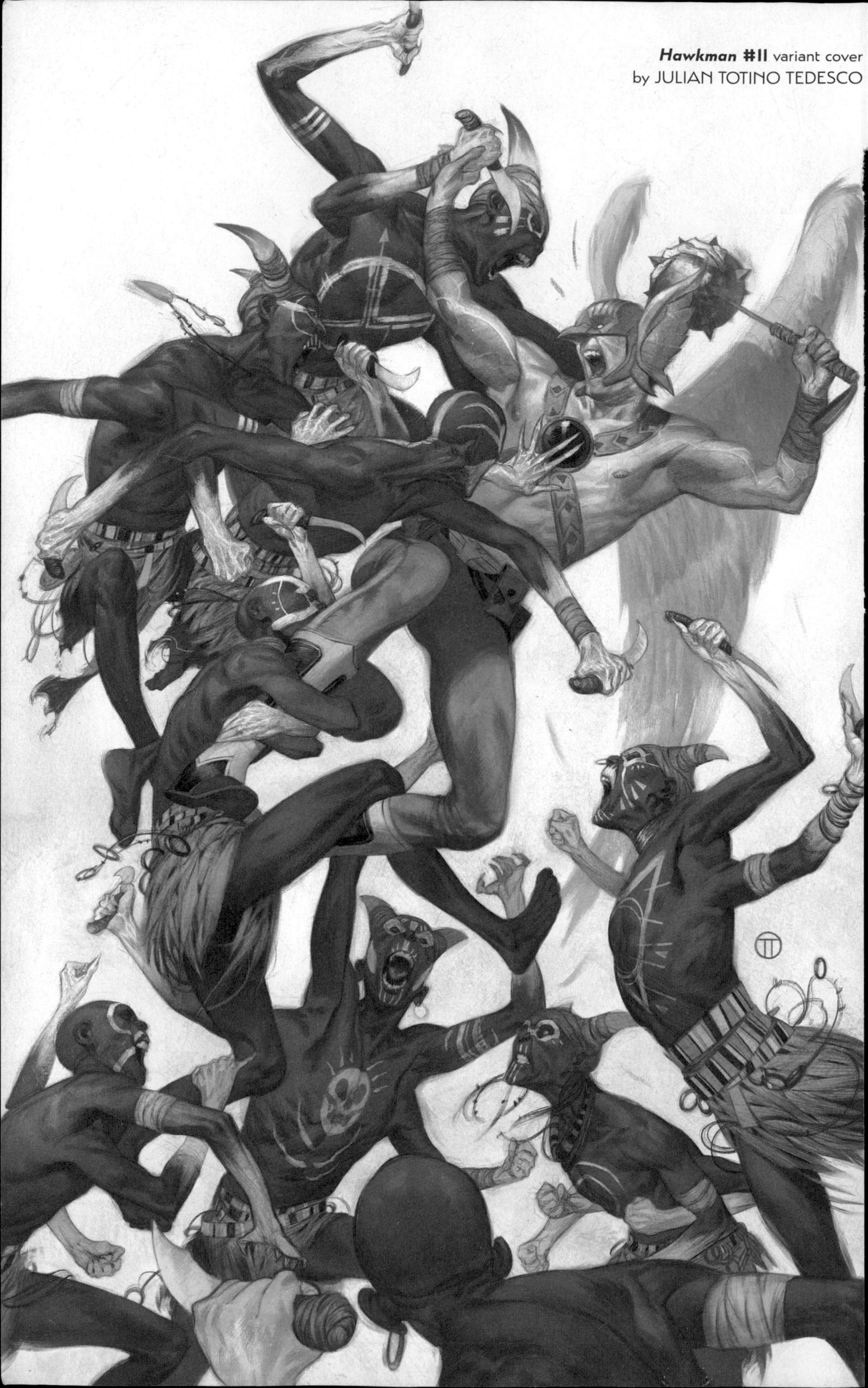

***Hawkman* #11** variant cover
by JULIAN TOTINO TEDESCO

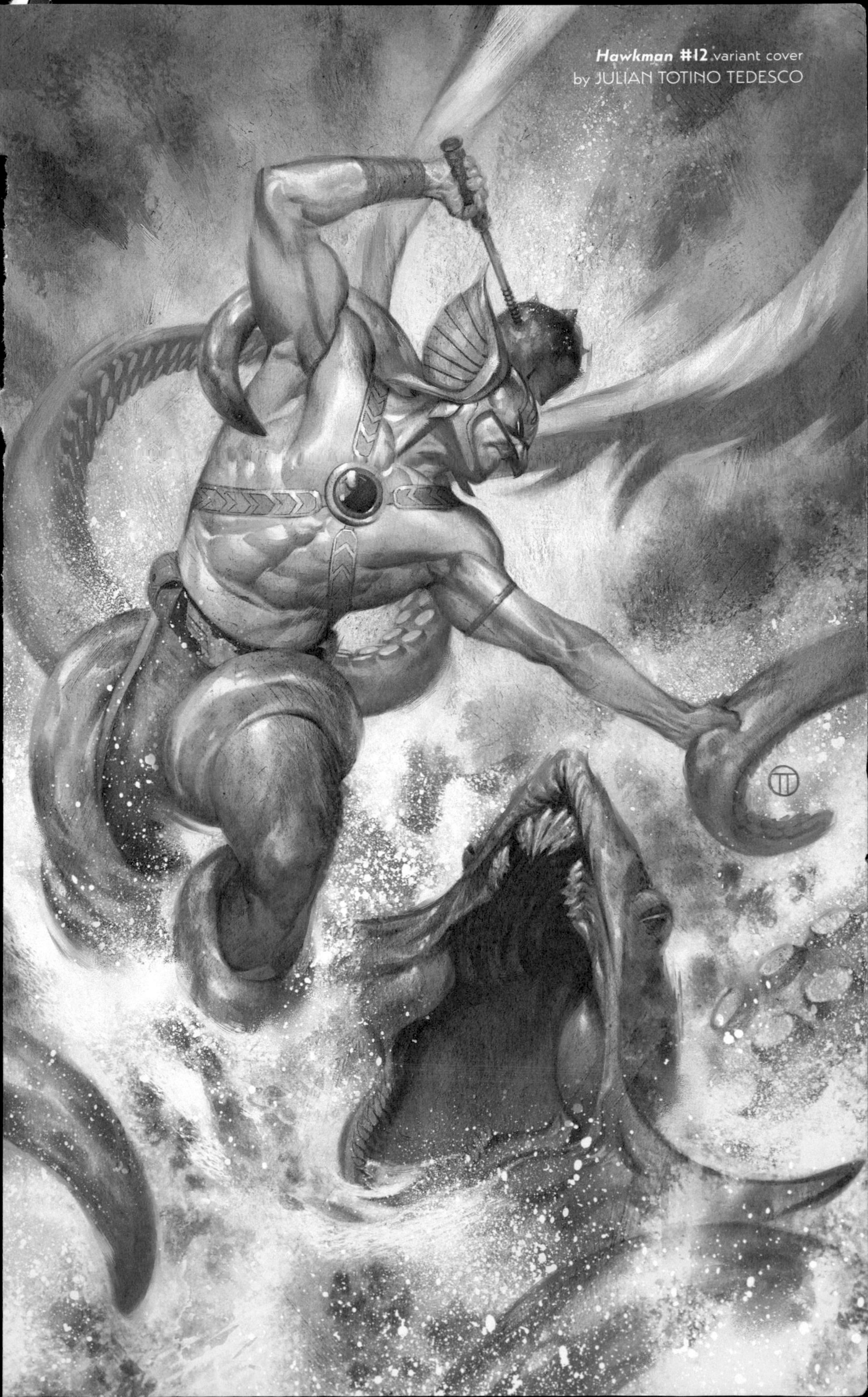

***Hawkman* #12** variant cover
by JULIAN TOTINO TEDESCO

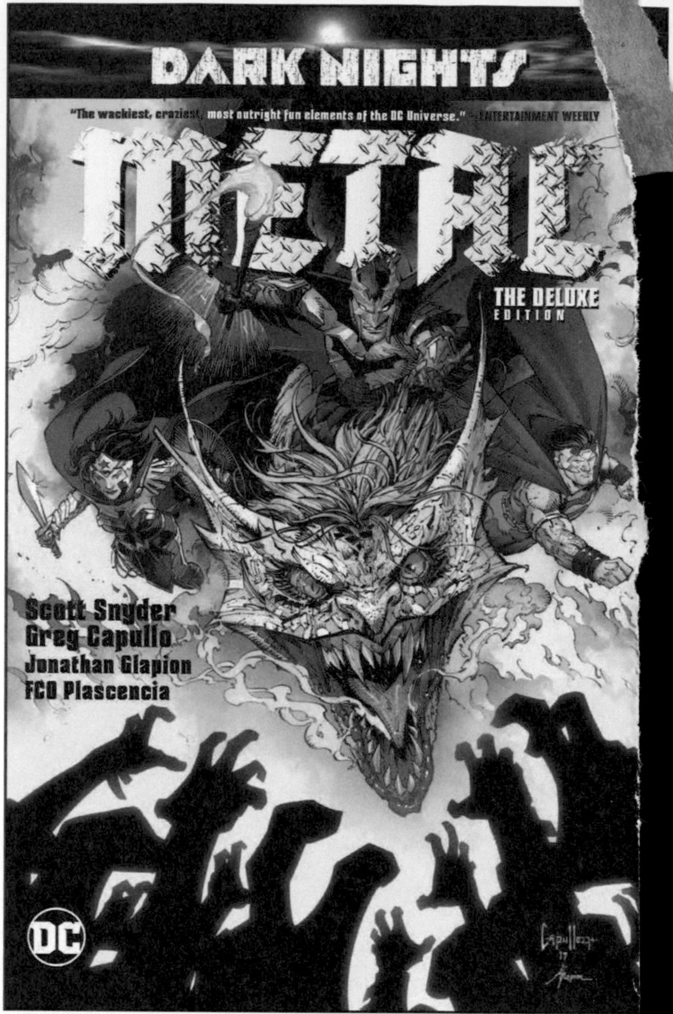
DARK NIGHTS
"The wackiest, craziest, most outright fun elements of the DC Universe." —ENTERTAINMENT WEEKLY
METAL
THE DELUXE EDITION
Scott Snyder
Greg Capullo
Jonathan Glapion
FCO Plascencia
DC

"This is the work of two men at the top of their games."
–THE NEW YORK TIMES

"Where nightmares and reality collide."
–THE WASHINGTON POST

"The Batman of your wildest nightmares."
–POLYGON

DARK NIGHTS:
METAL
SCOTT SNYDER
GREG CAPULLO

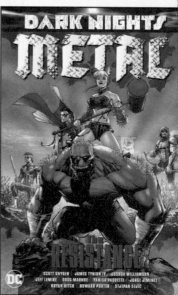

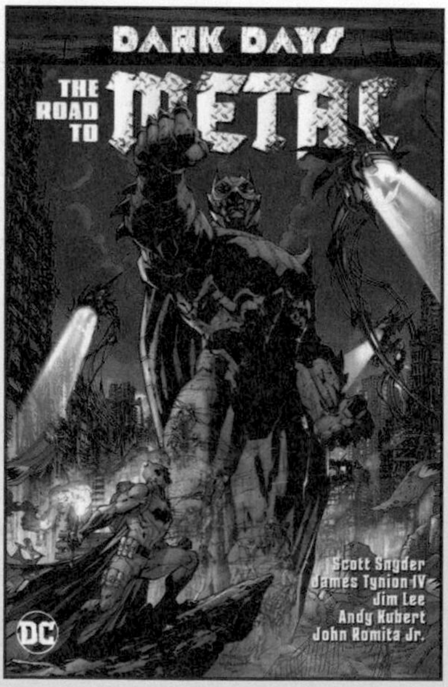
DARK DAYS
THE ROAD TO
METAL
Scott Snyder
James Tynion IV
Jim Lee
Andy Kubert
John Romita Jr.
DC

DARK DAYS:
THE ROAD TO METAL

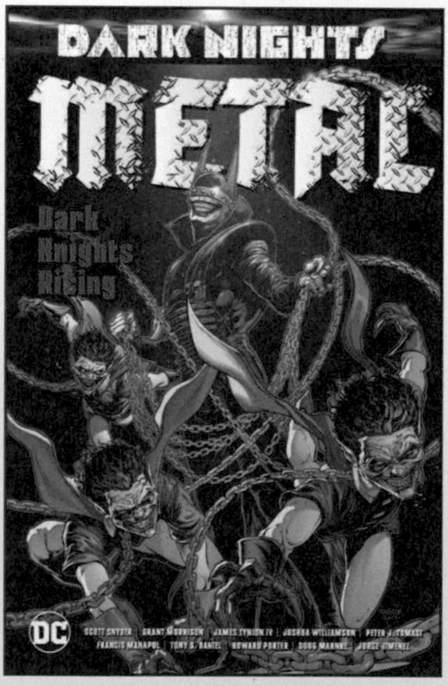
DARK NIGHTS
METAL
Dark Knights Rising
DC

DARK NIGHTS: METAL:
DARK KNIGHTS RISING

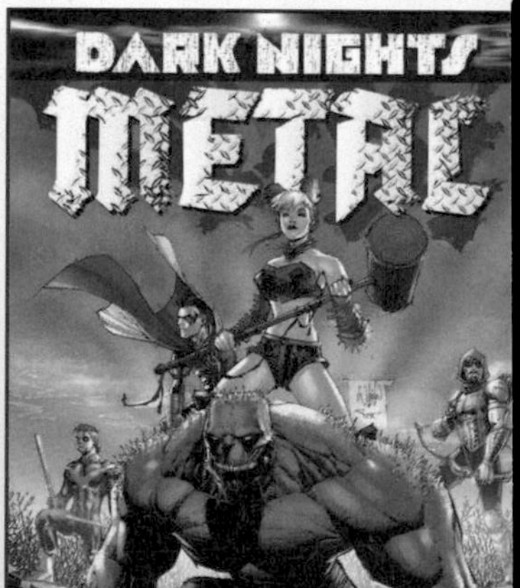
DARK NIGHTS
METAL
The RESISTANCE
DC

DARK NIGHTS: METAL:
THE RESISTANCE

Get more DC graphic novels wherever comics and books are sold!